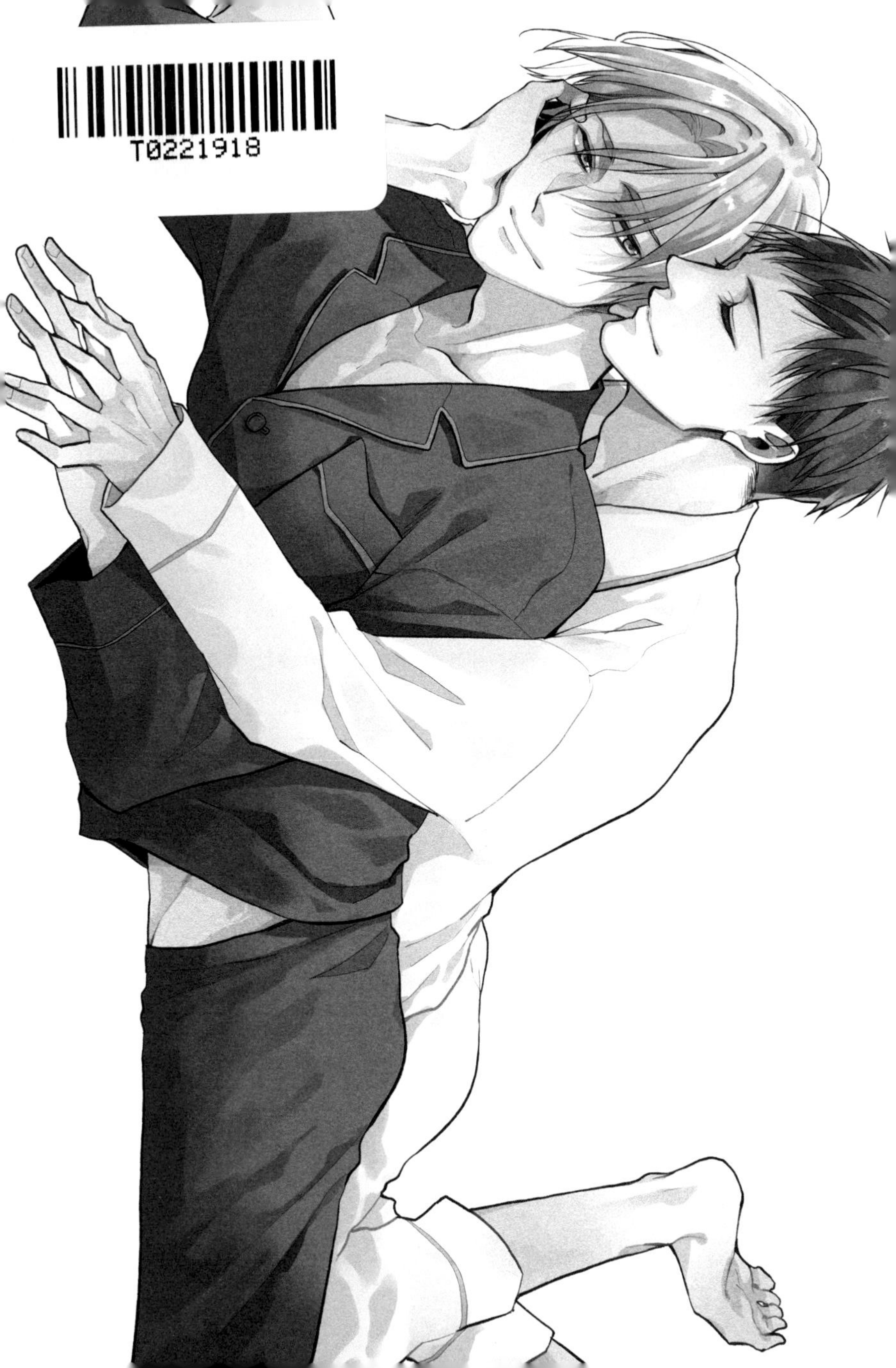

Contents

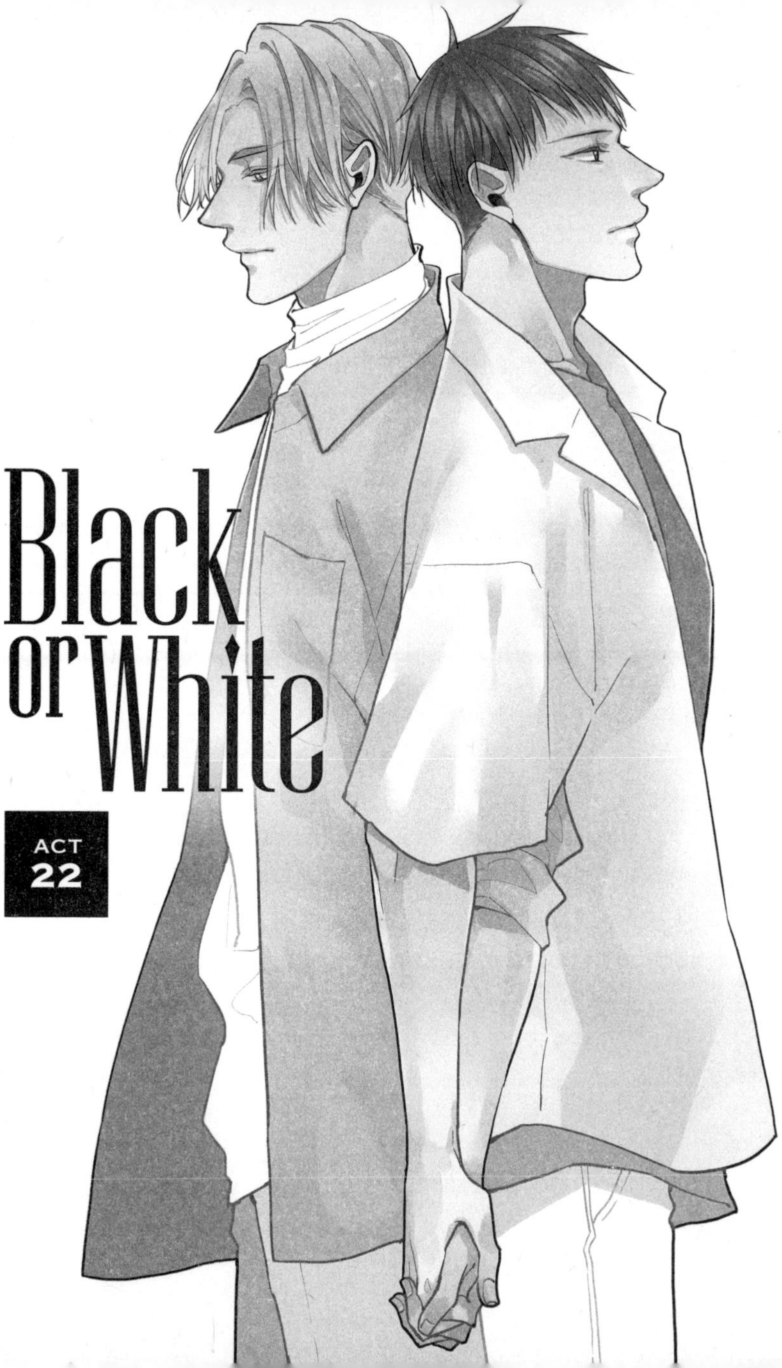
Black or White
ACT 22

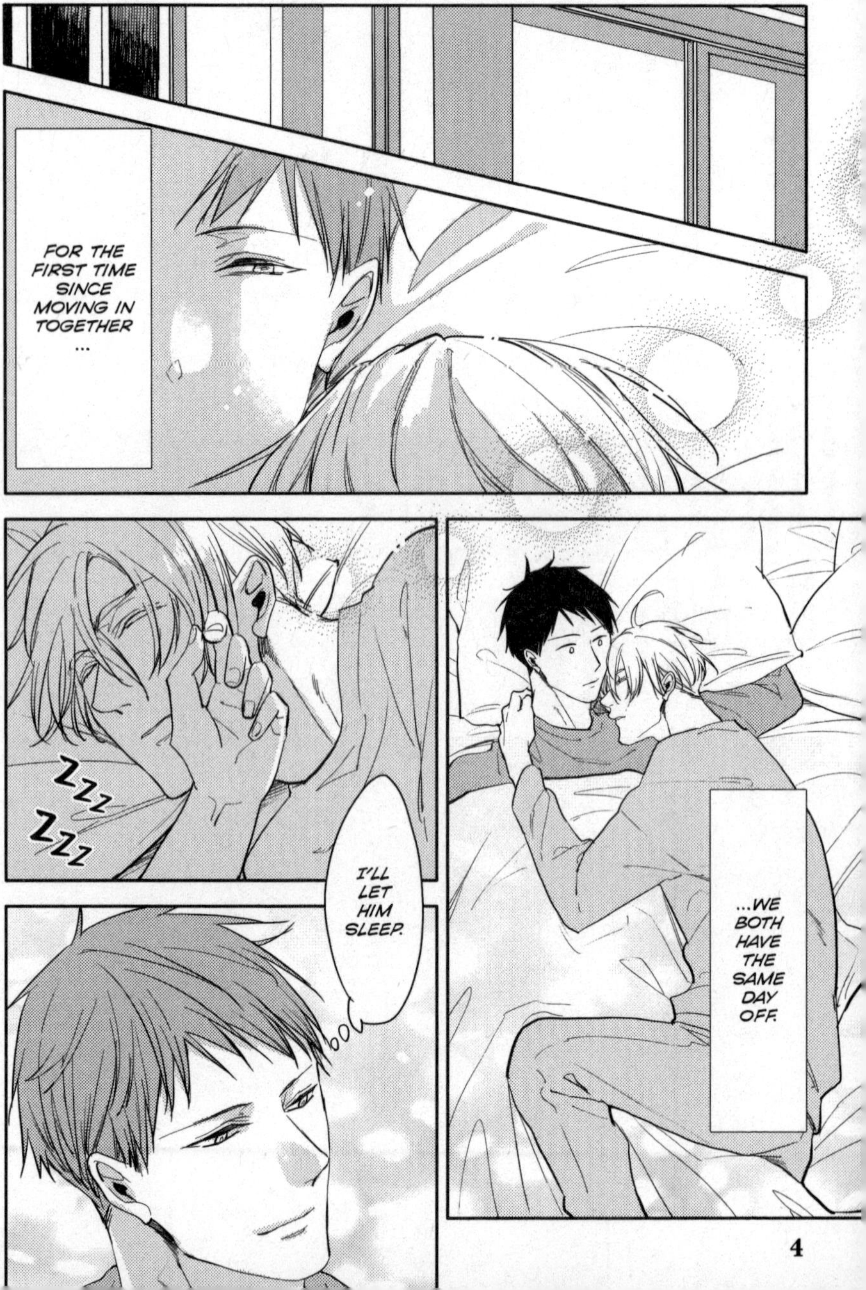
FOR THE FIRST TIME SINCE MOVING IN TOGETHER...
...WE BOTH HAVE THE SAME DAY OFF.
ZZZ
ZZZ
I'LL LET HIM SLEEP.

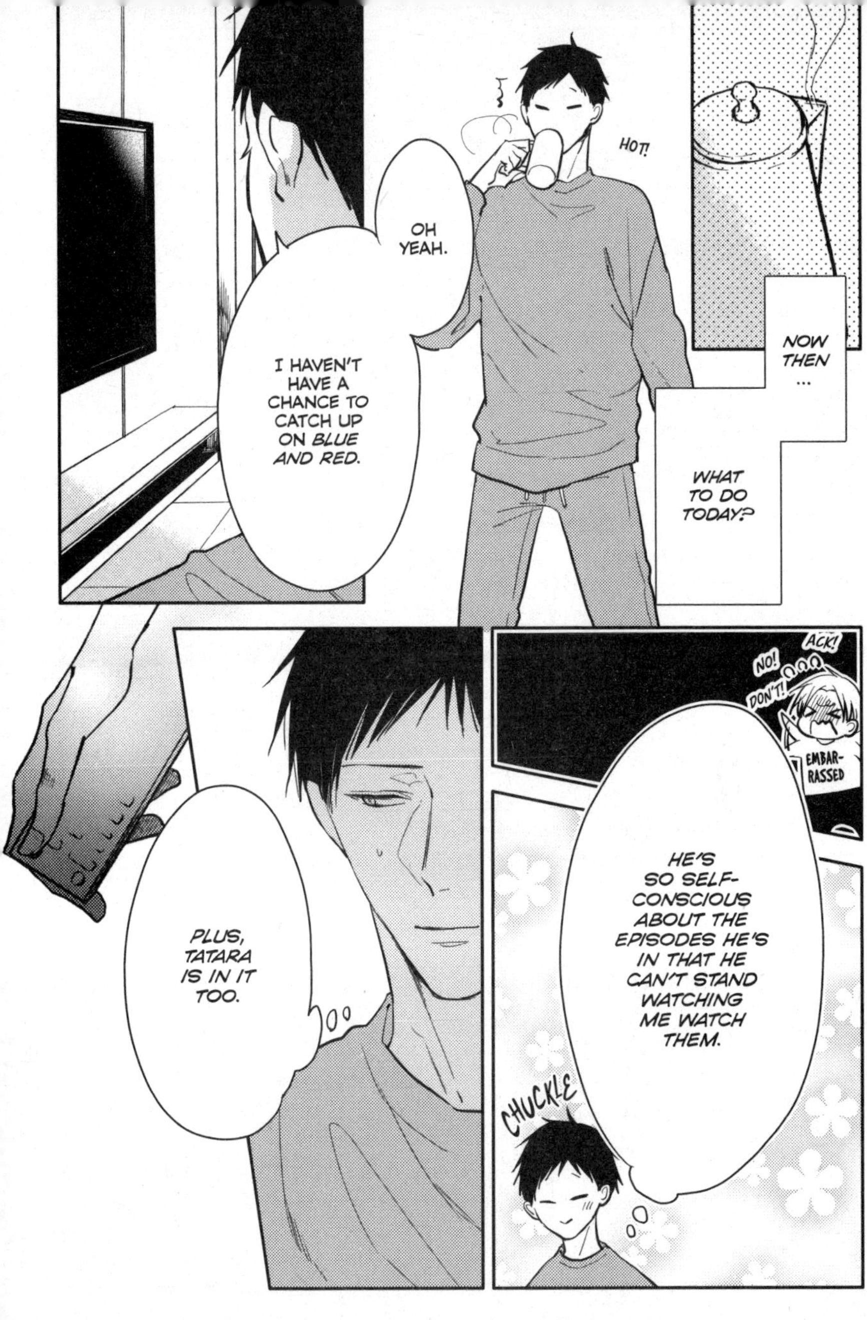
HOT!
NOW THEN ...
WHAT TO DO TODAY?
OH YEAH.
I HAVEN'T HAVE A CHANCE TO CATCH UP ON *BLUE AND RED.*
ACK!
NO! DON'T!
EMBARRASSED
HE'S SO SELF-CONSCIOUS ABOUT THE EPISODES HE'S IN THAT HE CAN'T STAND WATCHING ME WATCH THEM.
CHUCKLE
PLUS, TATARA IS IN IT TOO.

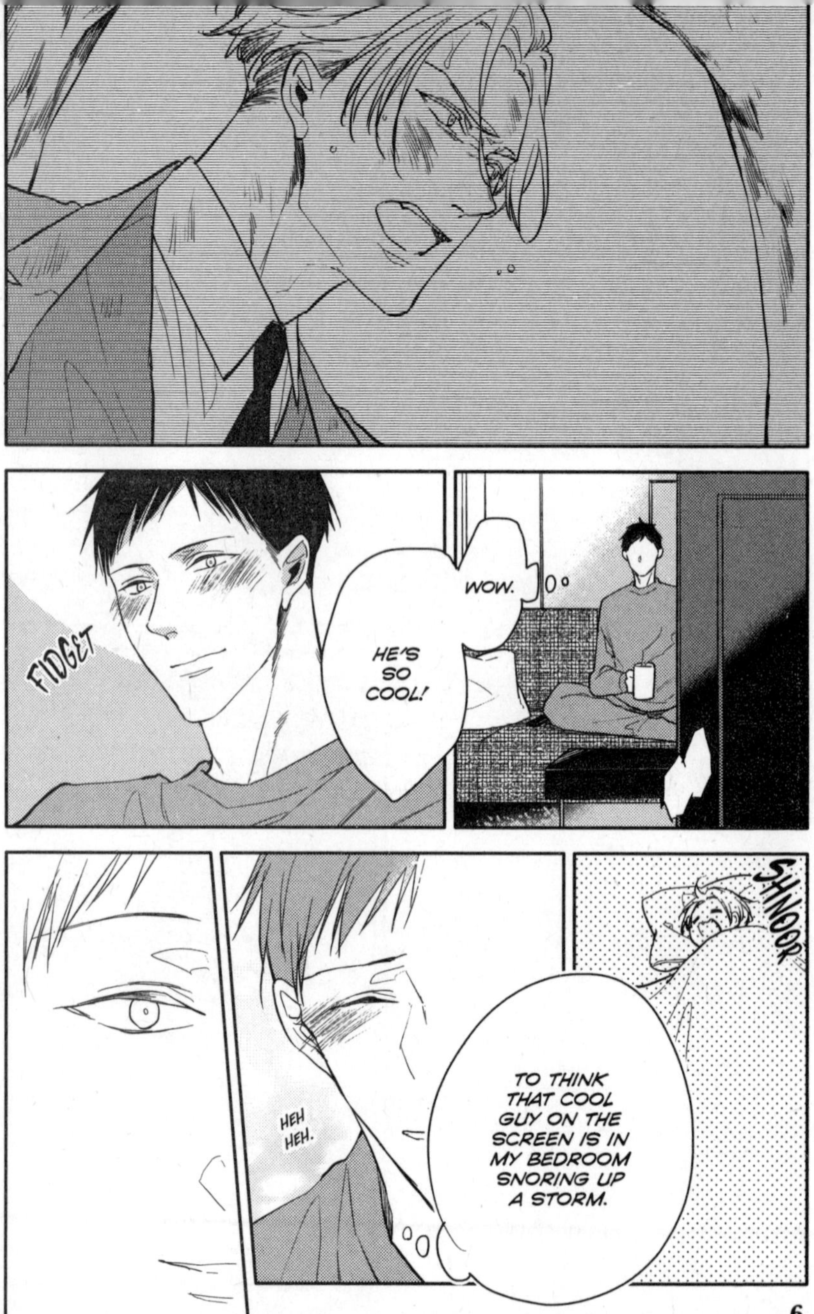
WOW.
HE'S SO COOL!
FIDGET
SHNOOR
TO THINK THAT COOL GUY ON THE SCREEN IS IN MY BEDROOM SNORING UP A STORM.
HEH HEH.

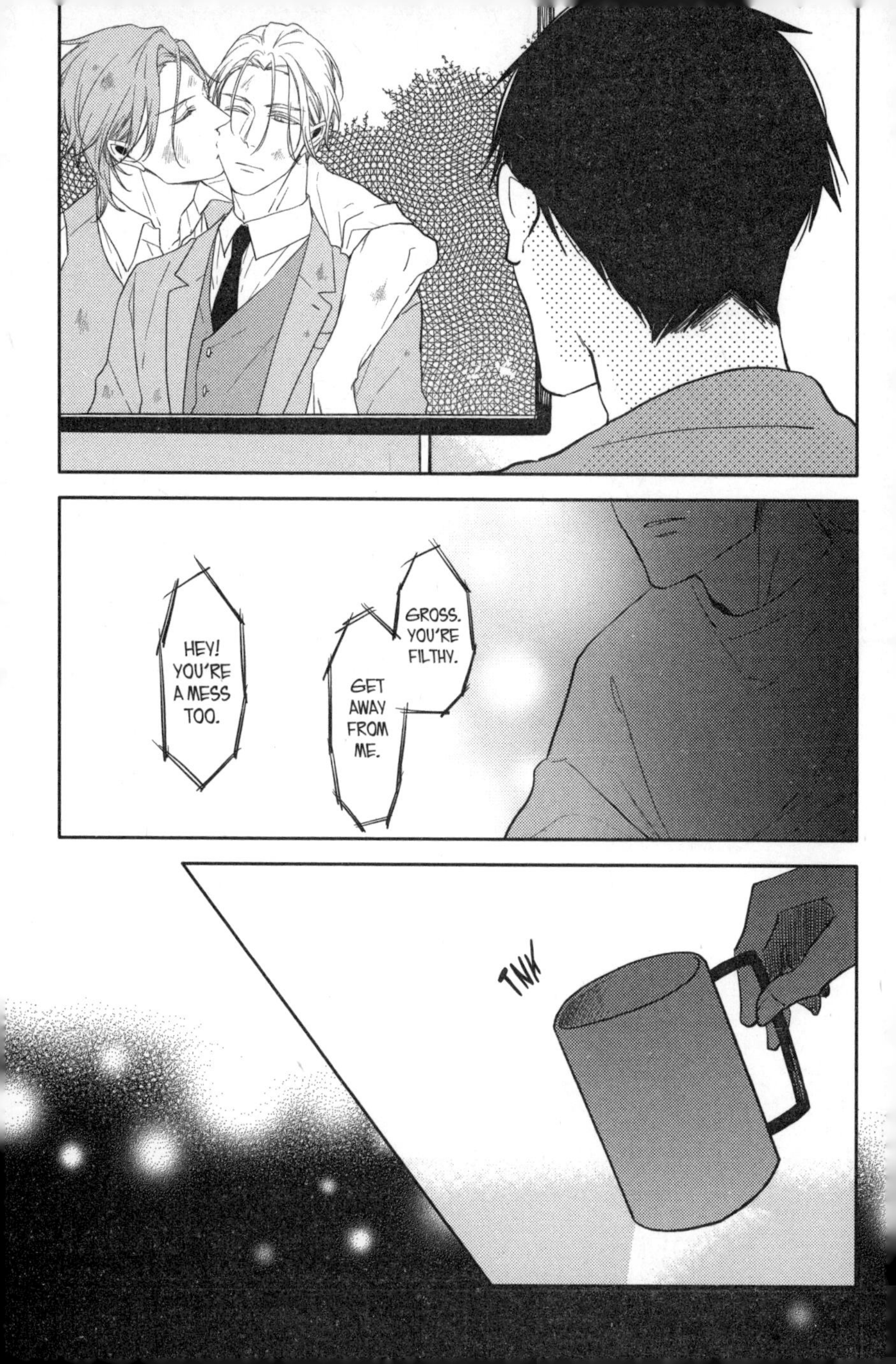
GROSS. YOU'RE FILTHY.
GET AWAY FROM ME.
HEY! YOU'RE A MESS TOO.
TNK

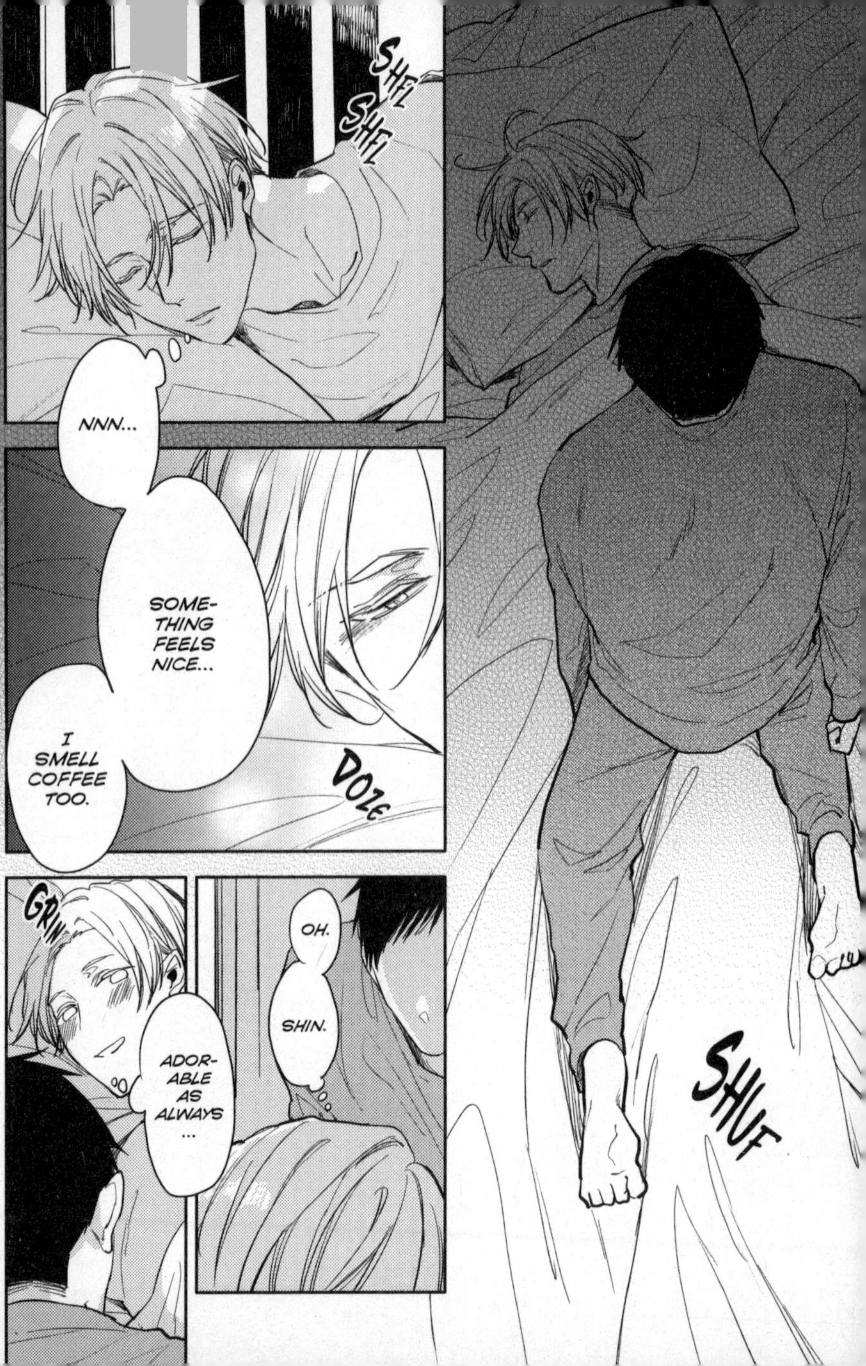
SHUF
SHEL SHEL
NNN...
SOME-THING FEELS NICE...
I SMELL COFFEE TOO.
DOZE
OH.
SHIN.
GRIN
ADORABLE AS ALWAYS...

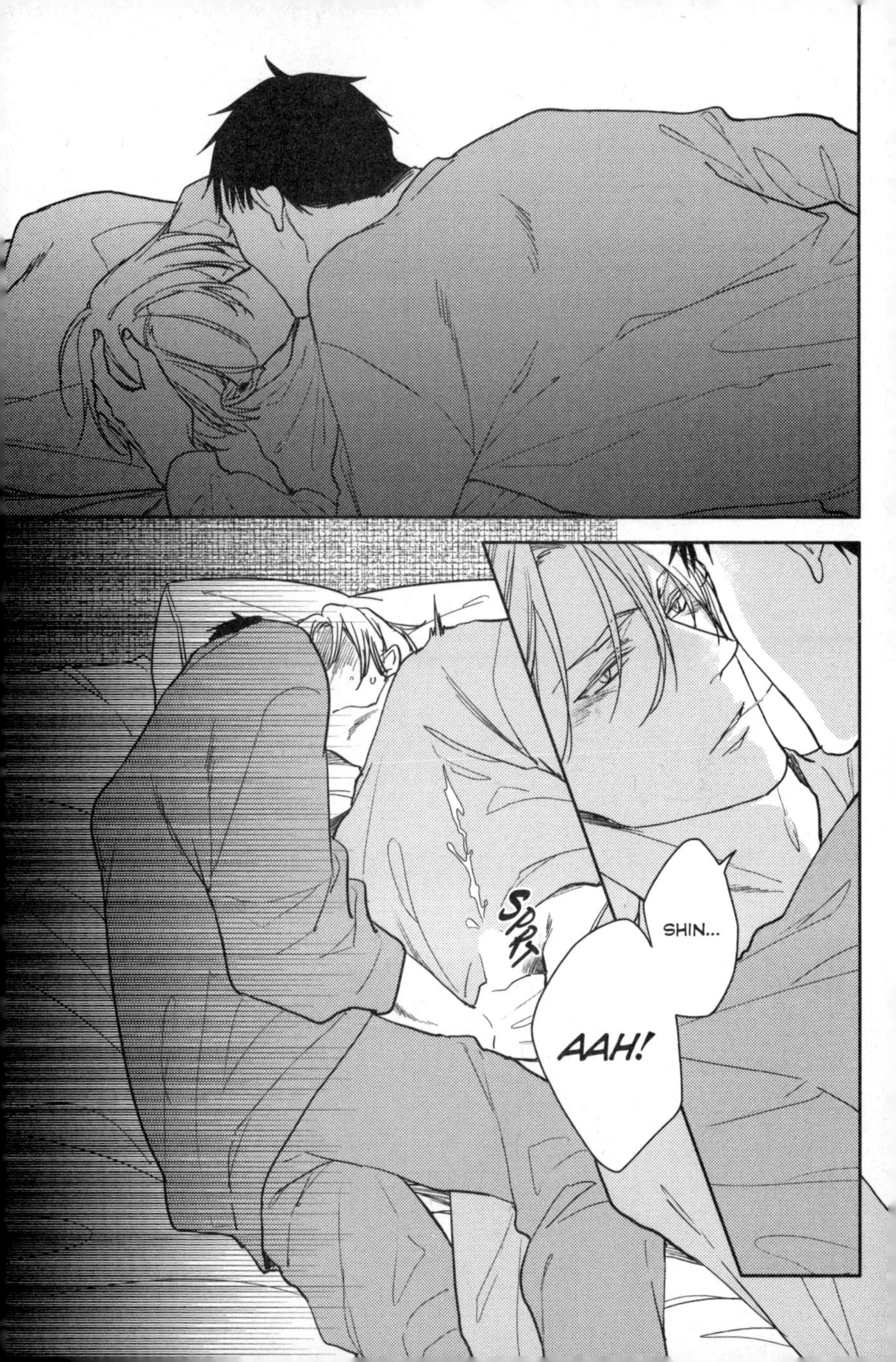
SPRT
SHIN...
AAH!

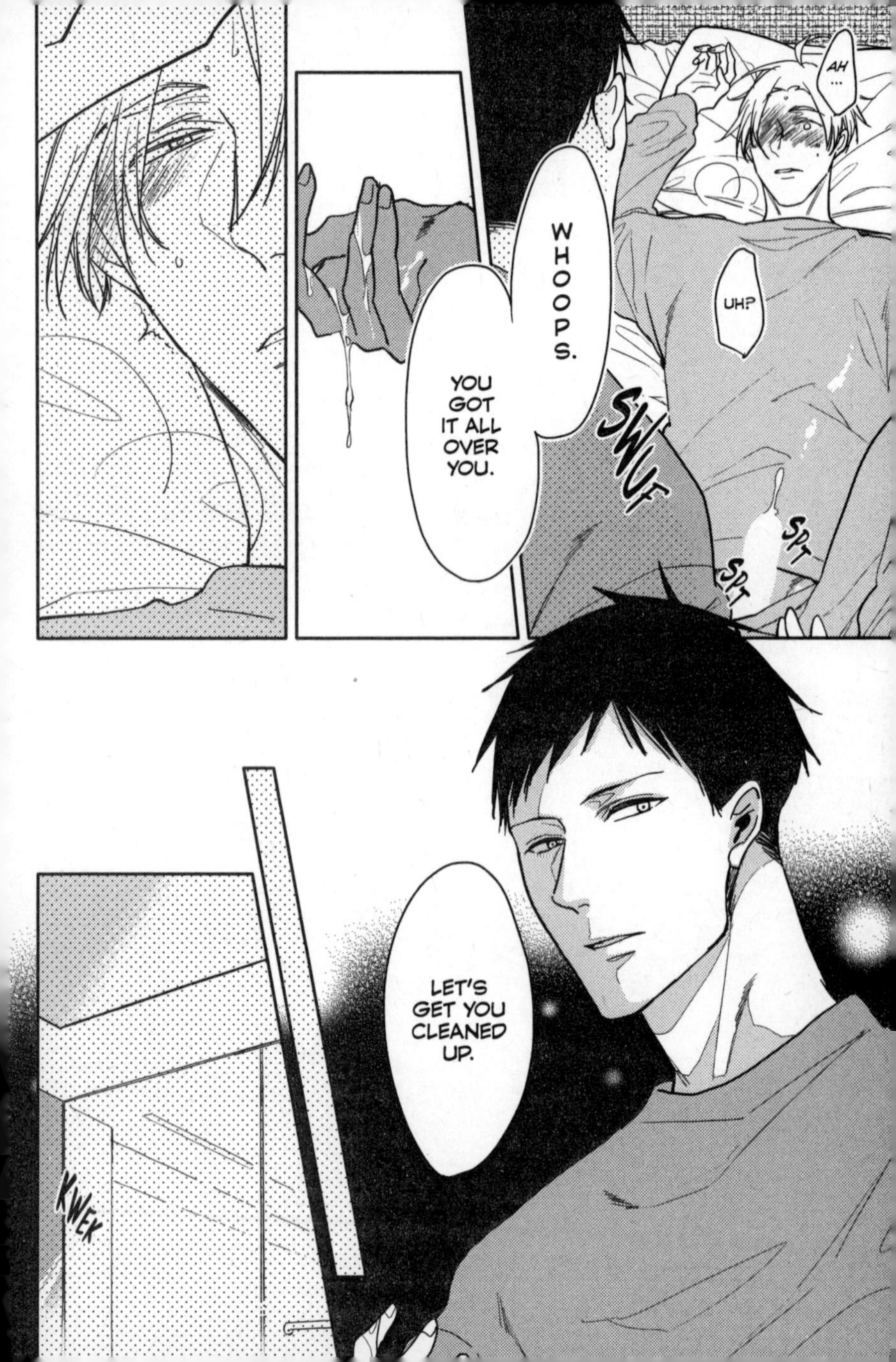
AH ...
UH?
WHOOPS.
YOU GOT IT ALL OVER YOU.
SWUF
SPT
SPT
LET'S GET YOU CLEANED UP.
KWEK

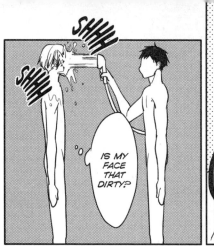

SHHH

SHHH

IS MY FACE THAT DIRTY?

SHHH

BLRPH.

HA HA.

IS THIS OUR FIRST TIME TAKING A MORNING SHOWER TOGETHER?

NOT THAT WE HAVEN'T ALREADY DONE SOME SERIOUSLY SEXY STUFF IN HERE.

KTNK

PLIP

PLIP

YEAH.

SHUK

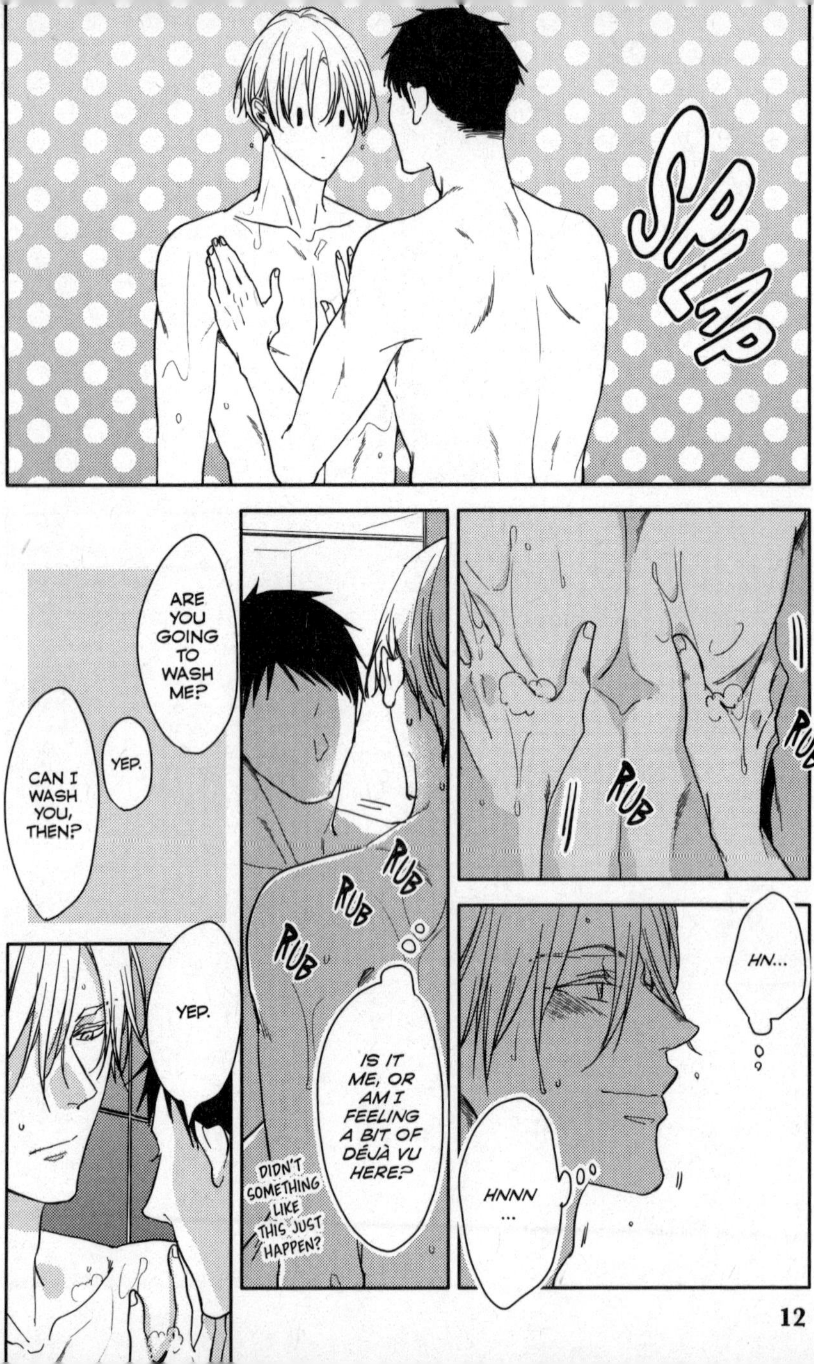
SPLAP
RUB
RUB
HN...
HNNN...
ARE YOU GOING TO WASH ME?
YEP.
RUB
RUB
RUB
IS IT ME, OR AM I FEELING A BIT OF DÉJÀ VU HERE?
DIDN'T SOMETHING LIKE THIS JUST HAPPEN?
CAN I WASH YOU, THEN?
YEP.

THRB

THRB

I KNOW IT HAPPENS ALL THE TIME, BUT...

OKAY.

FUF

...

...

FUF

FUF

IT'S A LITTLE EMBARRASSING THAT I'M ROCK HARD ALREADY.

BUT...

FUF

RUB

RUB

RUB

FUF

RUB

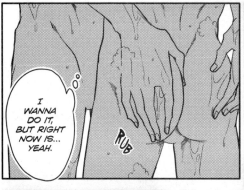

I WANNA DO IT, BUT RIGHT NOW IS... YEAH.

RUB

THIS IS NICE.

FUF

FWUF

FUF

FWUF

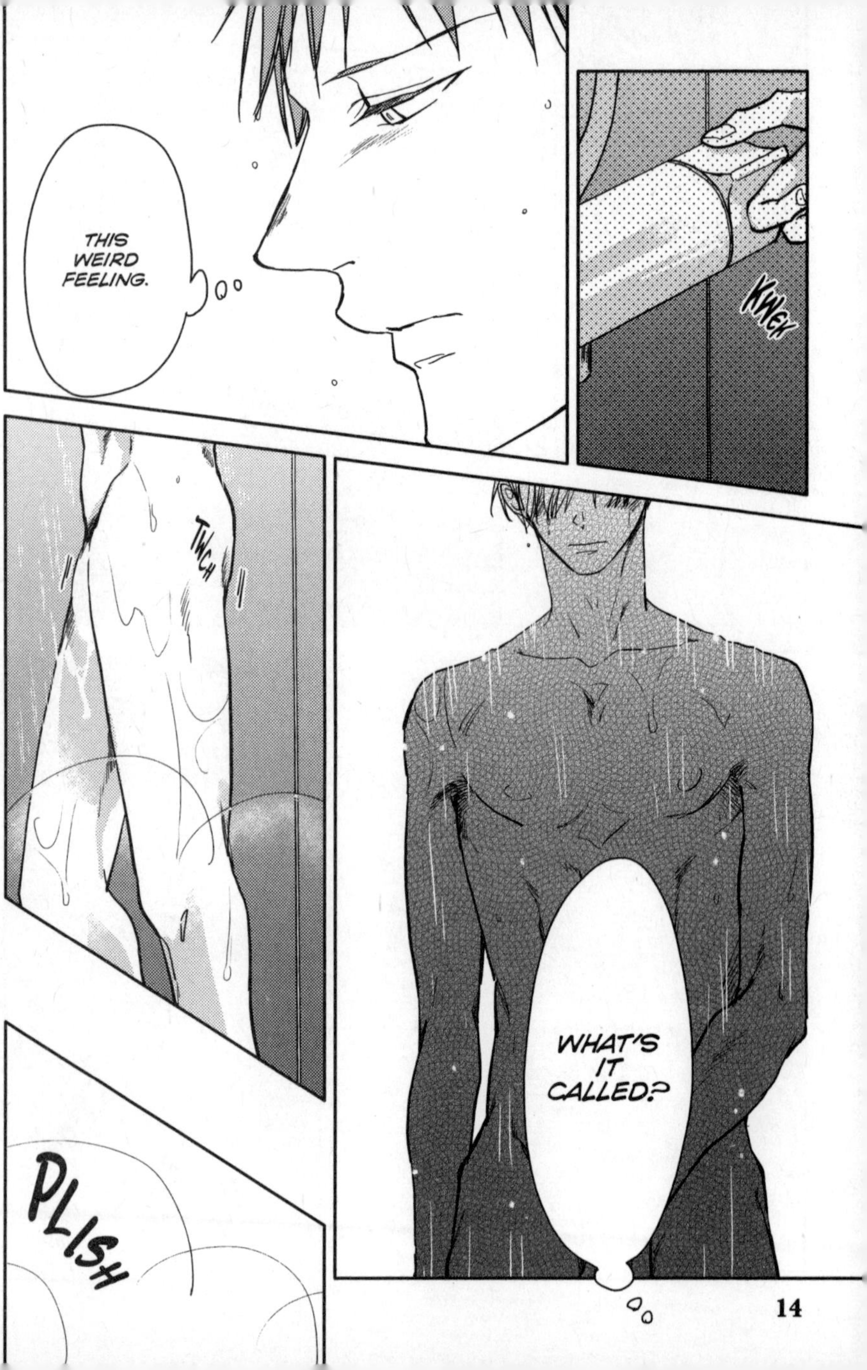
KWEK
THIS WEIRD FEELING.
WHAT'S IT CALLED?
TWCH
PLISH

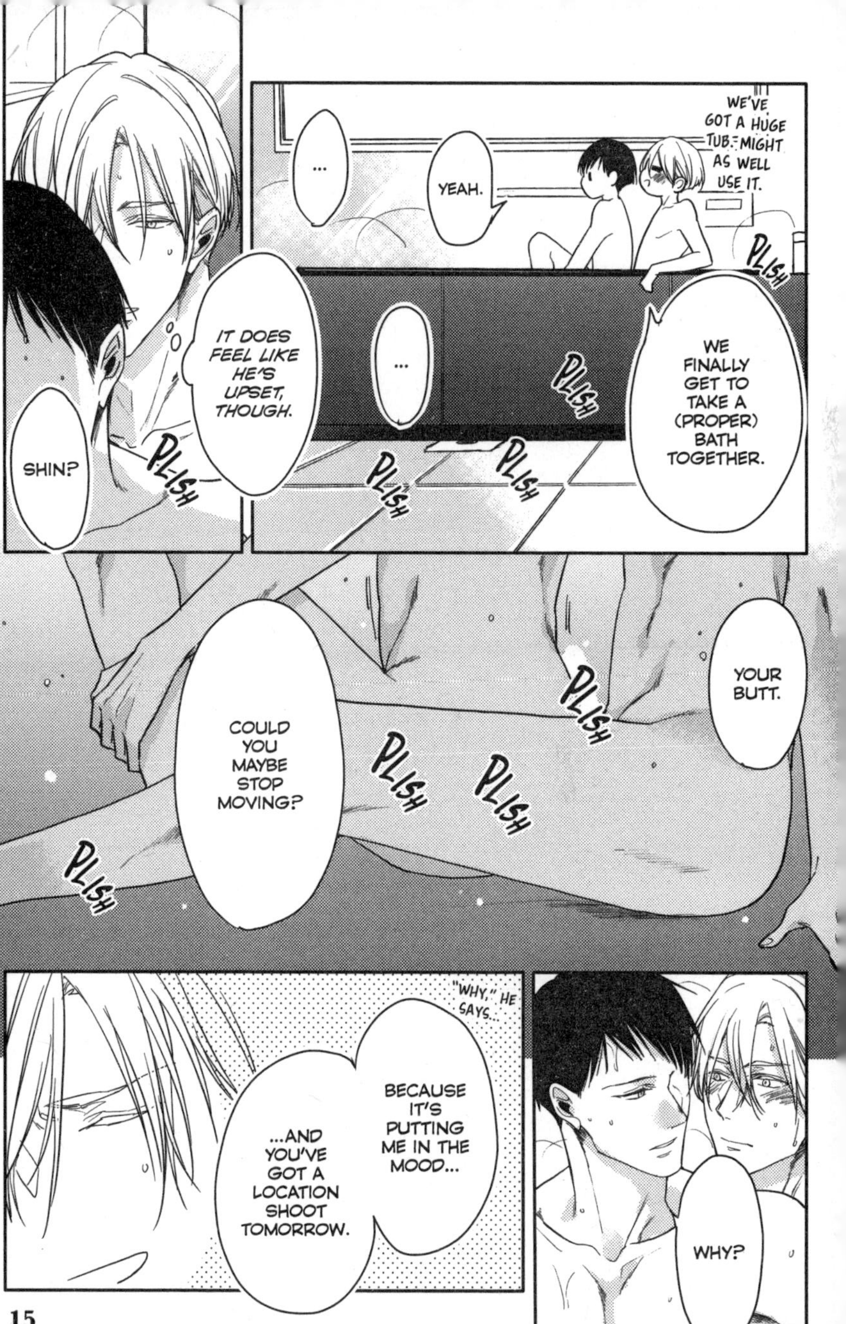
WE'VE GOT A HUGE TUB. MIGHT AS WELL USE IT.
PLISH
WE FINALLY GET TO TAKE A (PROPER) BATH TOGETHER.
YEAH.
...
PLISH
PLISH
PLISH
...
IT DOES FEEL LIKE HE'S UPSET, THOUGH.
PLISH
SHIN?
YOUR BUTT.
PLISH
PLISH
PLISH
COULD YOU MAYBE STOP MOVING?
PLISH
WHY?
"WHY," HE SAYS...
BECAUSE IT'S PUTTING ME IN THE MOOD...
...AND YOU'VE GOT A LOCATION SHOOT TOMORROW.

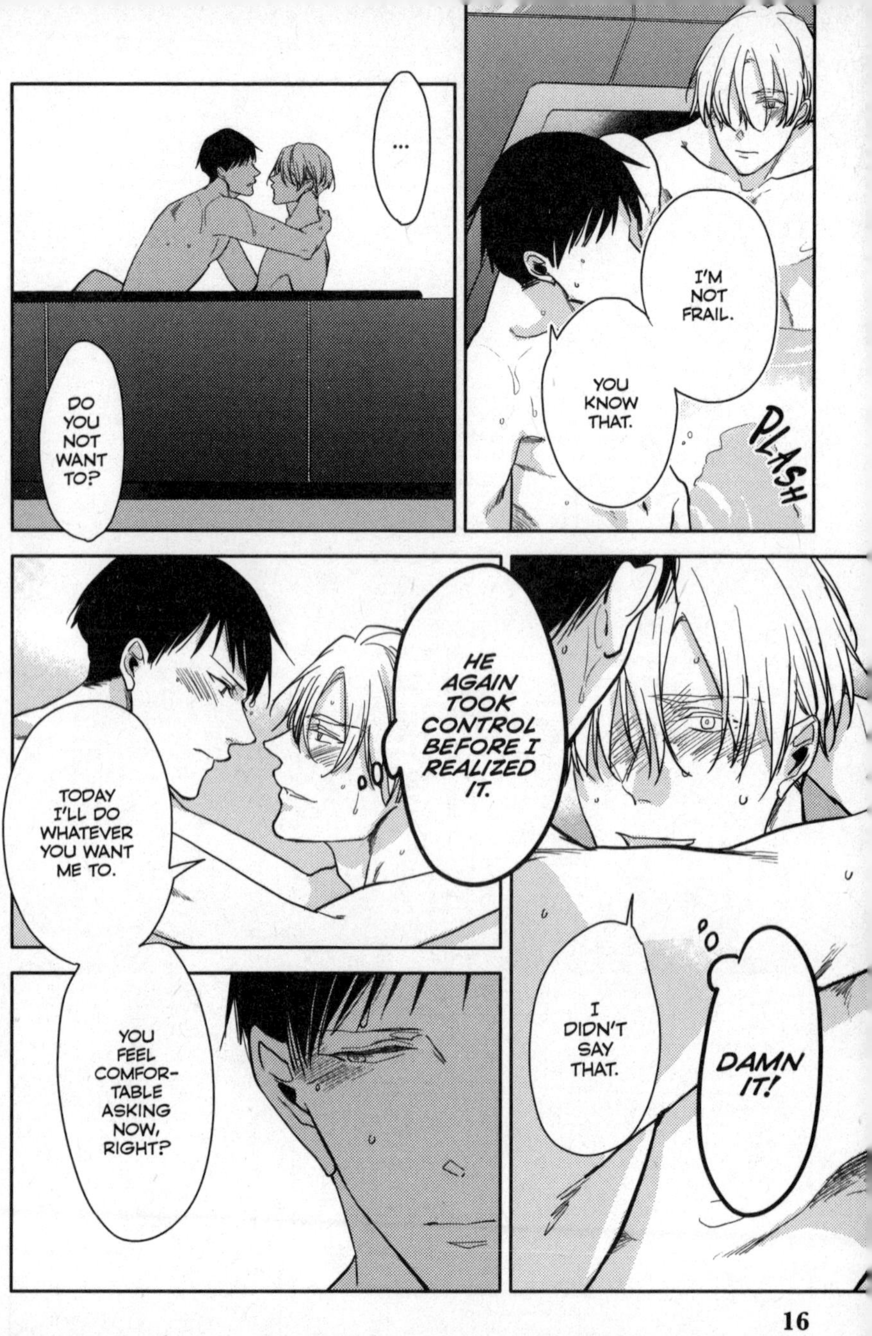
I'M NOT FRAIL.
YOU KNOW THAT.
PLASH
...
DO YOU NOT WANT TO?
DAMN IT!
I DIDN'T SAY THAT.
HE AGAIN TOOK CONTROL BEFORE I REALIZED IT.
TODAY I'LL DO WHATEVER YOU WANT ME TO.
YOU FEEL COMFORTABLE ASKING NOW, RIGHT?

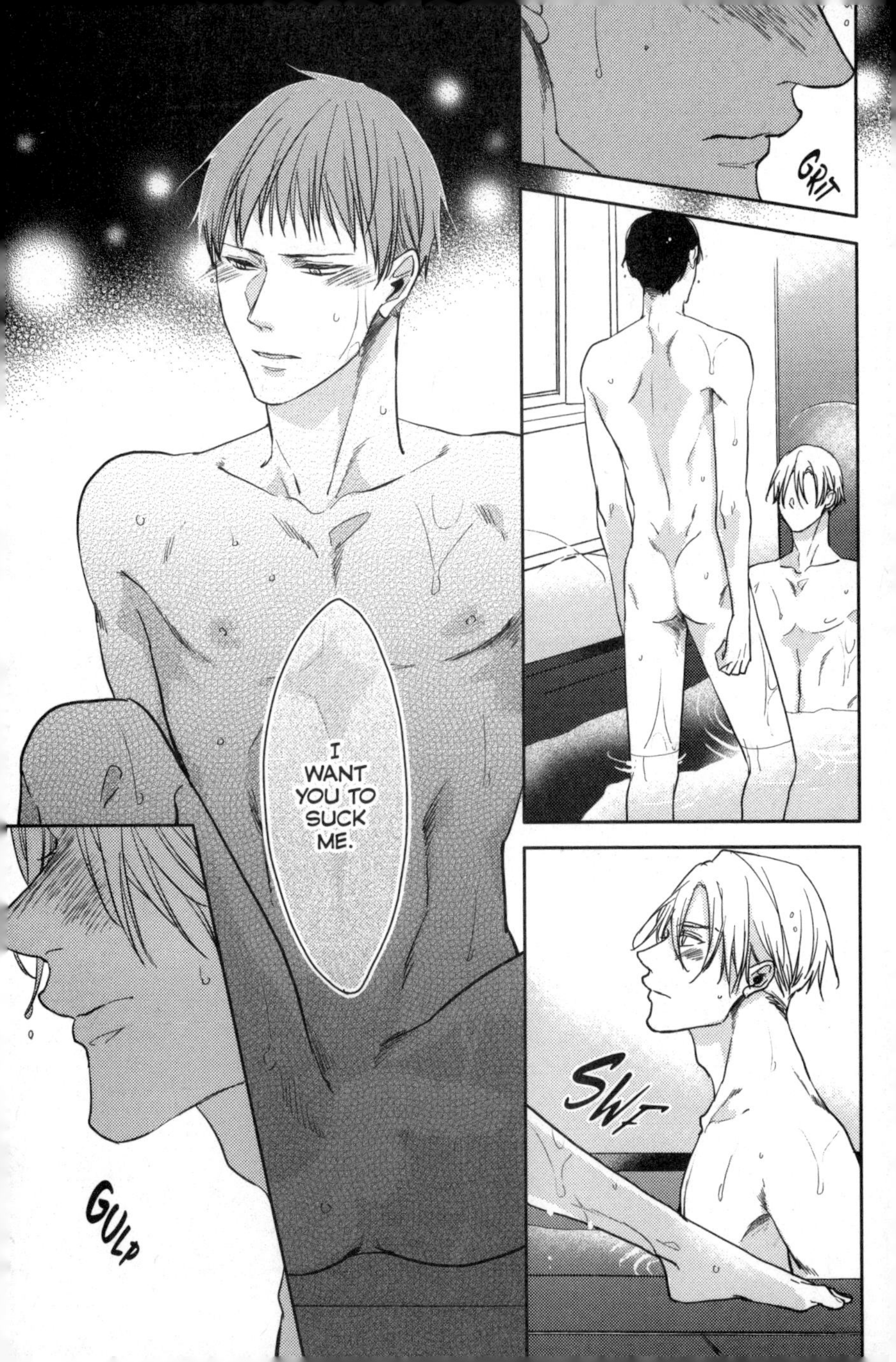
GRIT
SWF
I WANT YOU TO SUCK ME.
GULP

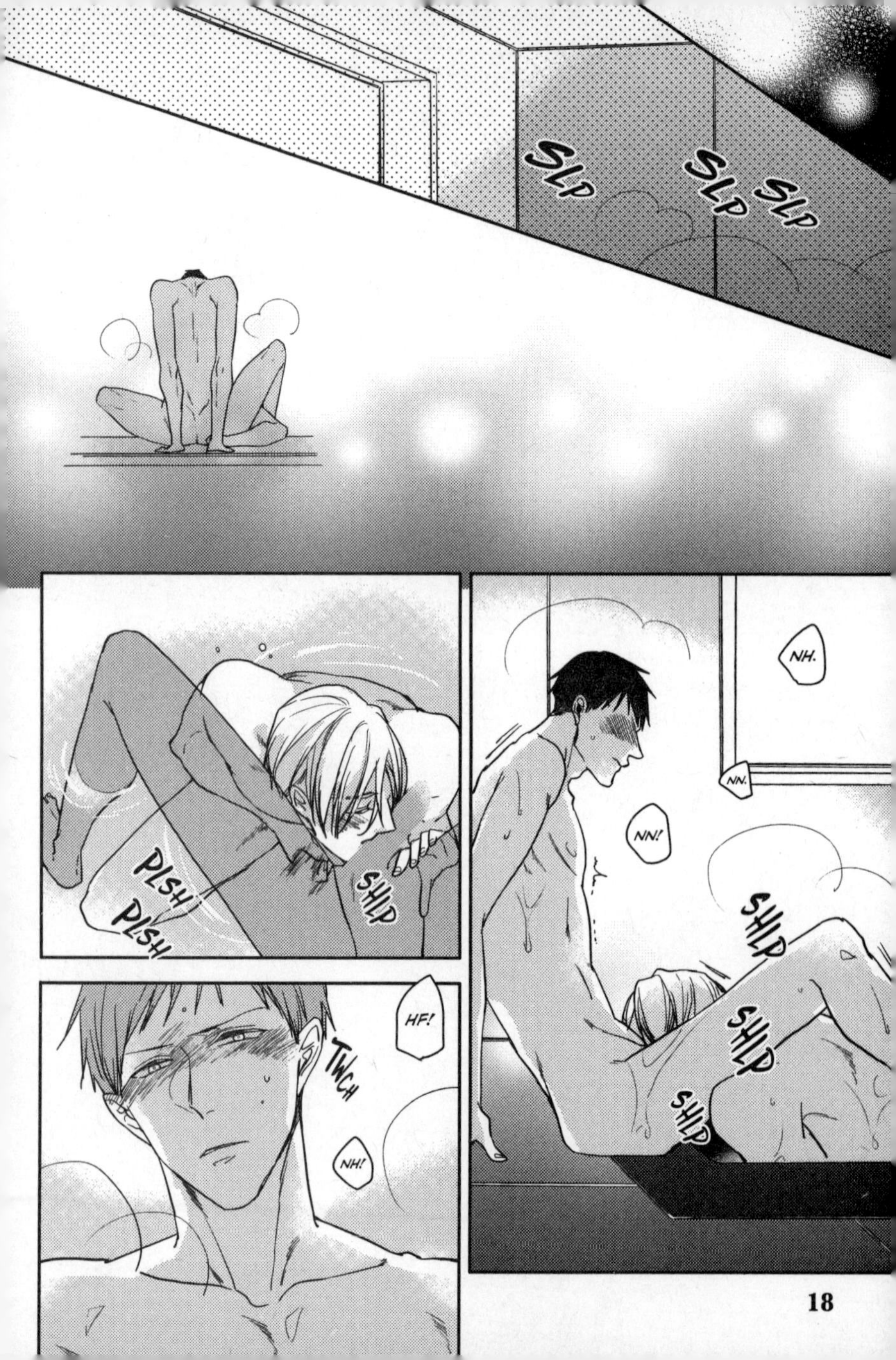
SLP
SLP
SLP
NH.
NN.
NN!
SHLP
SHLP
SHLP
PLSH
PLSH
SHLP
HF!
TWCH
NH!

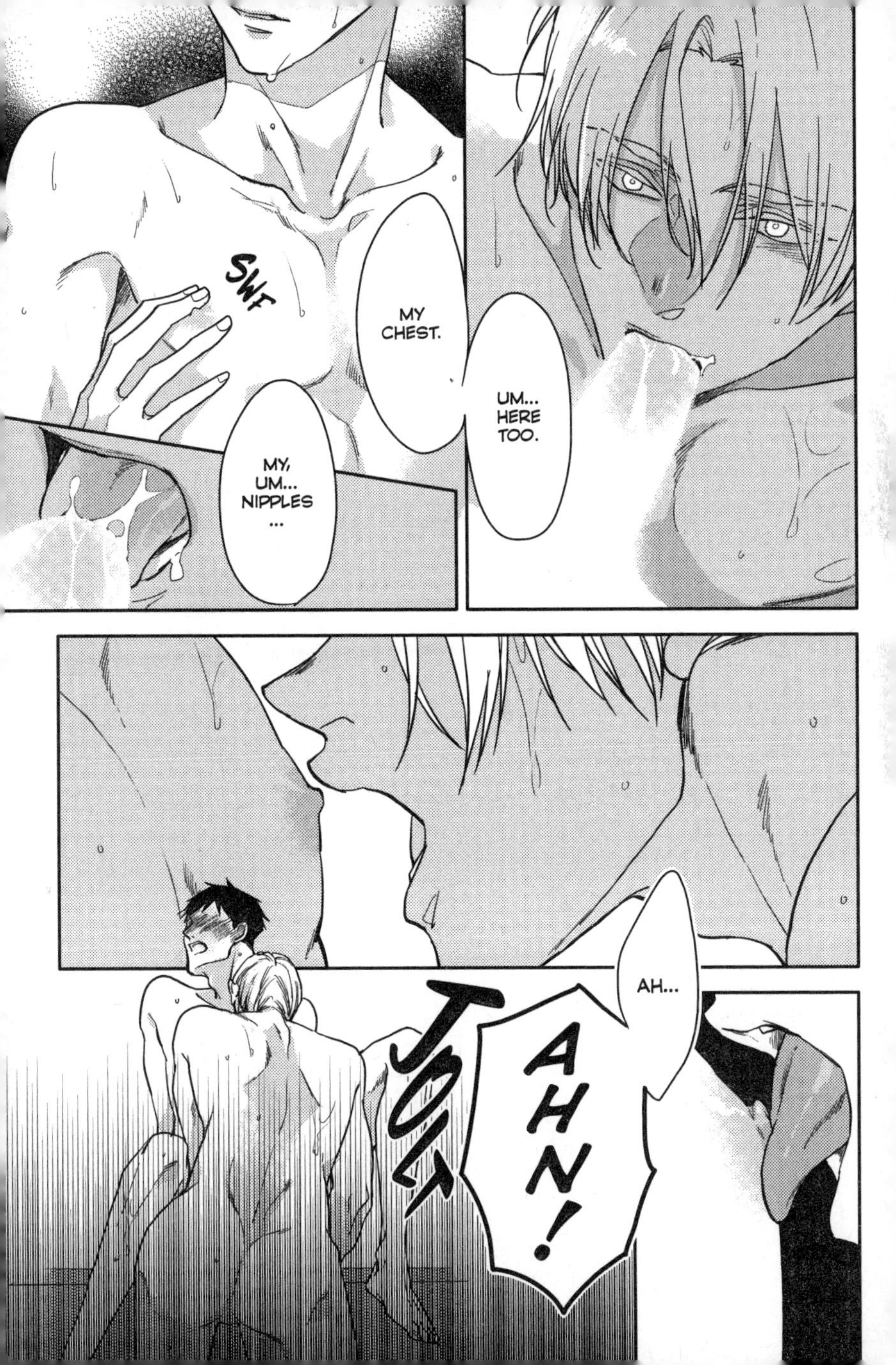
UM... HERE TOO.
MY CHEST.
SWF
MY, UM... NIPPLES ...
AH...
AHN!
JOLT

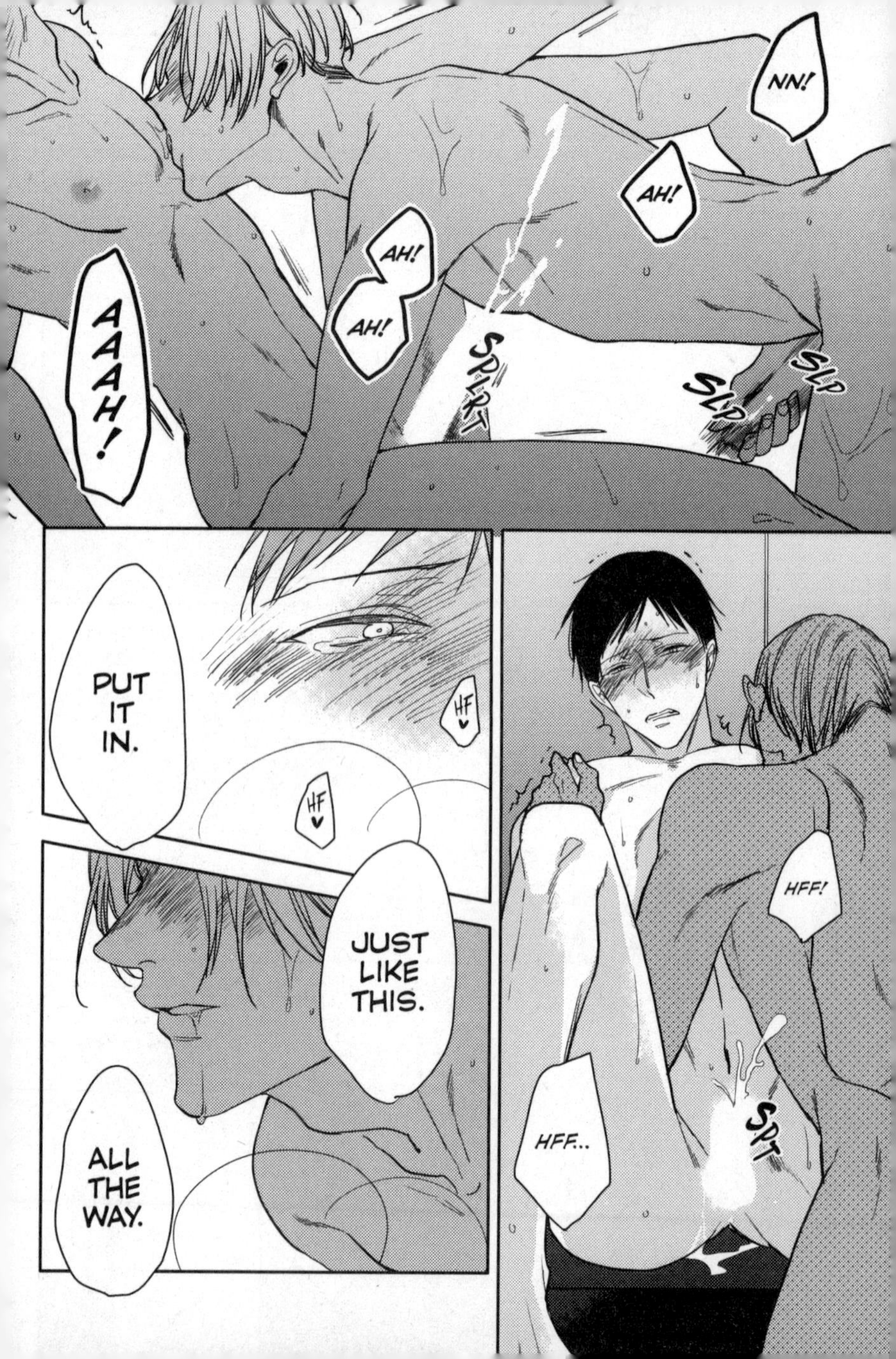
NN!
AH!
AH!
AH!
AAAAH!
SPLRT
SLP
SLP
HFF!
SPT
HFF...
HF
HF
PUT IT IN.
JUST LIKE THIS.
ALL THE WAY.

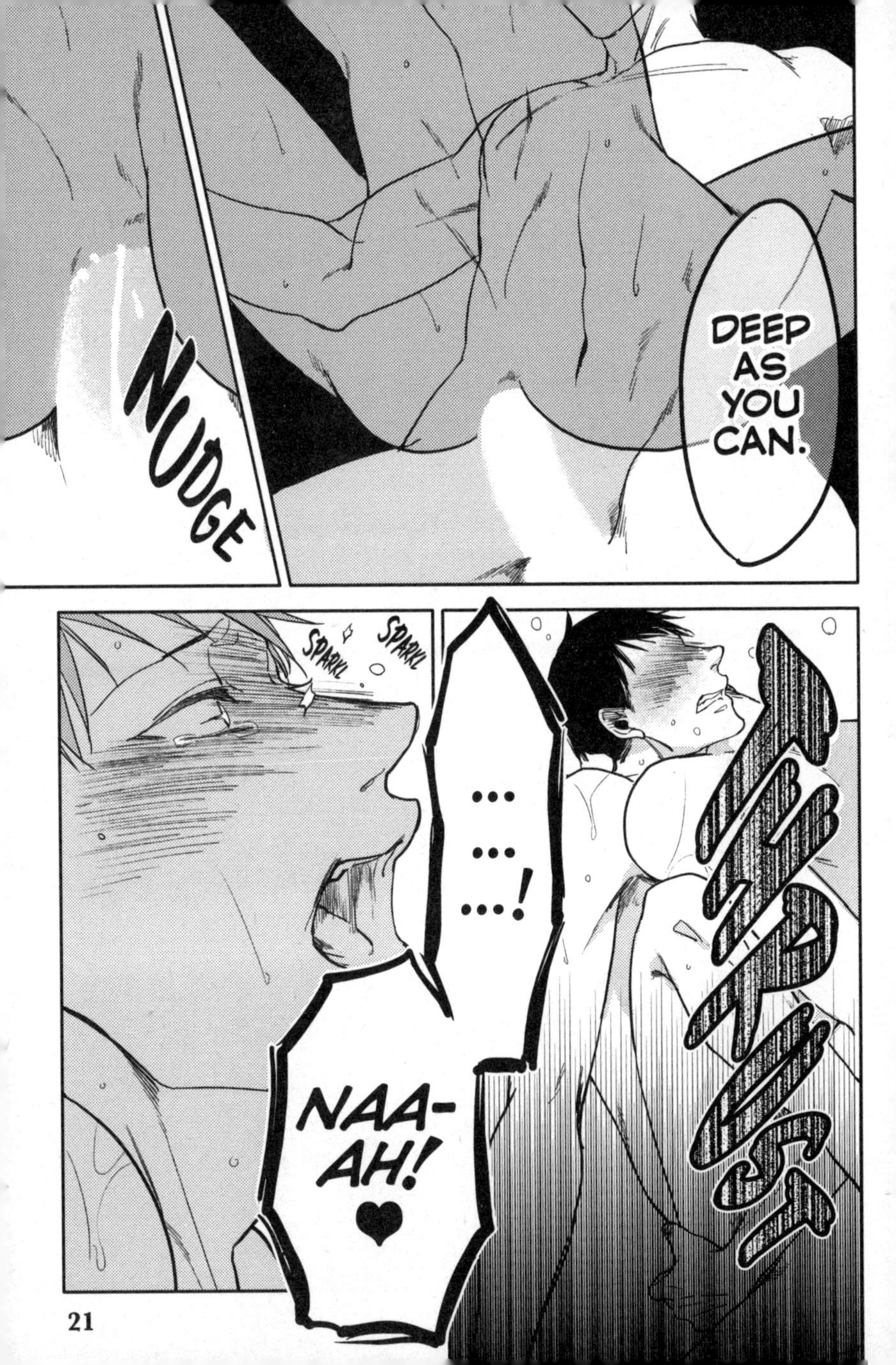
DEEP AS YOU CAN.
NUDGE
THRUST
SPARKL
SPARKL
... ...!
NAA-AH! ♥

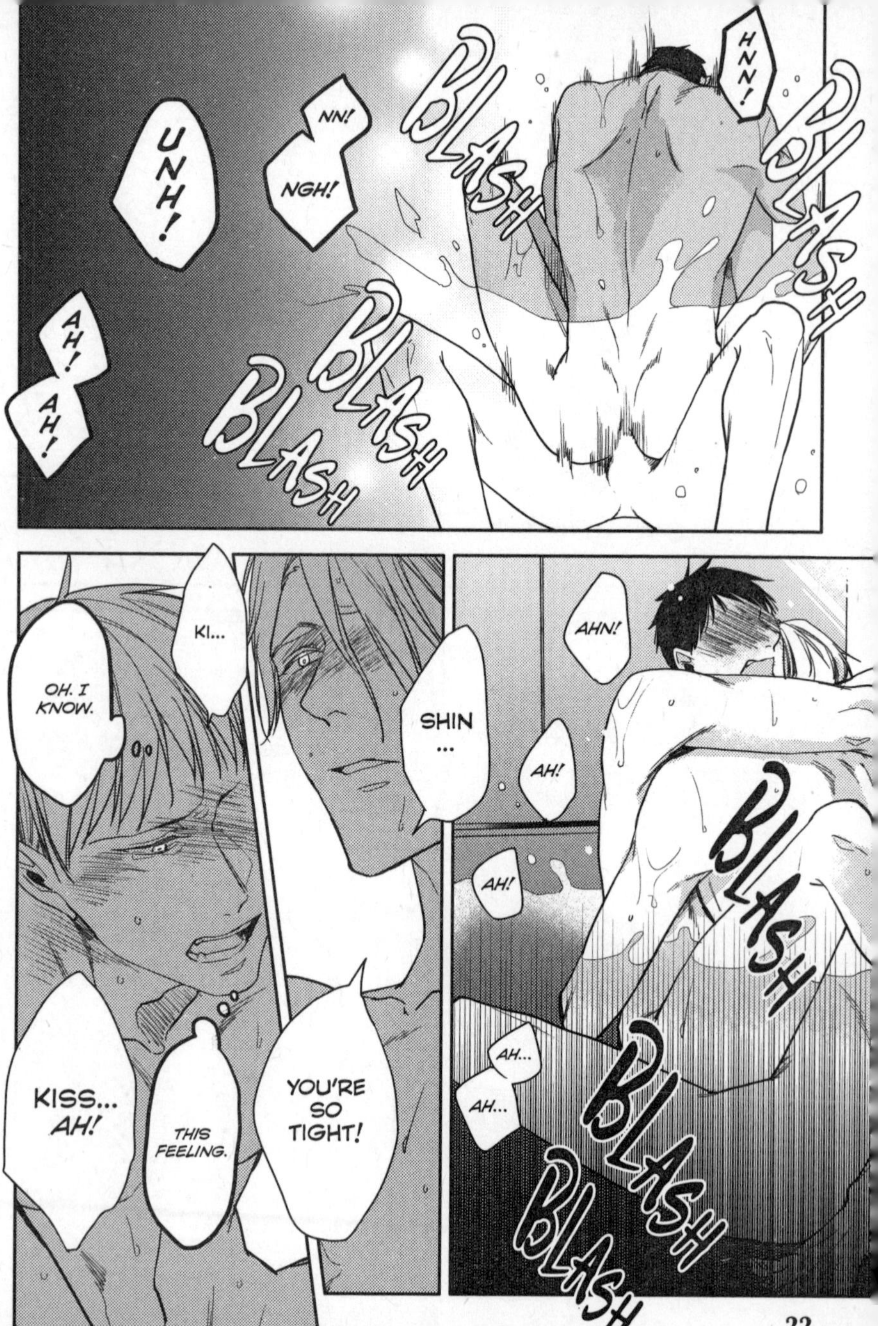
HNN!
BLASH
BLASH
NN! NGH!
UNH!
BLASH
BLASH
AH! AH!
AHN!
AH!
BLASH
AH!
AH... AH...
BLASH
BLASH
BLASH
KI...
SHIN ...
YOU'RE SO TIGHT!
OH. I KNOW.
KISS... AH!
THIS FEELING.

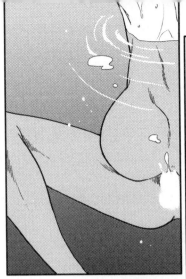

BLASH

IT'S
POSSES-
SIVENESS.

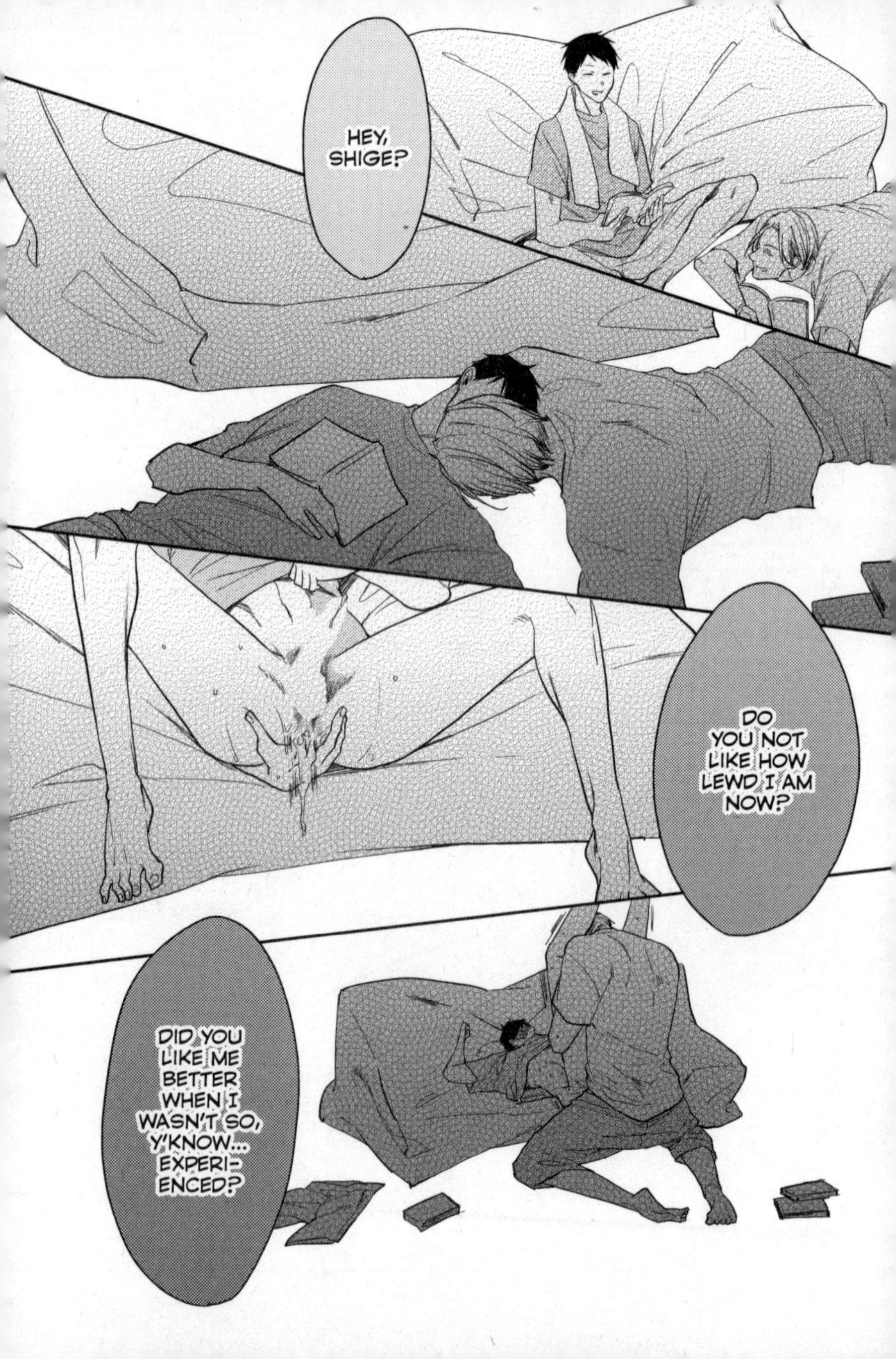
HEY, SHIGE?
DO YOU NOT LIKE HOW LEWD I AM NOW?
DID YOU LIKE ME BETTER WHEN I WASN'T SO, Y'KNOW... EXPERI-ENCED?

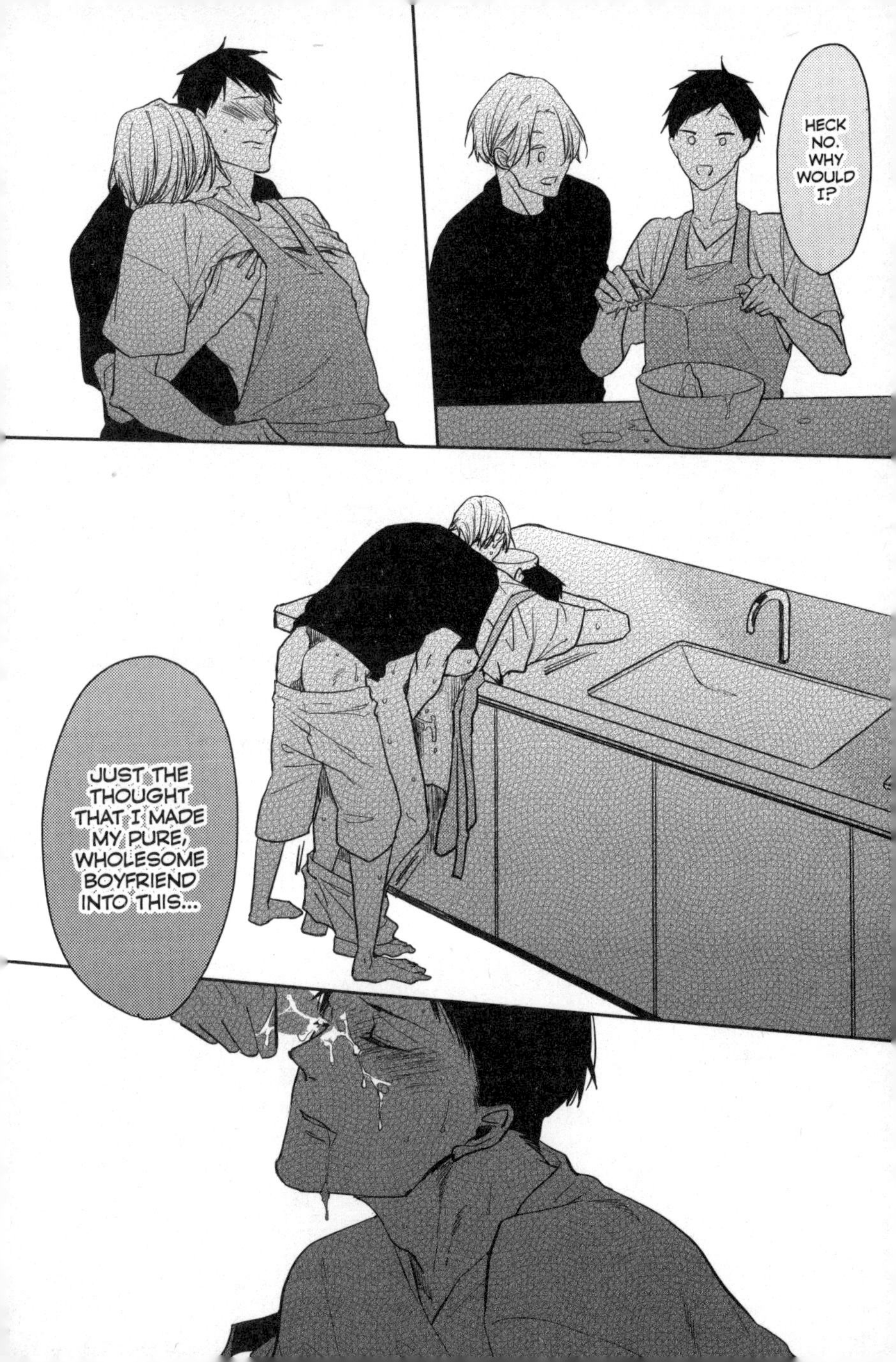
HECK NO. WHY WOULD I?
JUST THE THOUGHT THAT I MADE MY PURE, WHOLESOME BOYFRIEND INTO THIS...

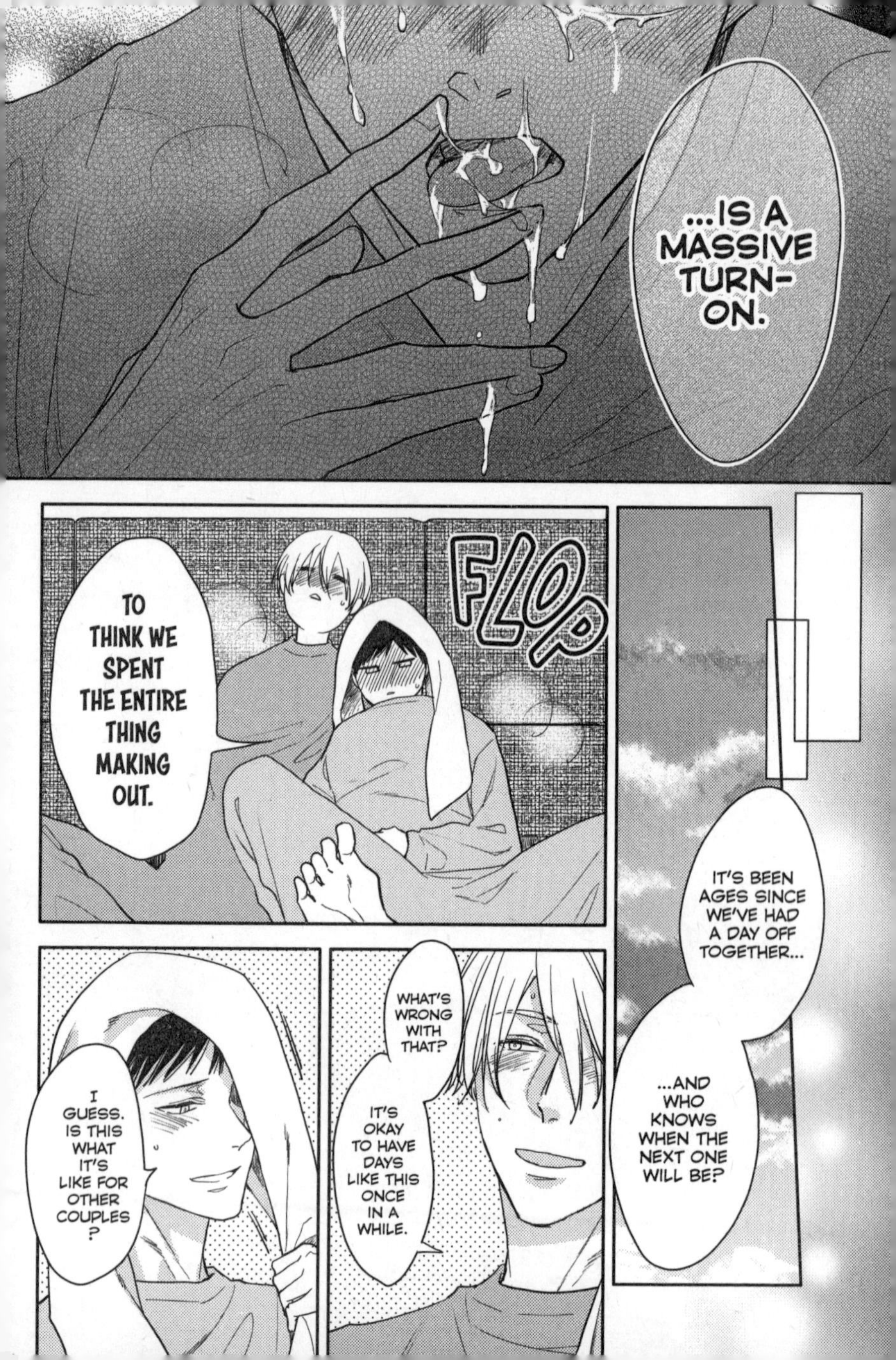
...IS A MASSIVE TURN-ON.
IT'S BEEN AGES SINCE WE'VE HAD A DAY OFF TOGETHER...
...AND WHO KNOWS WHEN THE NEXT ONE WILL BE?
FLOP
TO THINK WE SPENT THE ENTIRE THING MAKING OUT.
WHAT'S WRONG WITH THAT?
IT'S OKAY TO HAVE DAYS LIKE THIS ONCE IN A WHILE.
I GUESS. IS THIS WHAT IT'S LIKE FOR OTHER COUPLES?

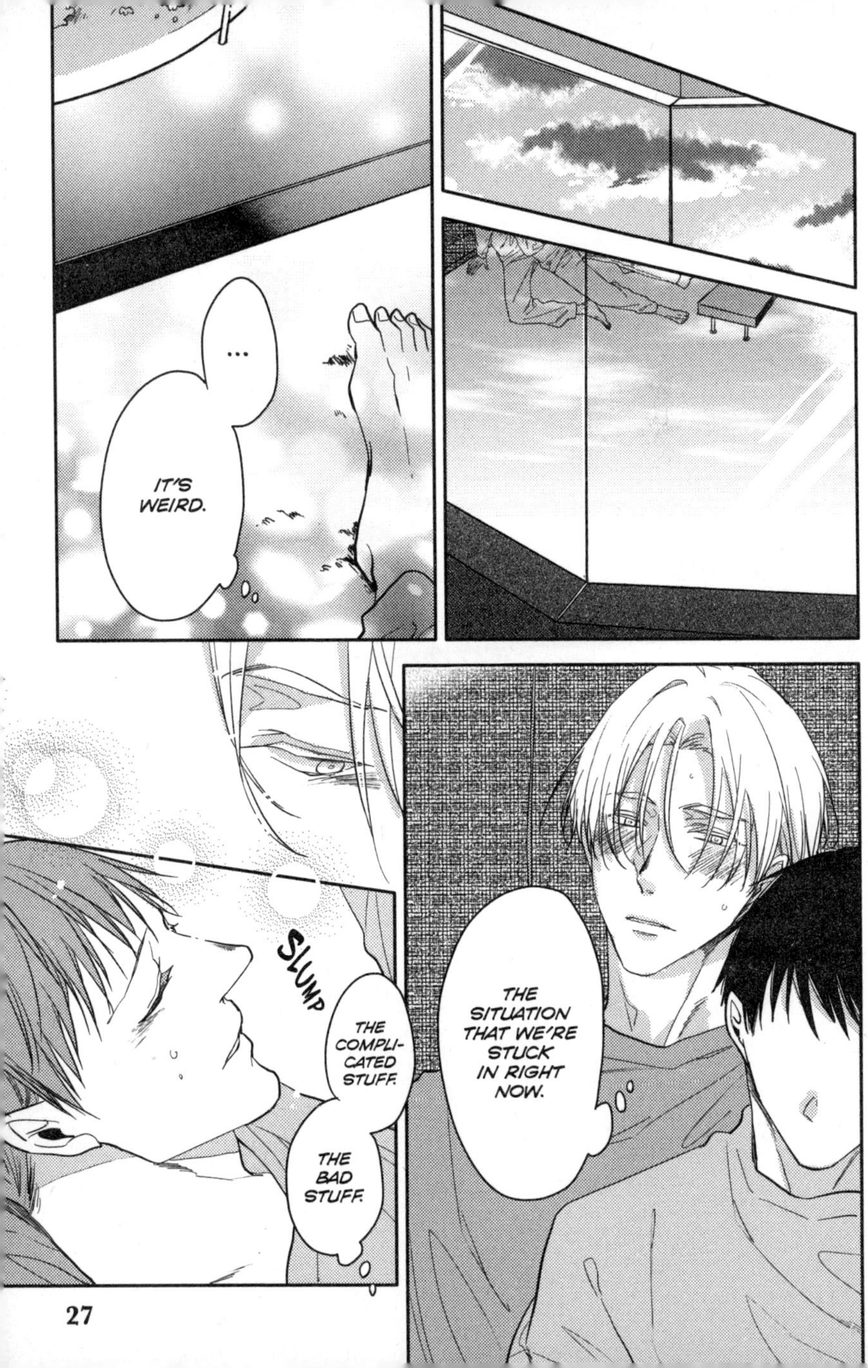
...
IT'S WEIRD.
THE SITUATION THAT WE'RE STUCK IN RIGHT NOW.
SLUMP
THE COMPLICATED STUFF.
THE BAD STUFF.

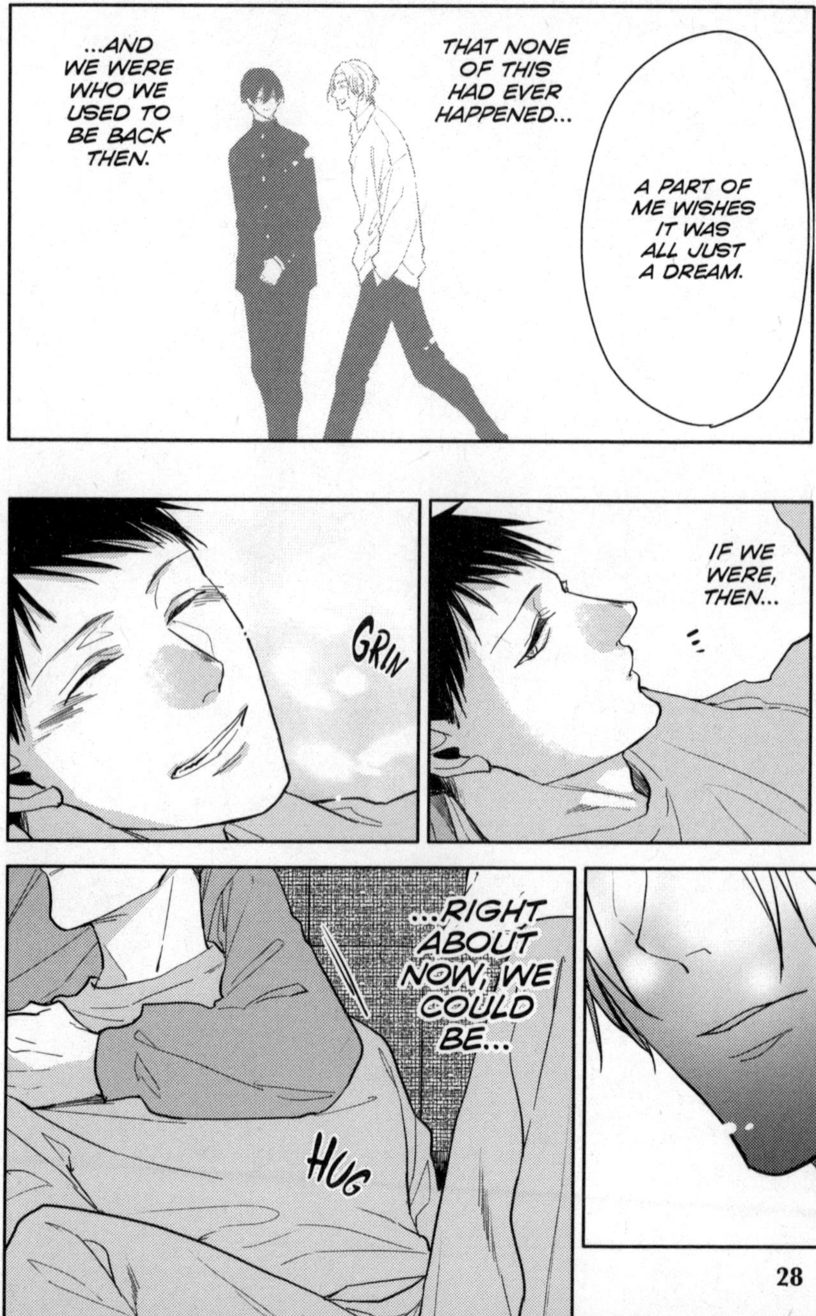
A PART OF ME WISHES IT WAS ALL JUST A DREAM.
THAT NONE OF THIS HAD EVER HAPPENED...
...AND WE WERE WHO WE USED TO BE BACK THEN.
IF WE WERE, THEN...
GRIN
...RIGHT ABOUT NOW, WE COULD BE...
HUG

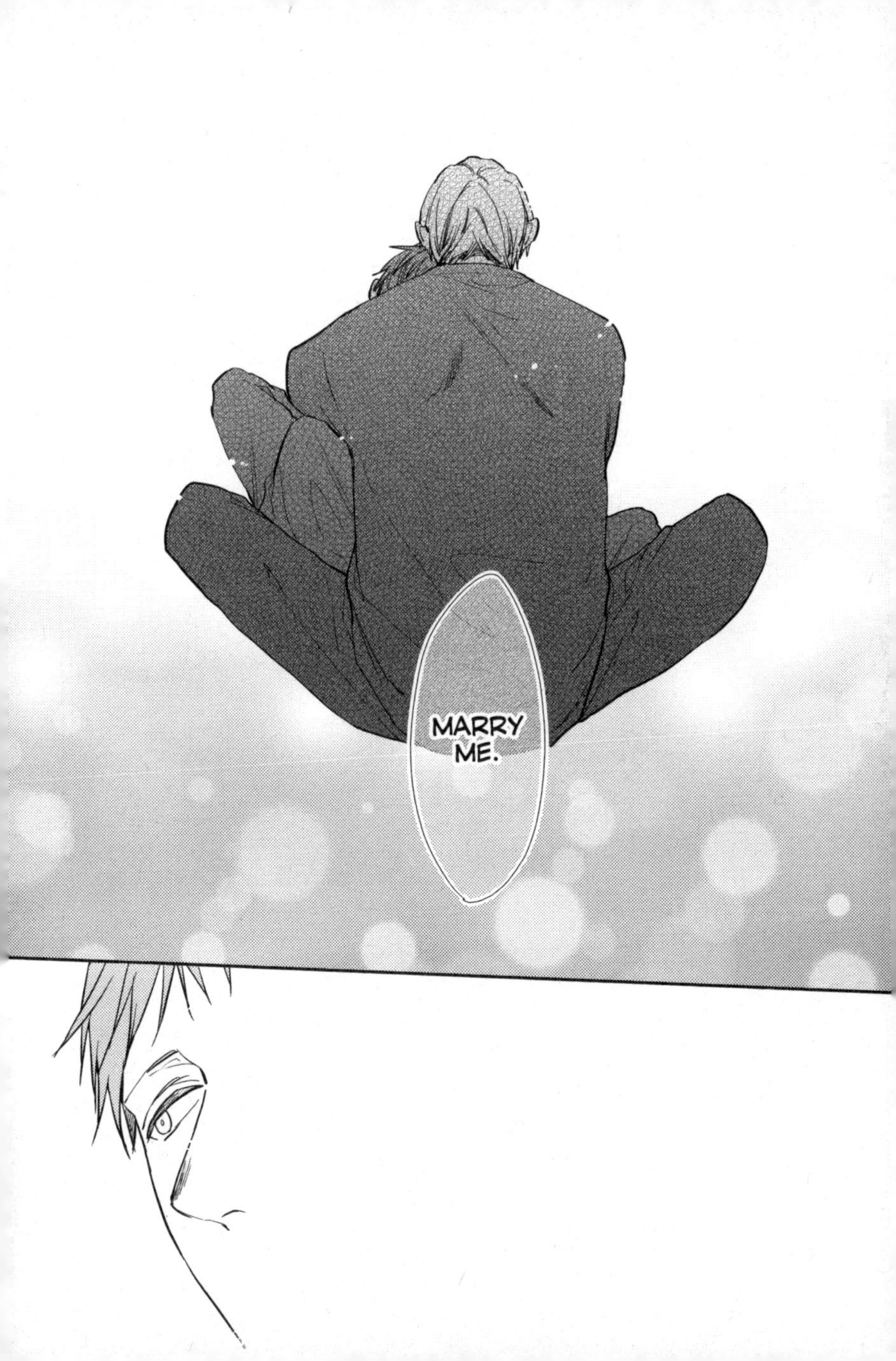
MARRY ME.

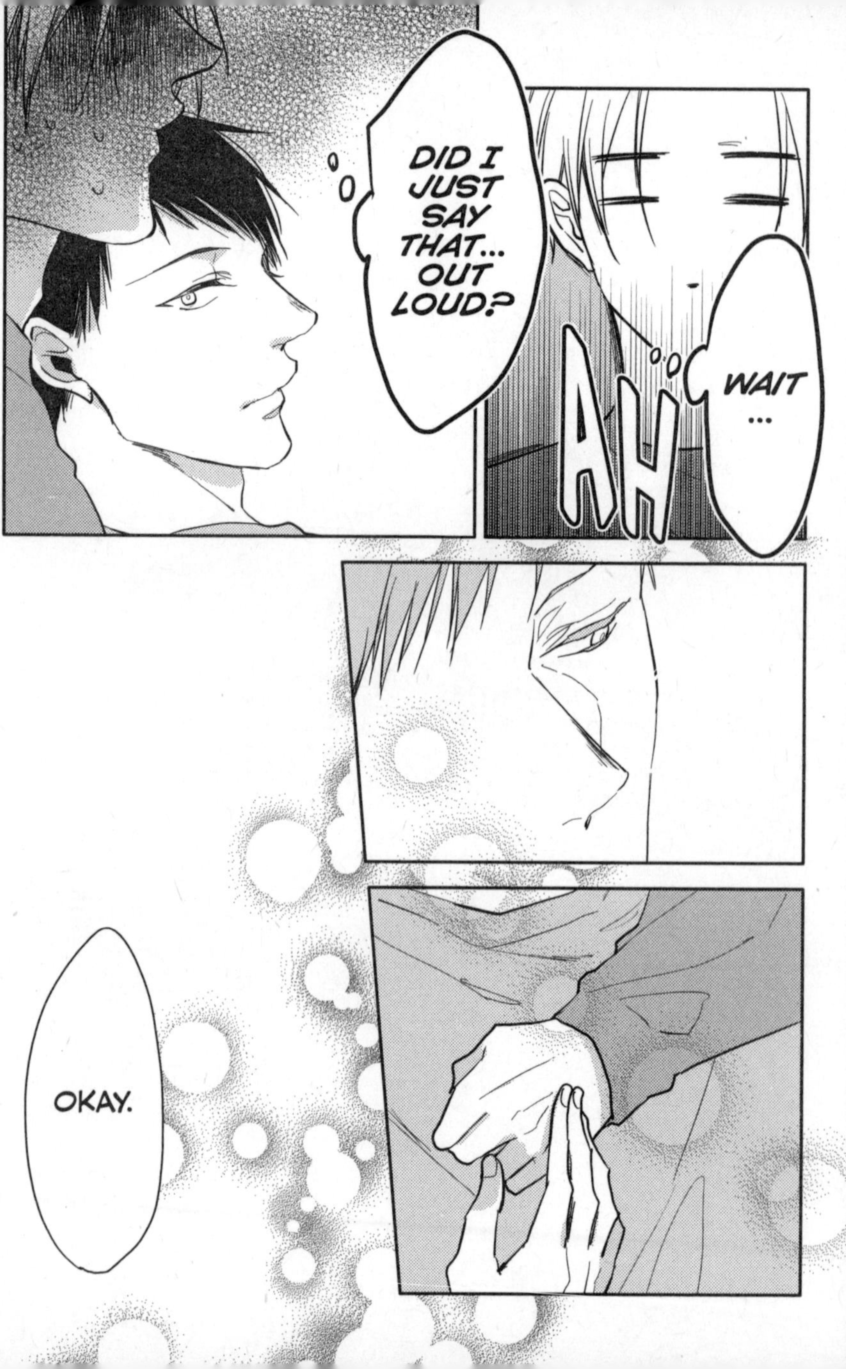
WAIT ...
AH
DID I JUST SAY THAT... OUT LOUD?
OKAY.

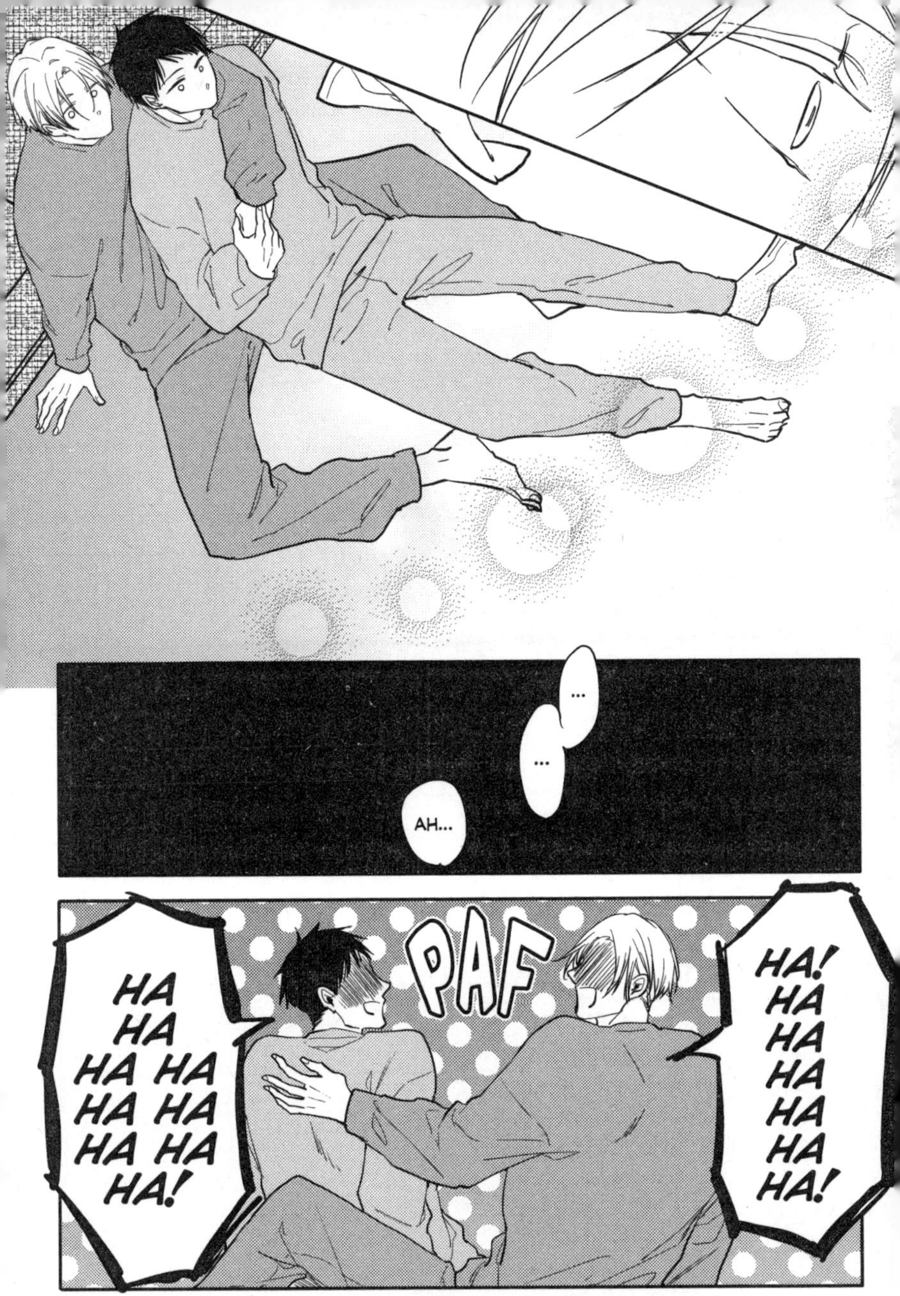
...
...
AH...
HA! HA HA HA HA HA HA HA!
PAF
HA HA HA HA HA HA HA HA HA!

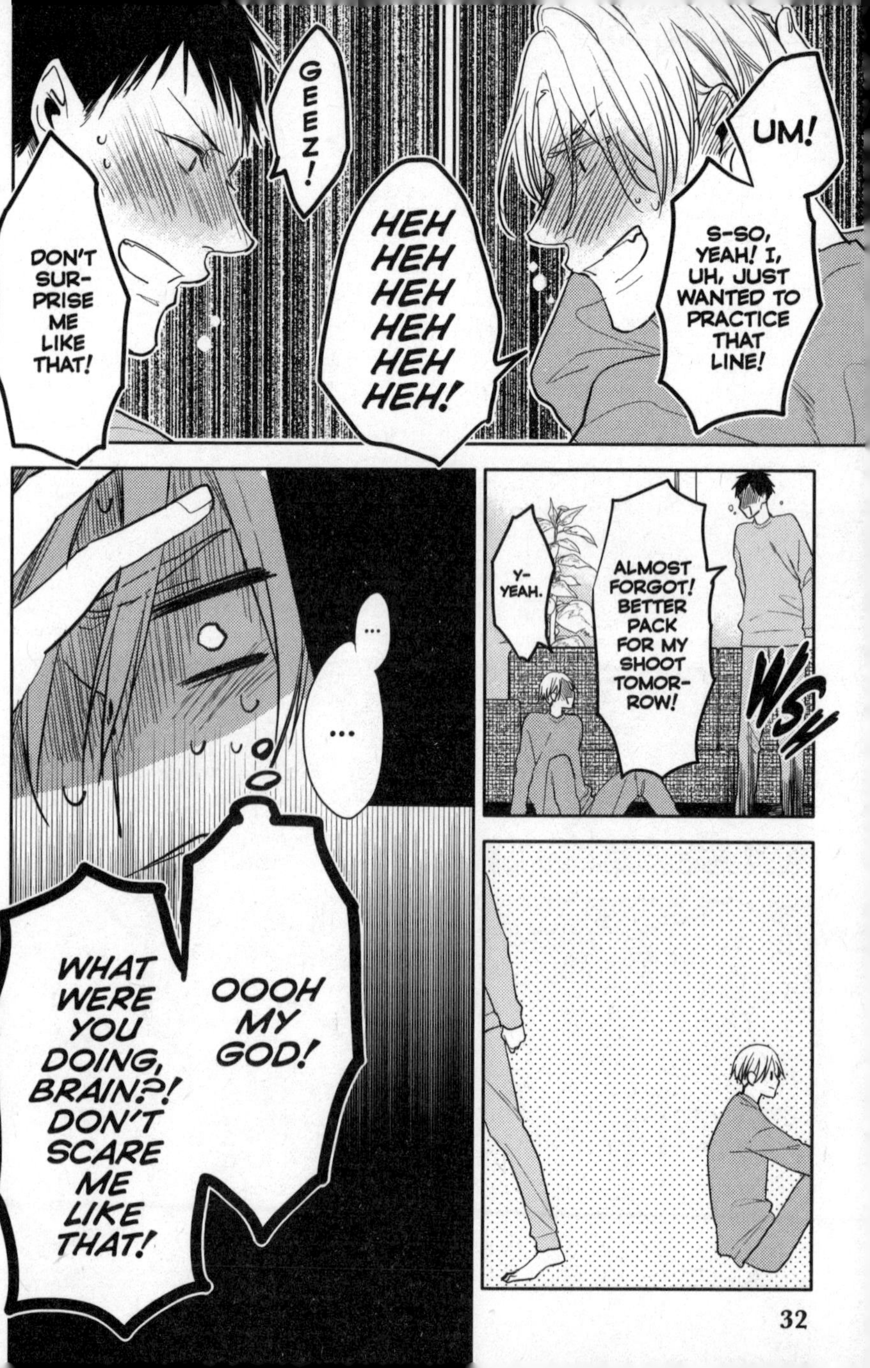
UM!
S-SO, YEAH! I, UH, JUST WANTED TO PRACTICE THAT LINE!
HEH HEH HEH HEH HEH HEH HEH!
GEEZ!
DON'T SUR-PRISE ME LIKE THAT!
ALMOST FORGOT! BETTER PACK FOR MY SHOOT TOMOR-ROW!
Y-YEAH.
WSH
...
...
OOOH MY GOD!
WHAT WERE YOU DOING, BRAIN?! DON'T SCARE ME LIKE THAT!

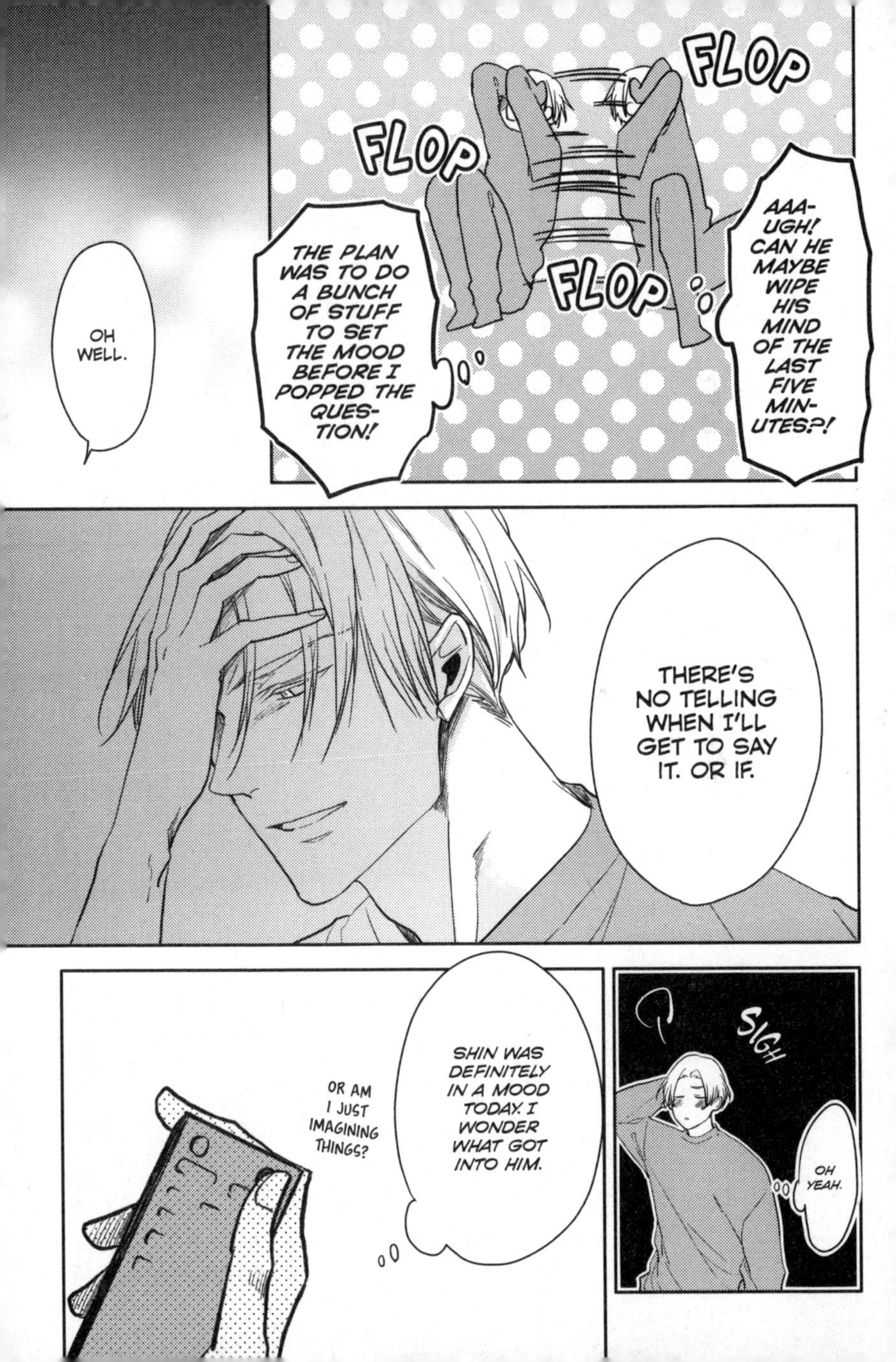
FLOP
FLOP
AAA-UGH! CAN HE MAYBE WIPE HIS MIND OF THE LAST FIVE MIN-UTES?!
FLOP
THE PLAN WAS TO DO A BUNCH OF STUFF TO SET THE MOOD BEFORE I POPPED THE QUES-TION!
OH WELL.
THERE'S NO TELLING WHEN I'LL GET TO SAY IT. OR IF.
SIGH
OH YEAH.
SHIN WAS DEFINITELY IN A MOOD TODAY. I WONDER WHAT GOT INTO HIM.
OR AM I JUST IMAGINING THINGS?

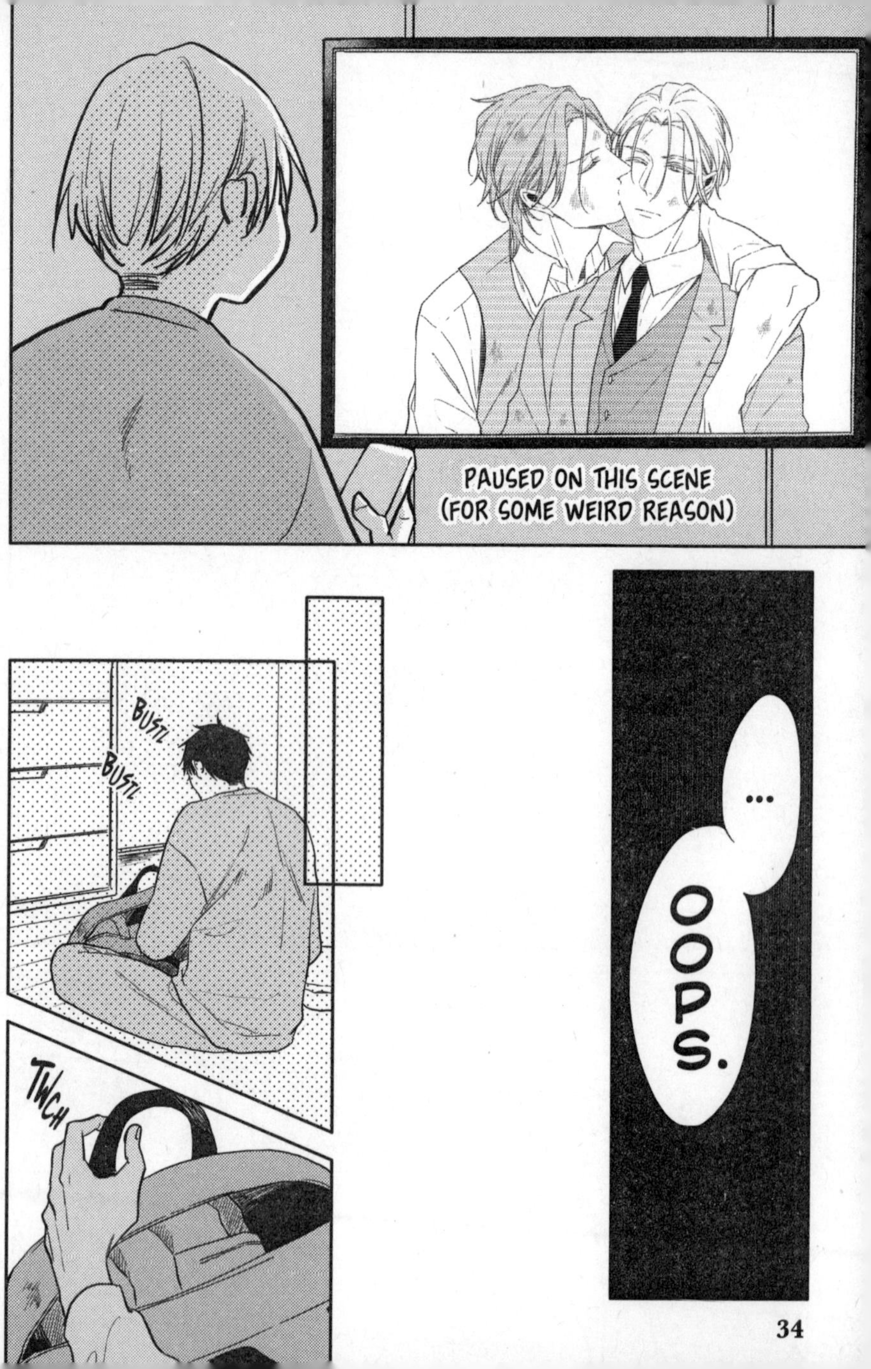

PAUSED ON THIS SCENE (FOR SOME WEIRD REASON)
...
OOPS.
BUSTL
BUSTL
TWCH

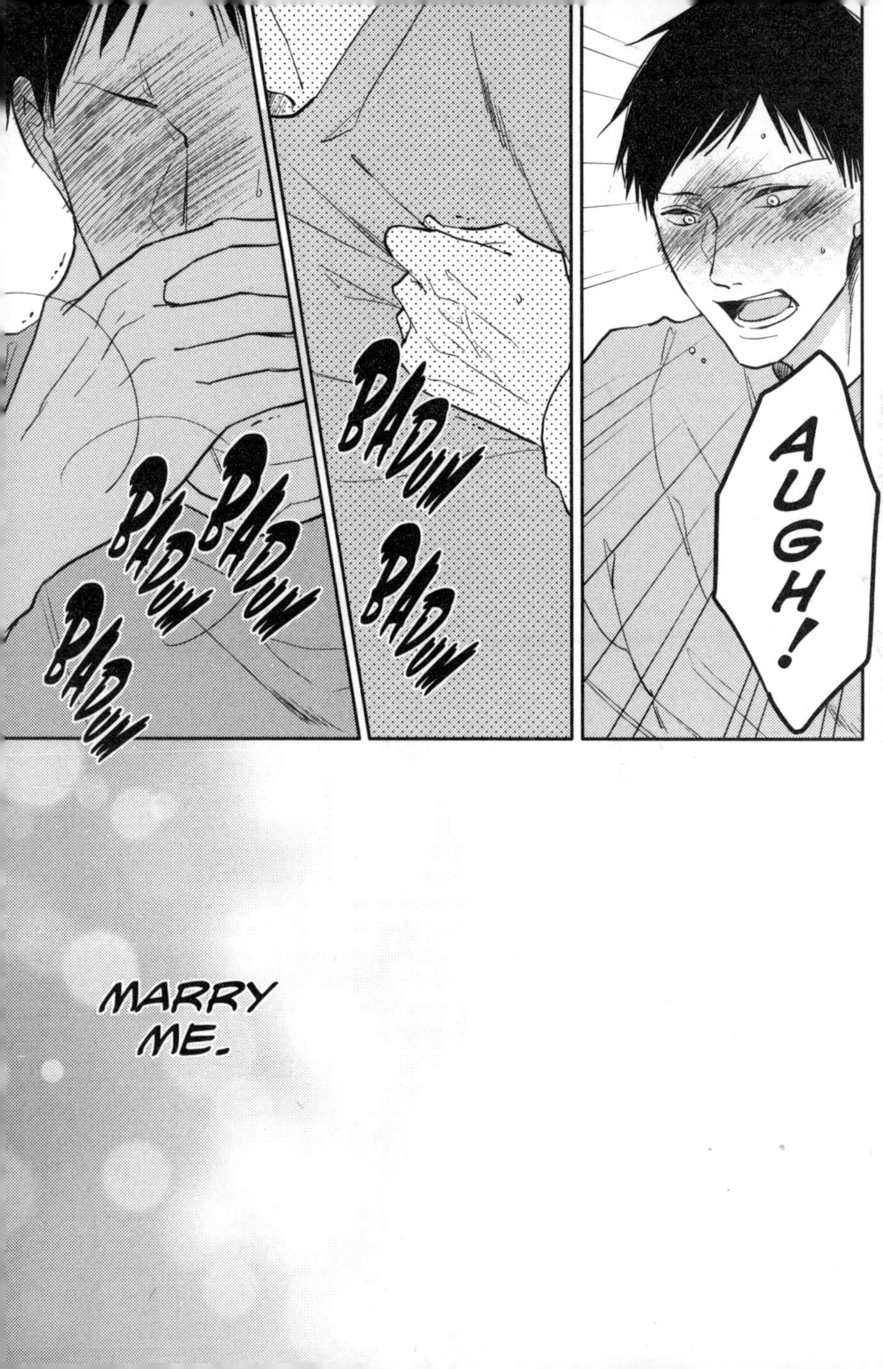
AUGH!
BADUM BADUM
BADUM BADUM BADUM BADUM
MARRY ME.

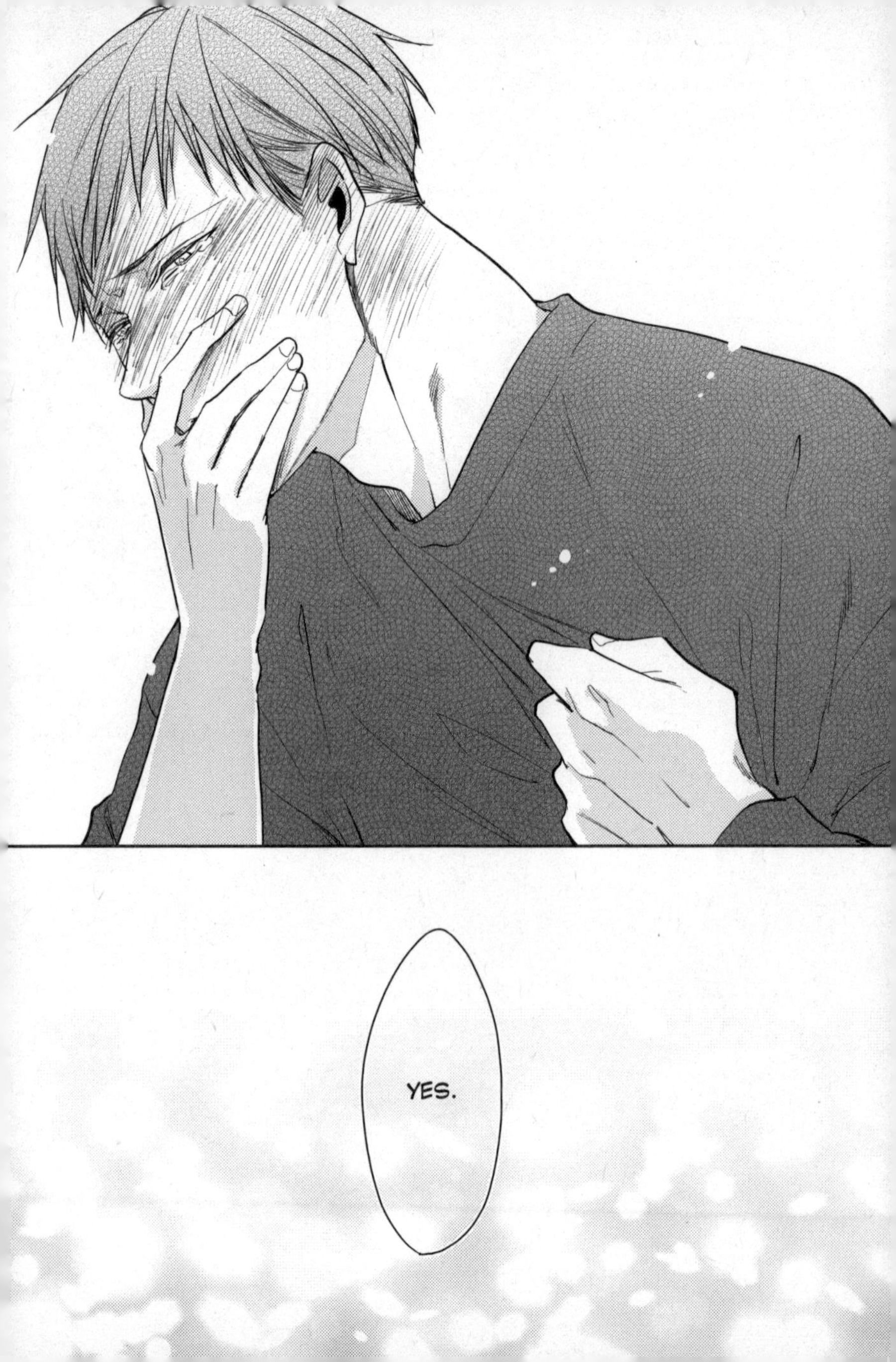
YES.

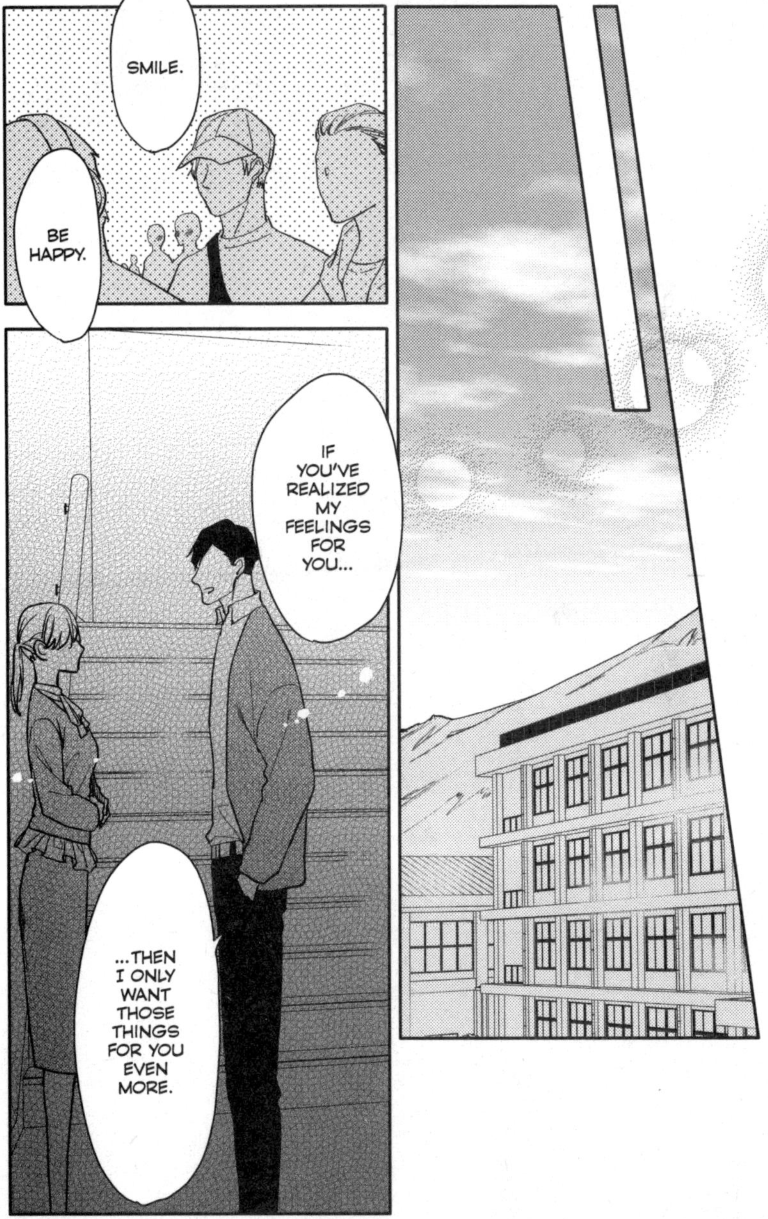
SMILE.
BE HAPPY.
IF YOU'VE REALIZED MY FEELINGS FOR YOU...
...THEN I ONLY WANT THOSE THINGS FOR YOU EVEN MORE.

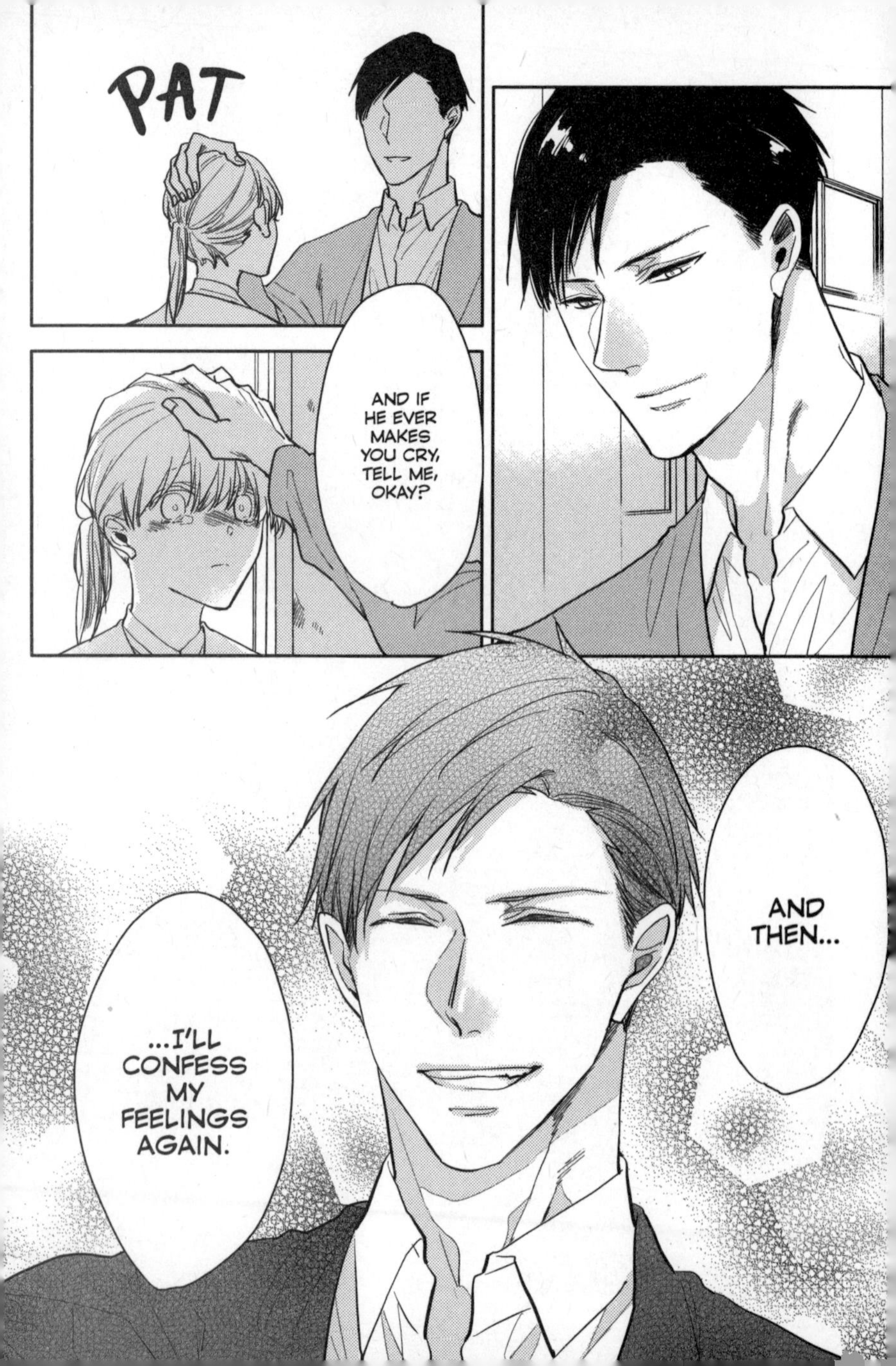
PAT
AND IF HE EVER MAKES YOU CRY, TELL ME, OKAY?
AND THEN...
...I'LL CONFESS MY FEELINGS AGAIN.

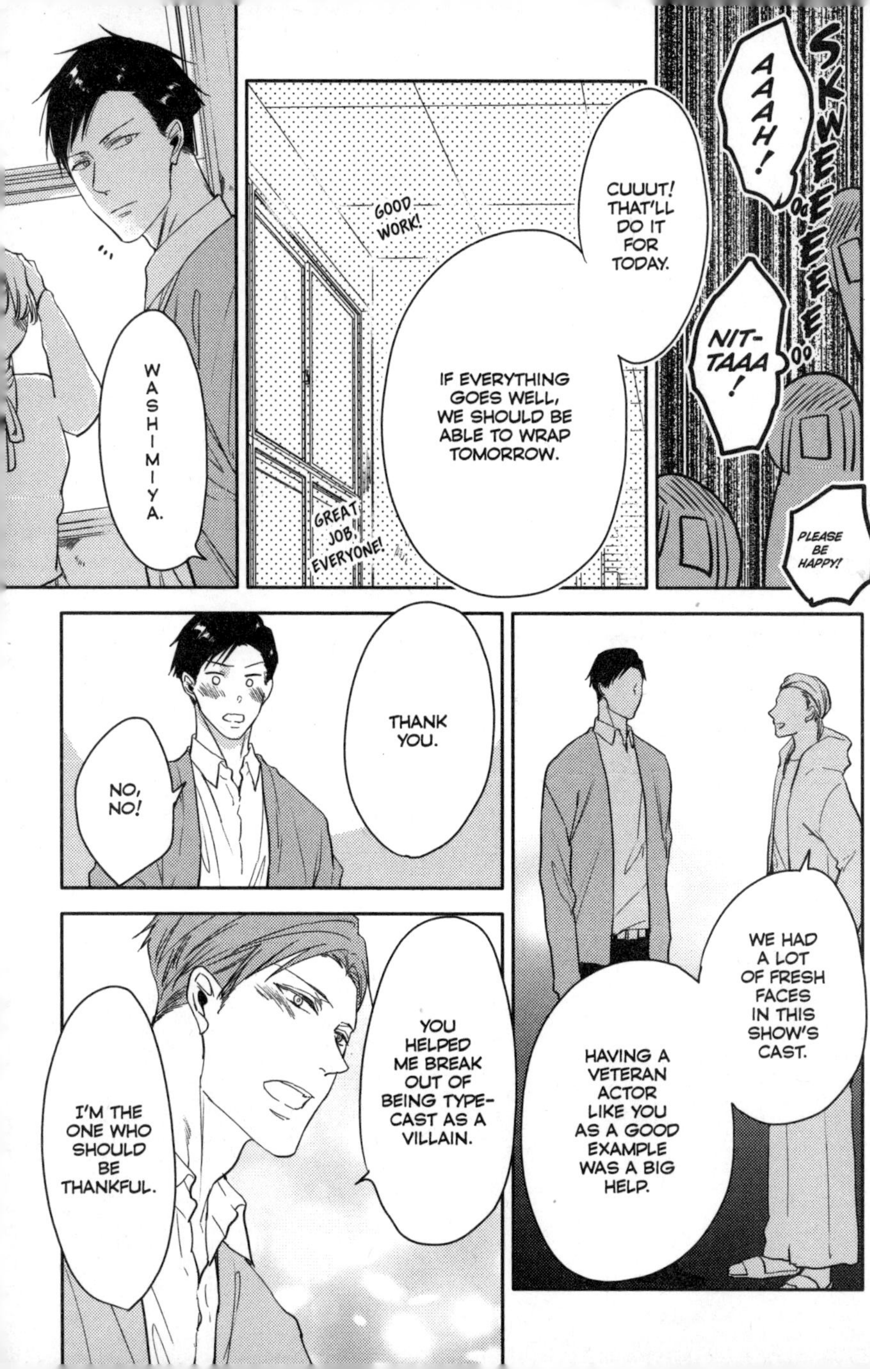
SKWEEEEEE
AAAH!
NIT-TAAA!
PLEASE BE HAPPY!
CUUUT! THAT'LL DO IT FOR TODAY.
IF EVERYTHING GOES WELL, WE SHOULD BE ABLE TO WRAP TOMORROW.
GOOD WORK!
GREAT JOB, EVERYONE!
...
WASHIMIYA.
WE HAD A LOT OF FRESH FACES IN THIS SHOW'S CAST.
HAVING A VETERAN ACTOR LIKE YOU AS A GOOD EXAMPLE WAS A BIG HELP.
THANK YOU.
NO, NO!
YOU HELPED ME BREAK OUT OF BEING TYPE-CAST AS A VILLAIN.
I'M THE ONE WHO SHOULD BE THANKFUL.

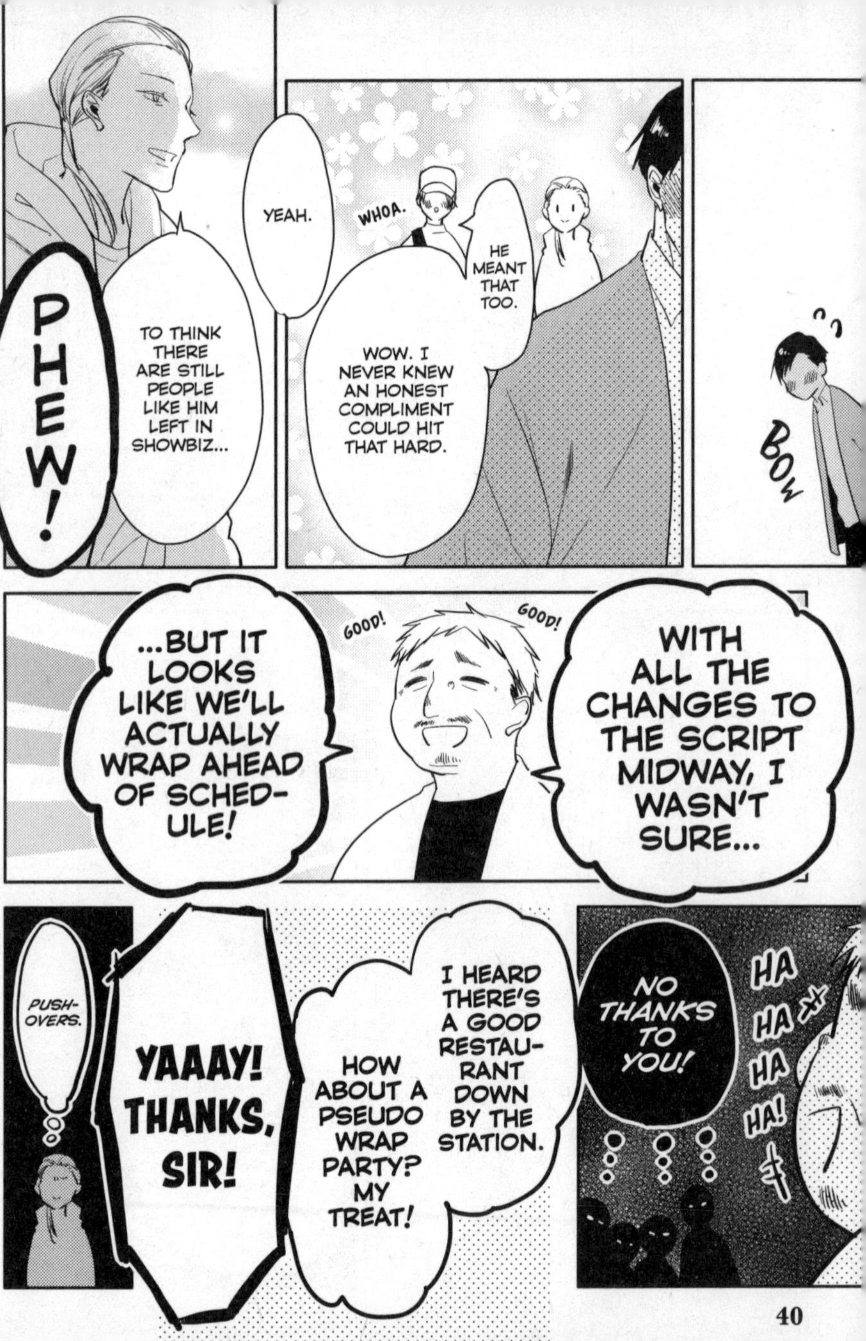
BOW
WHOA.
WOW. I NEVER KNEW AN HONEST COMPLIMENT COULD HIT THAT HARD.
HE MEANT THAT TOO.
YEAH.
TO THINK THERE ARE STILL PEOPLE LIKE HIM LEFT IN SHOWBIZ...
PHEW!
WITH ALL THE CHANGES TO THE SCRIPT MIDWAY, I WASN'T SURE...
GOOD! GOOD!
...BUT IT LOOKS LIKE WE'LL ACTUALLY WRAP AHEAD OF SCHED-ULE!
HA HA HA HA!
NO THANKS TO YOU!
I HEARD THERE'S A GOOD RESTAU-RANT DOWN BY THE STATION.
HOW ABOUT A PSEUDO WRAP PARTY? MY TREAT!
YAAAY! THANKS, SIR!
PUSH-OVERS.

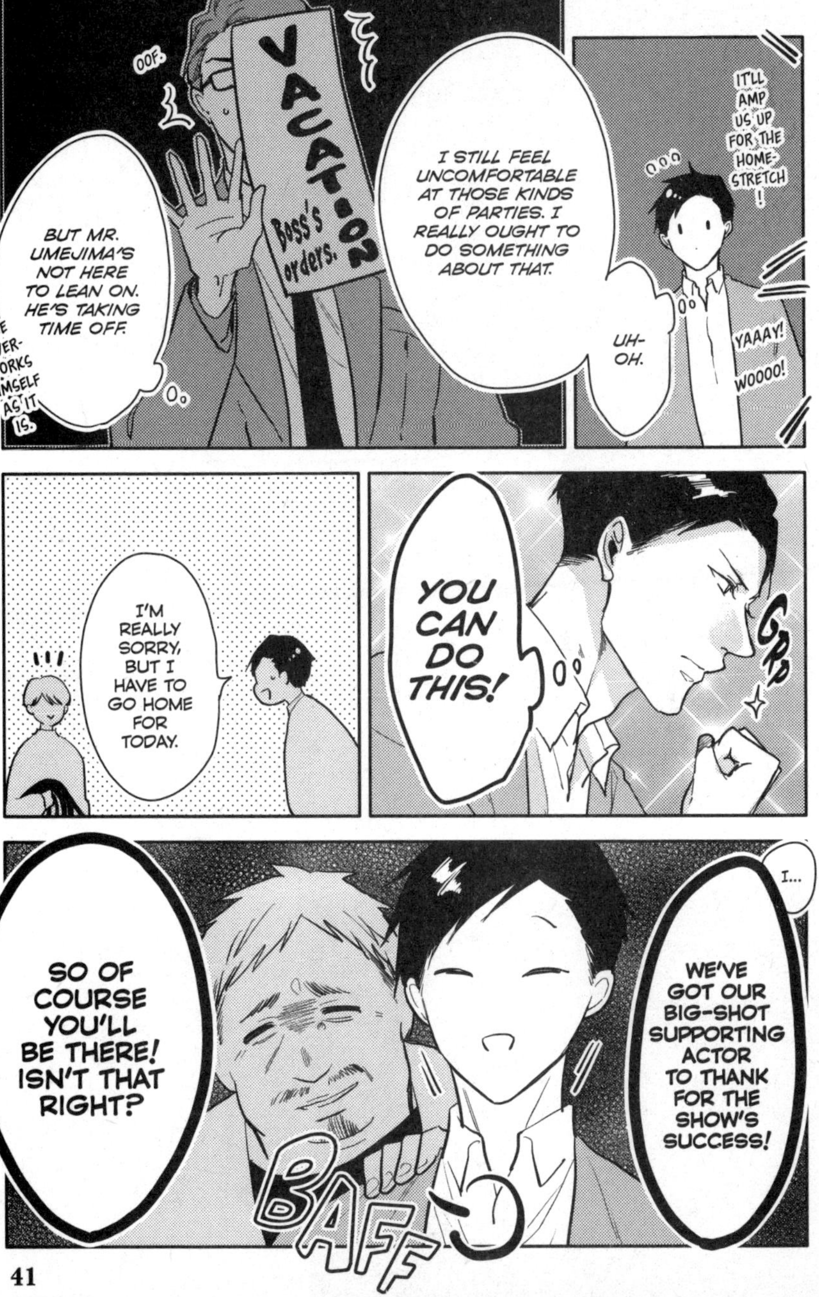
IT'LL AMP US UP FOR THE HOME-STRETCH!
UH-OH.
YAAAY!
WOOOO!
I STILL FEEL UNCOMFORTABLE AT THOSE KINDS OF PARTIES. I REALLY OUGHT TO DO SOMETHING ABOUT THAT.
VACAT
Boss's orders.
OOF.
BUT MR. UMEJIMA'S NOT HERE TO LEAN ON. HE'S TAKING TIME OFF.
HE OVERWORKS HIMSELF AS IT IS.
YOU CAN DO THIS!
GRP
I'M REALLY SORRY, BUT I HAVE TO GO HOME FOR TODAY.
I...
WE'VE GOT OUR BIG-SHOT SUPPORTING ACTOR TO THANK FOR THE SHOW'S SUCCESS!
SO OF COURSE YOU'LL BE THERE! ISN'T THAT RIGHT?
BAFF

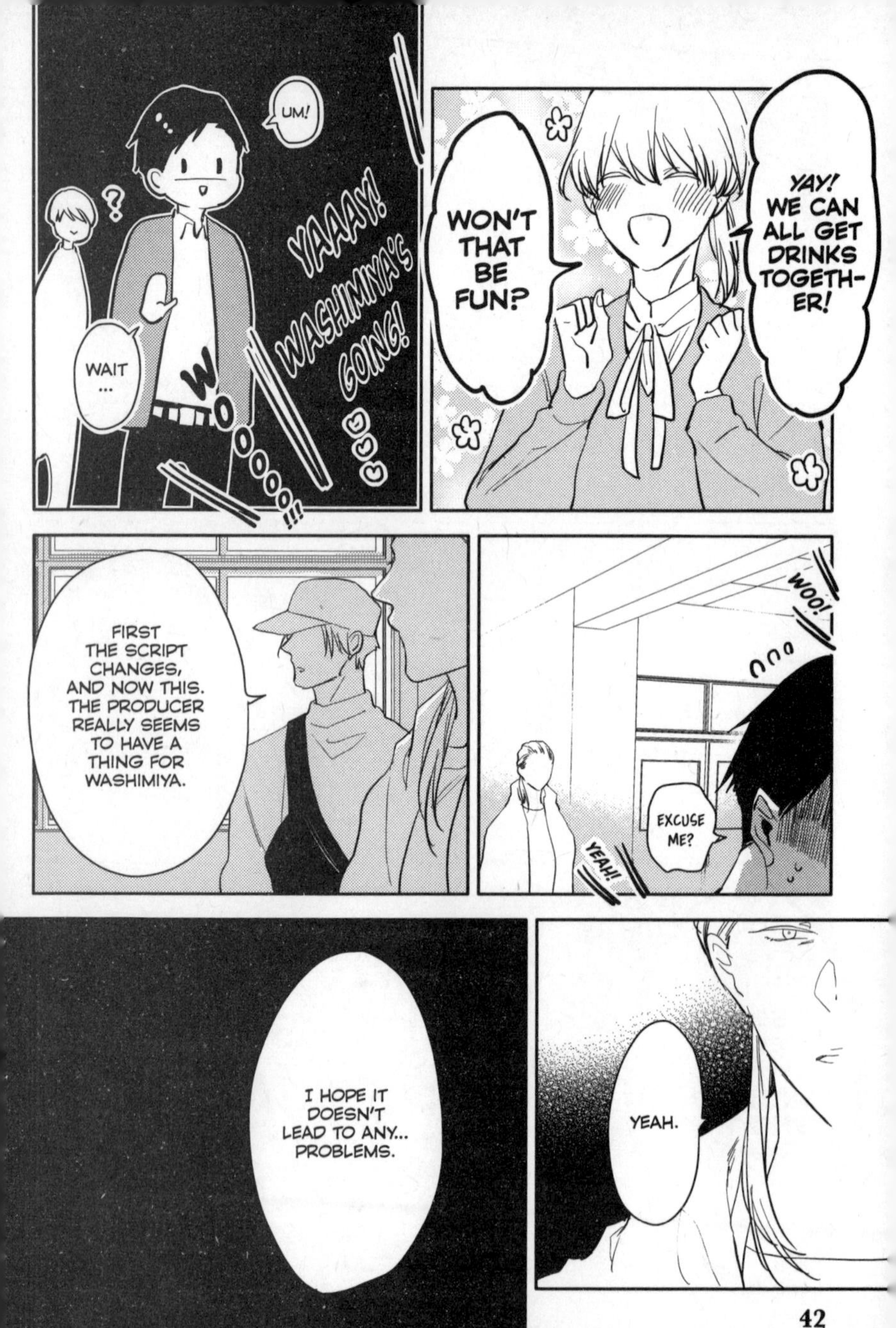

YAY! WE CAN ALL GET DRINKS TOGETH-ER!
WON'T THAT BE FUN?
UM!
YAAAY! WASHIMIYA'S GOING!
?
WOOOOOO!!
WAIT ...
WOO!
OOO
EXCUSE ME?
YEAH!
FIRST THE SCRIPT CHANGES, AND NOW THIS. THE PRODUCER REALLY SEEMS TO HAVE A THING FOR WASHIMIYA.
YEAH.
I HOPE IT DOESN'T LEAD TO ANY... PROBLEMS.

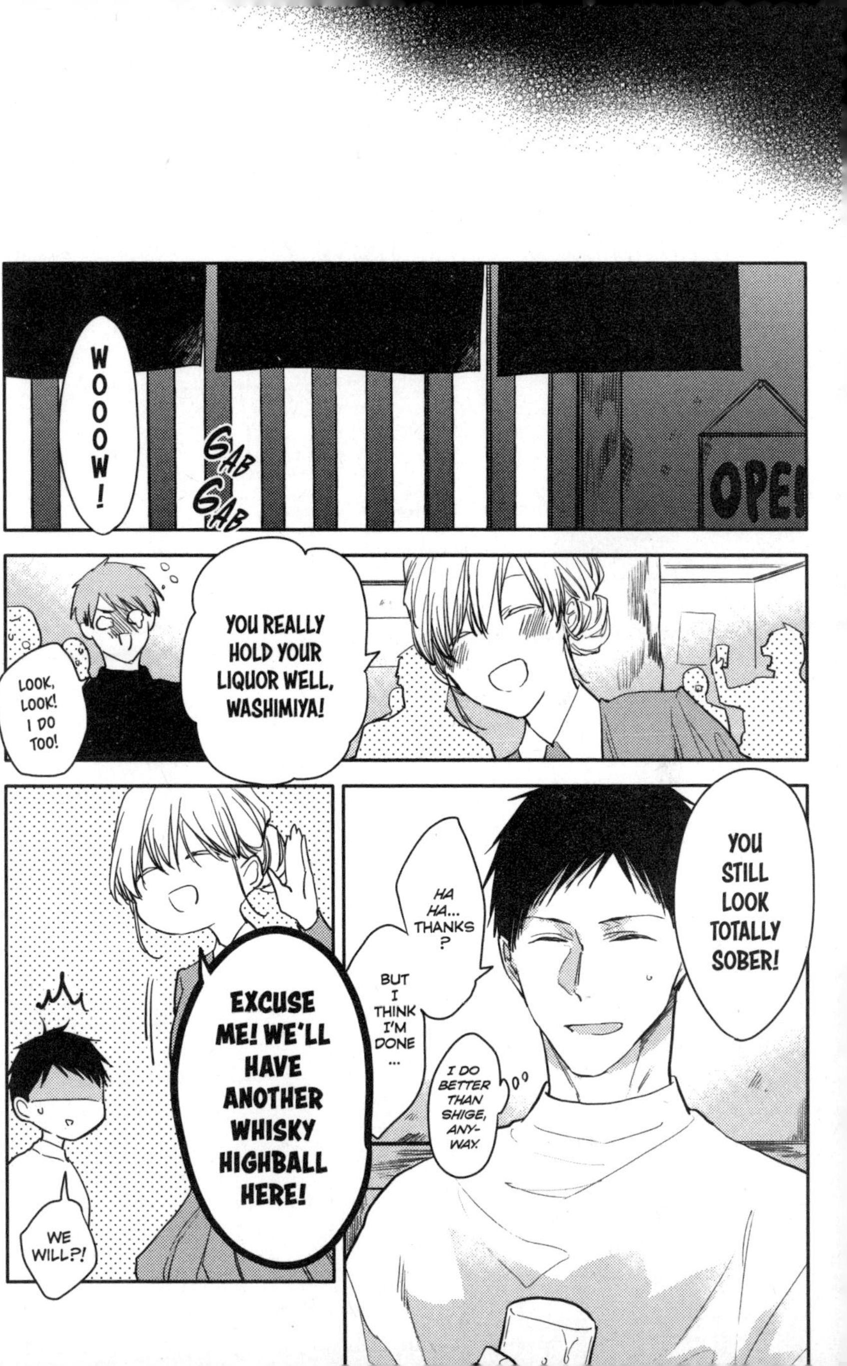
GAB GAB
WOOOOW!
YOU REALLY HOLD YOUR LIQUOR WELL, WASHIMIYA!
LOOK, LOOK! I DO TOO!
YOU STILL LOOK TOTALLY SOBER!
HA HA... THANKS?
BUT I THINK I'M DONE...
I DO BETTER THAN SHIGE, ANYWAY.
EXCUSE ME! WE'LL HAVE ANOTHER WHISKY HIGHBALL HERE!
WE WILL?!

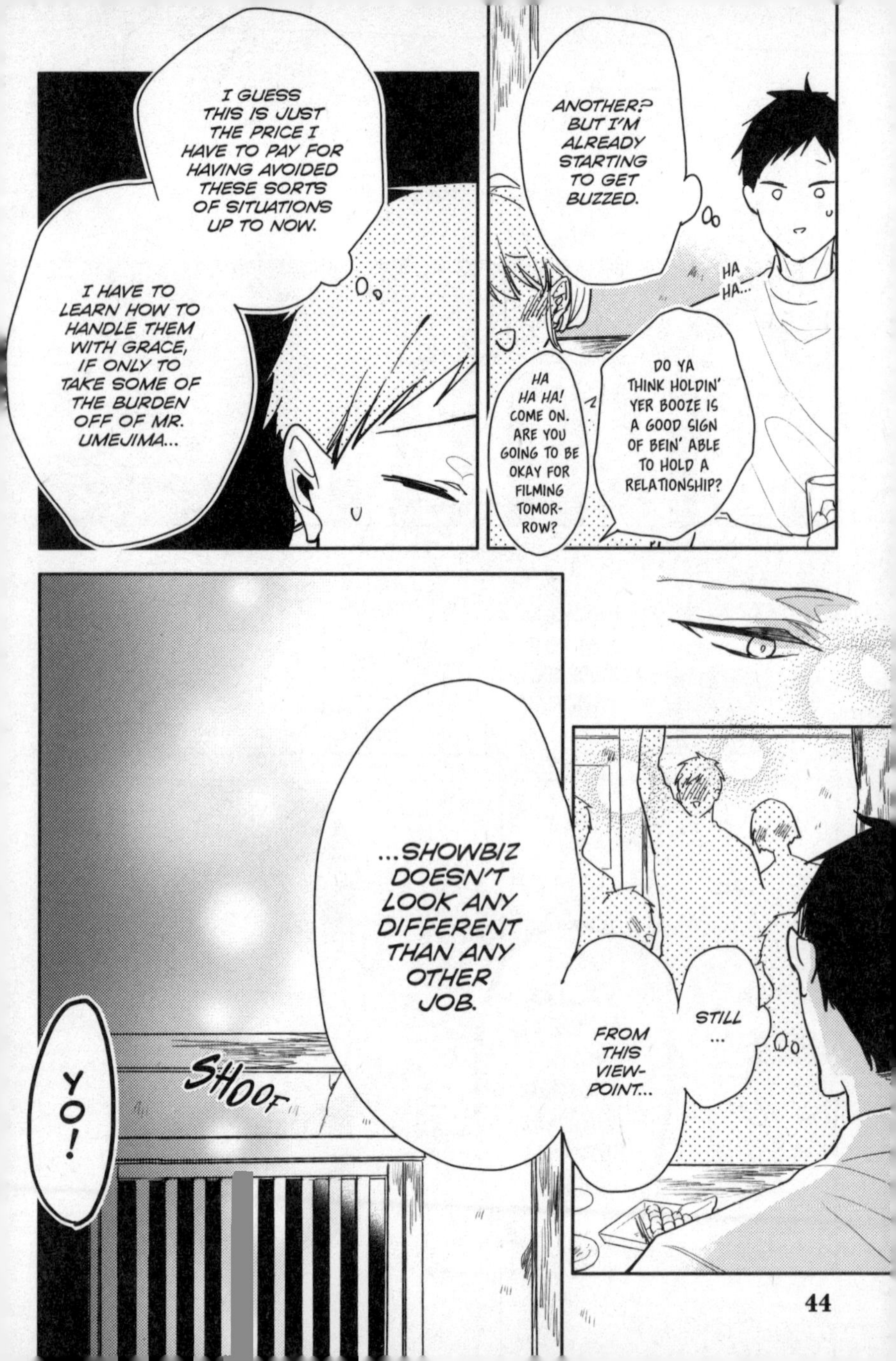
ANOTHER? BUT I'M ALREADY STARTING TO GET BUZZED.
HA HA...
DO YA THINK HOLDIN' YER BOOZE IS A GOOD SIGN OF BEIN' ABLE TO HOLD A RELATIONSHIP?
HA HA HA! COME ON. ARE YOU GOING TO BE OKAY FOR FILMING TOMOR-ROW?
I GUESS THIS IS JUST THE PRICE I HAVE TO PAY FOR HAVING AVOIDED THESE SORTS OF SITUATIONS UP TO NOW.
I HAVE TO LEARN HOW TO HANDLE THEM WITH GRACE, IF ONLY TO TAKE SOME OF THE BURDEN OFF OF MR. UMEJIMA...
STILL...
FROM THIS VIEW-POINT...
...SHOWBIZ DOESN'T LOOK ANY DIFFERENT THAN ANY OTHER JOB.
YO!
SHOOF

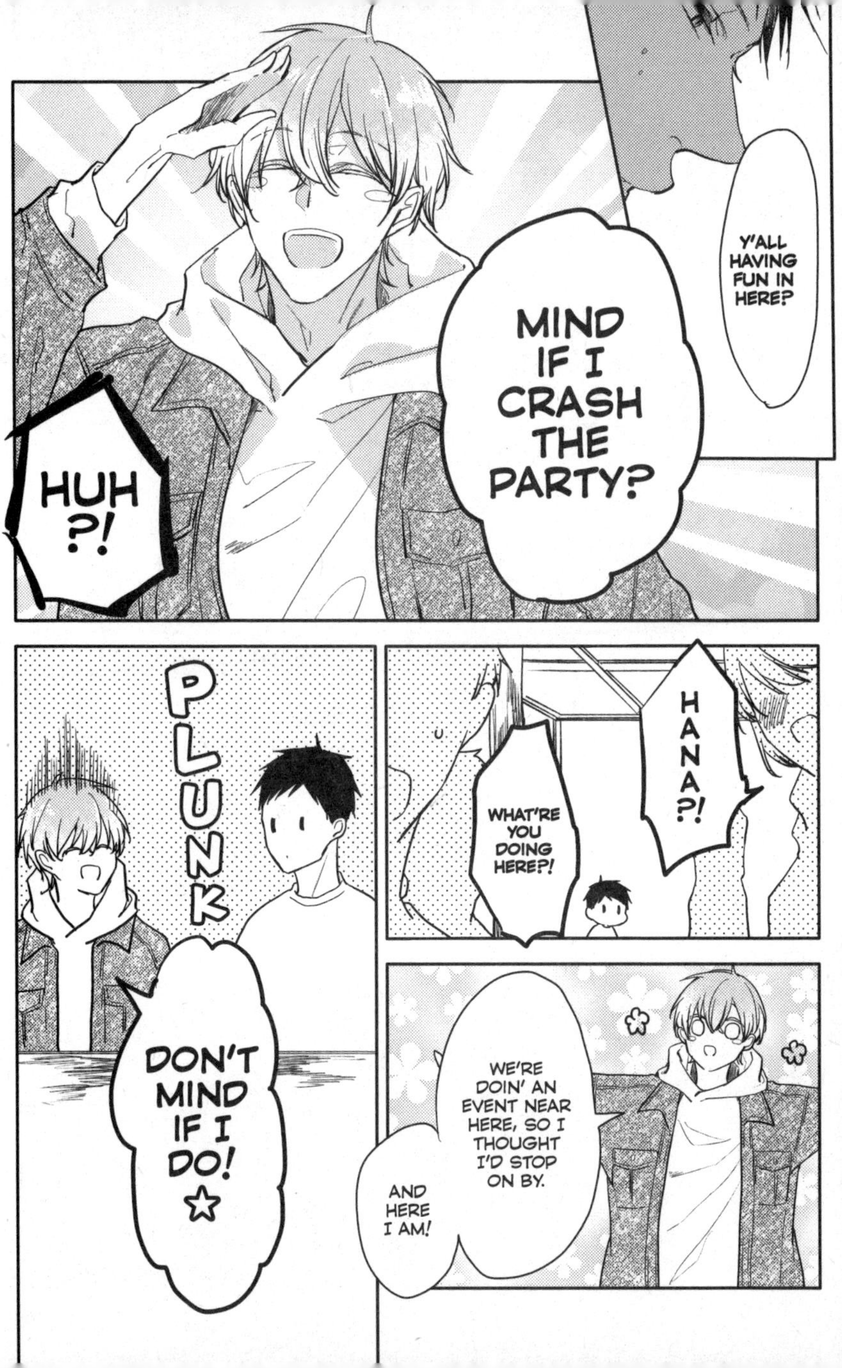
Y'ALL HAVING FUN IN HERE?
MIND IF I CRASH THE PARTY?
HUH?!
HANA?!
WHAT'RE YOU DOING HERE?!
WE'RE DOIN' AN EVENT NEAR HERE, SO I THOUGHT I'D STOP ON BY.
AND HERE I AM!
PLUNK
DON'T MIND IF I DO! ☆

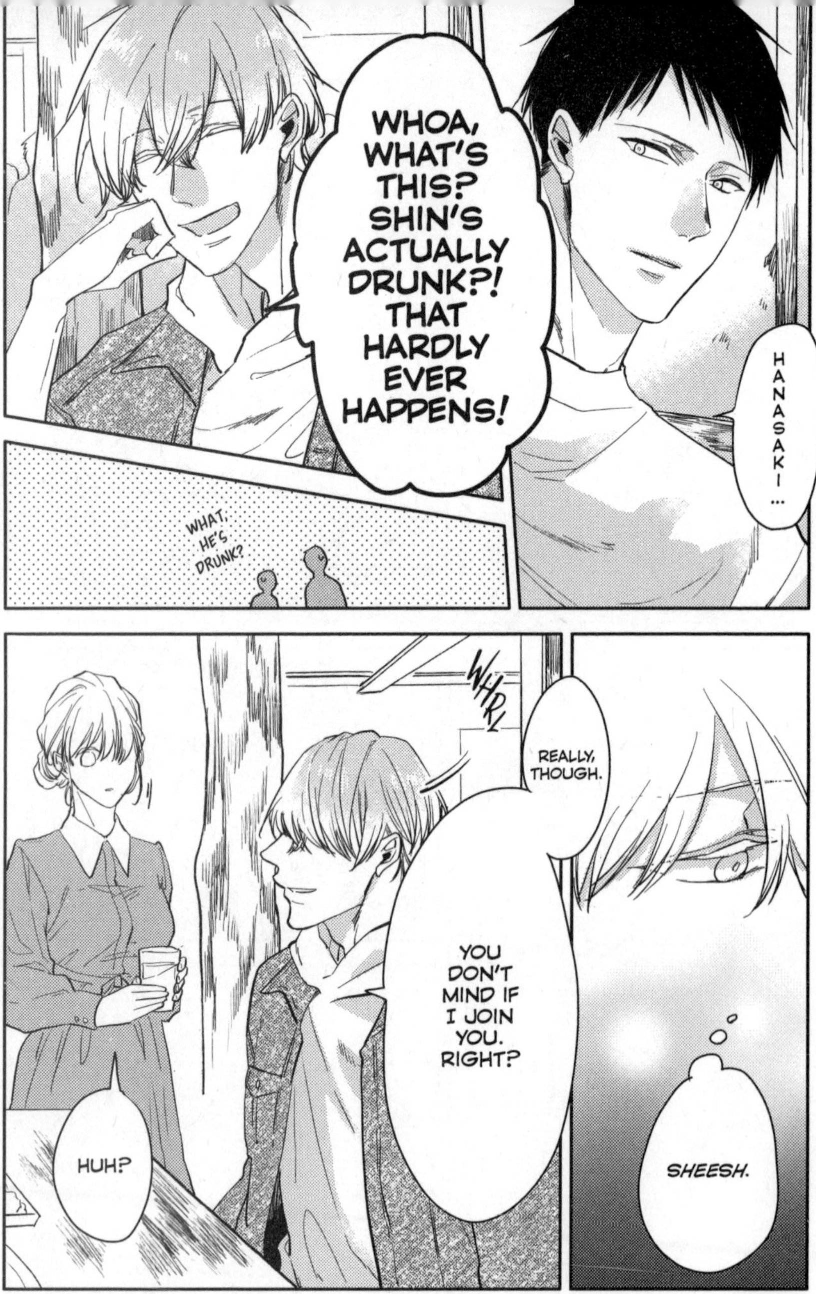
HANASAKI...
WHOA, WHAT'S THIS? SHIN'S ACTUALLY DRUNK?! THAT HARDLY EVER HAPPENS!
WHAT, HE'S DRUNK?
REALLY, THOUGH.
YOU DON'T MIND IF I JOIN YOU. RIGHT?
SHEESH.
WHRL
HUH?

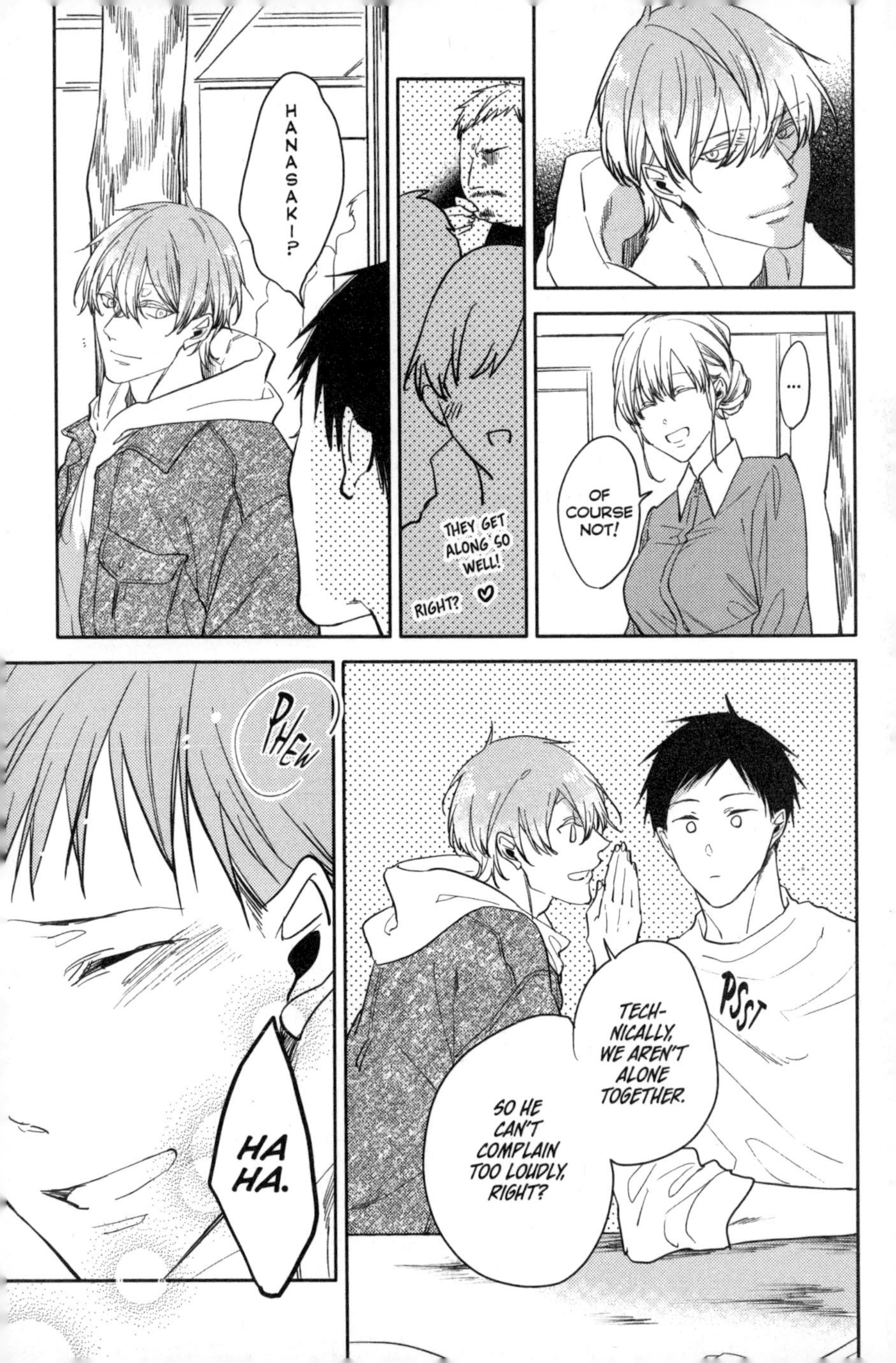
...
OF COURSE NOT!
THEY GET ALONG SO WELL!
RIGHT? ♥
HANASAKI!?
PSST
TECH-NICALLY, WE AREN'T ALONE TOGETHER.
SO HE CAN'T COMPLAIN TOO LOUDLY, RIGHT?
PHEW
HA HA.

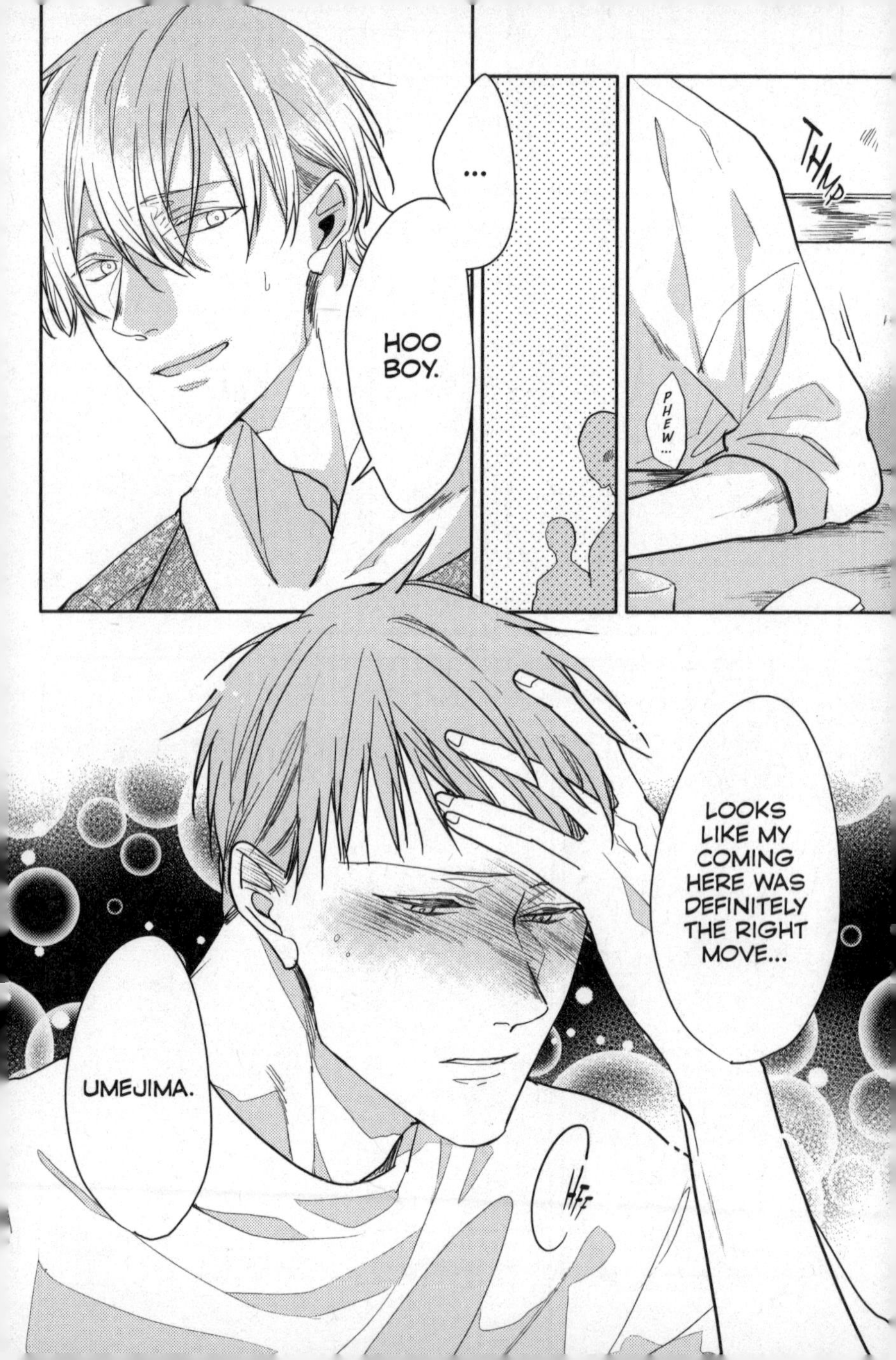
THMP
PHEW...
...
HOO BOY.
LOOKS LIKE MY COMING HERE WAS DEFINITELY THE RIGHT MOVE...
HFF
UMEJIMA.

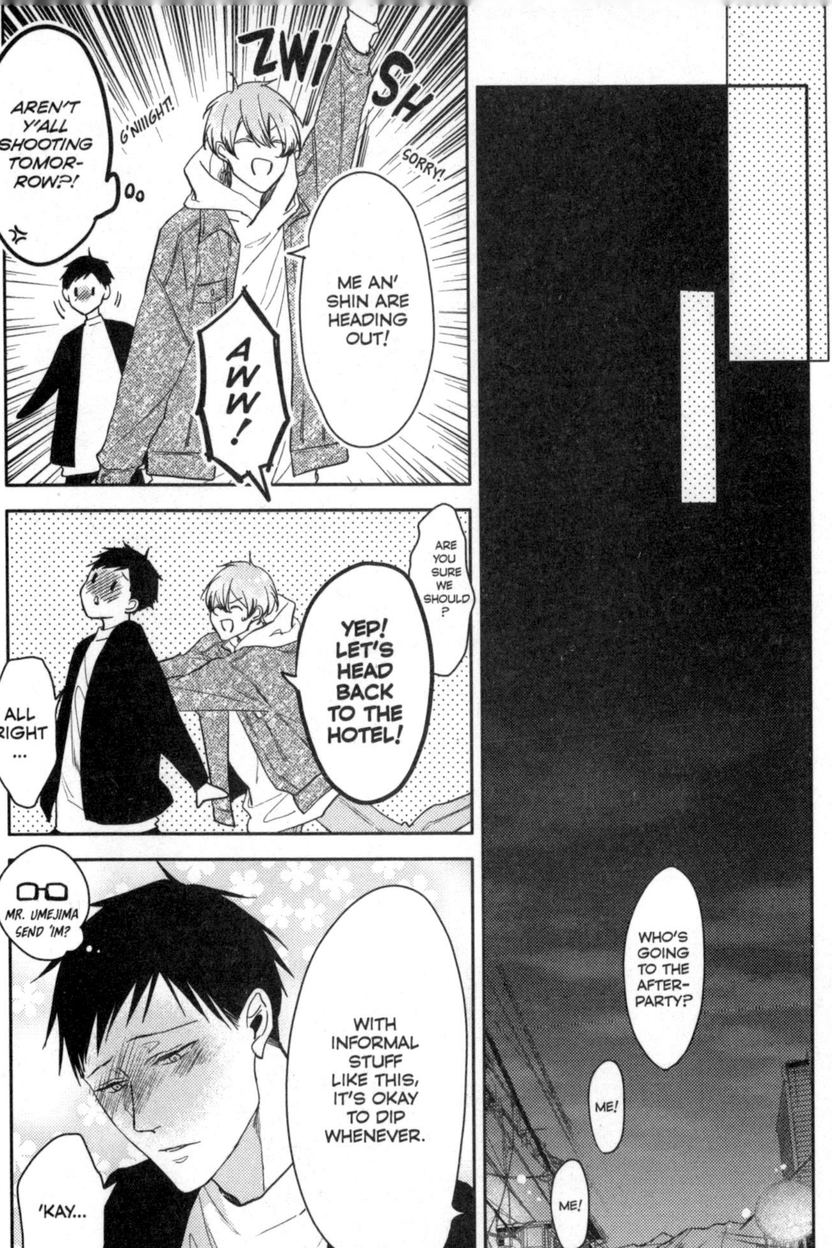
WHO'S GOING TO THE AFTER-PARTY?
ME!
ME!
ZWISH
SORRY!
ME AN' SHIN ARE HEADING OUT!
G'NIIIGHT!
AREN'T Y'ALL SHOOTING TOMORROW?!
AWW!
ARE YOU SURE WE SHOULD?
YEP! LET'S HEAD BACK TO THE HOTEL!
ALL RIGHT...
WITH INFORMAL STUFF LIKE THIS, IT'S OKAY TO DIP WHENEVER.
MR. UMEJIMA SEND 'IM?
'KAY...

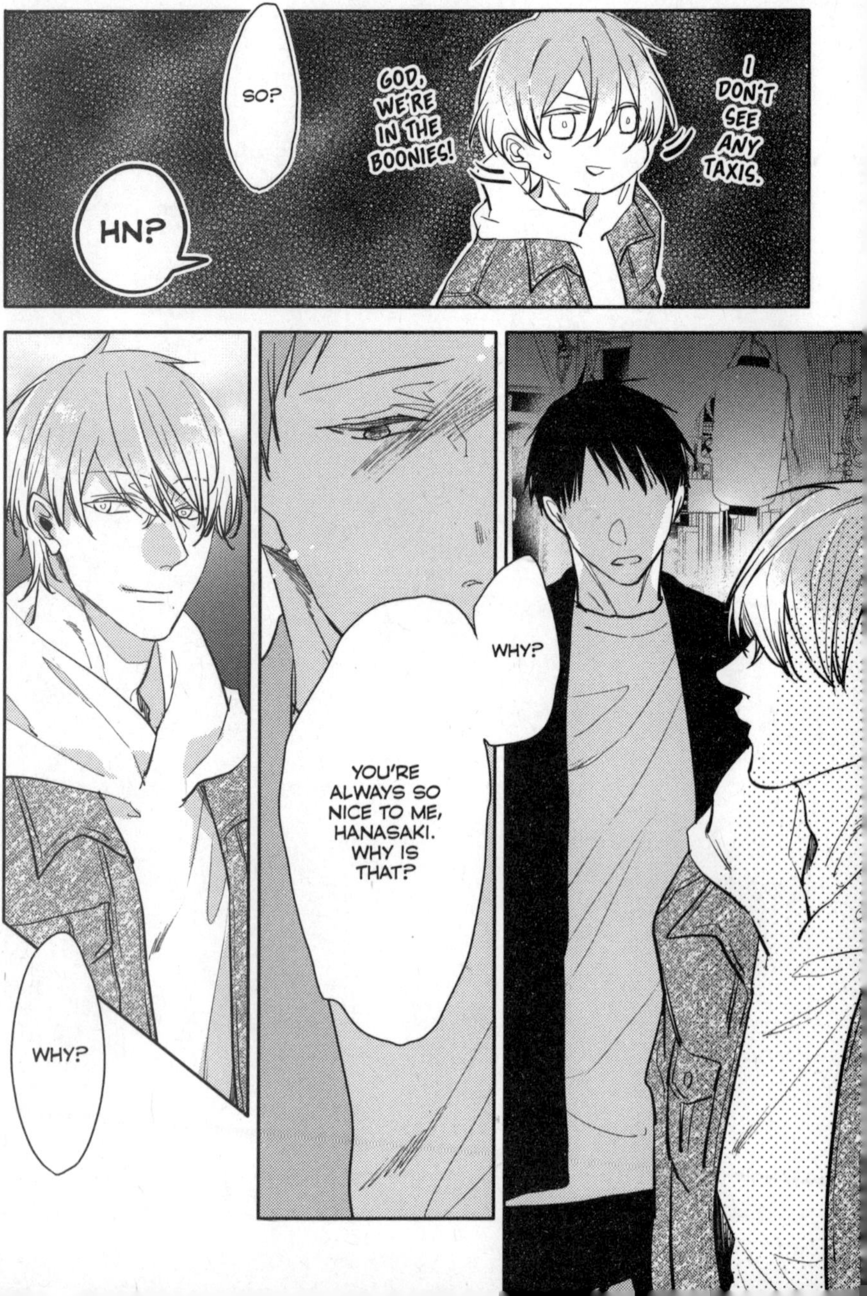
I DON'T SEE ANY TAXIS.
GOD, WE'RE IN THE BOONIES!
SO?
HN?
WHY?
YOU'RE ALWAYS SO NICE TO ME, HANASAKI. WHY IS THAT?
WHY?

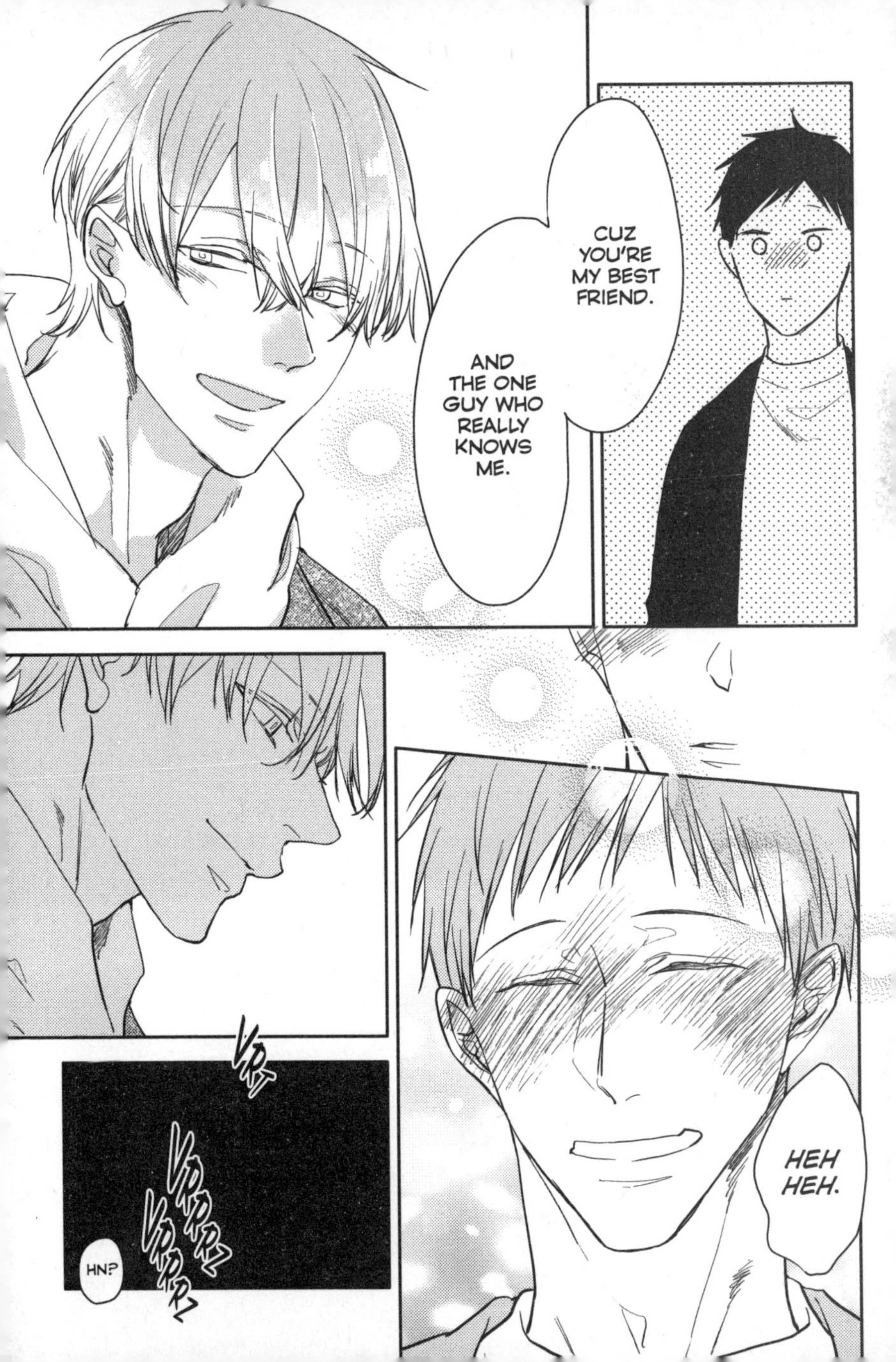
CUZ YOU'RE MY BEST FRIEND.
AND THE ONE GUY WHO REALLY KNOWS ME.
HEH HEH.
VRT
VRRRRZ
VRRRRZ
HN?

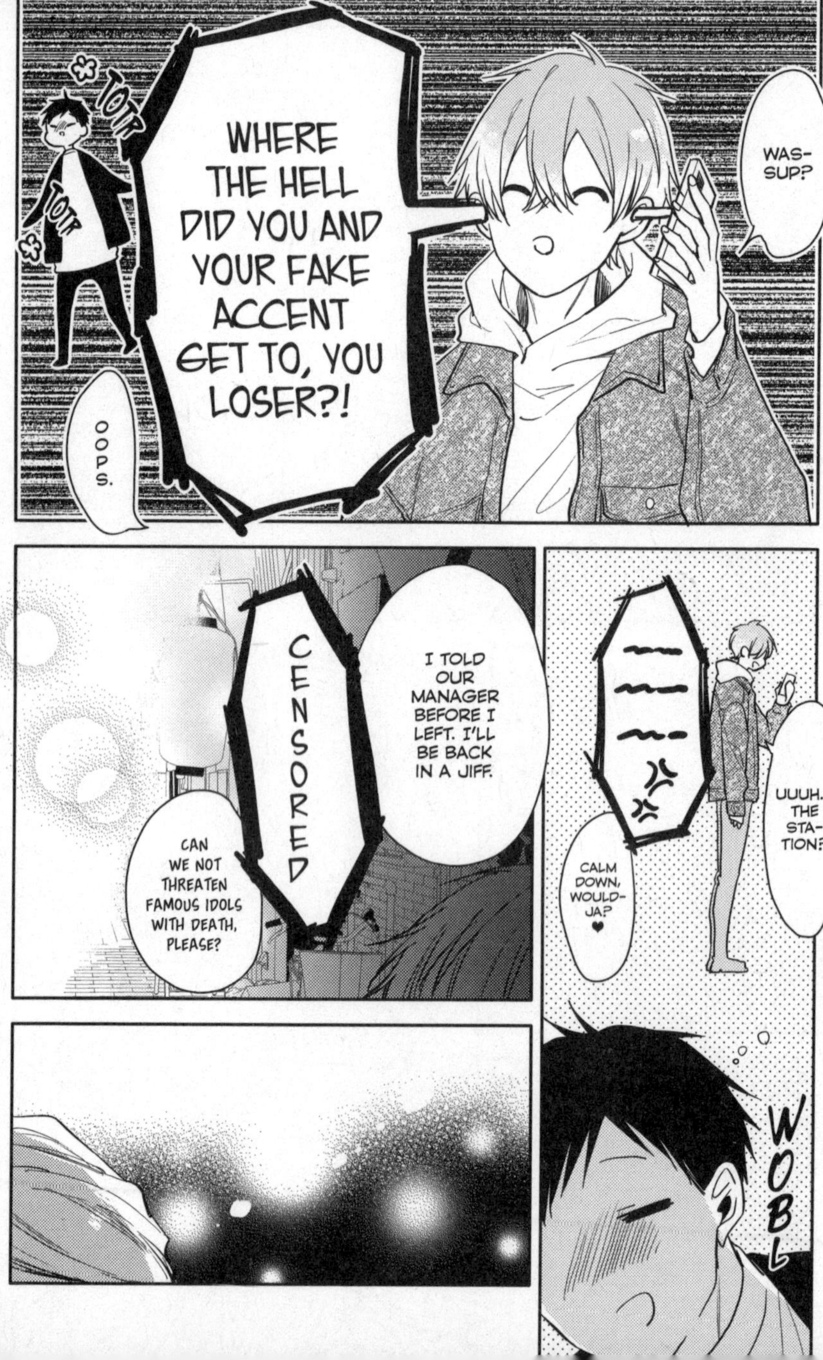
WAS-SUP?
WHERE THE HELL DID YOU AND YOUR FAKE ACCENT GET TO, YOU LOSER?!
TOTR
TOTR
OOPS.
UUUH... THE STA-TION?
CALM DOWN, WOULD-JA? ♥
I TOLD OUR MANAGER BEFORE I LEFT. I'LL BE BACK IN A JIFF.
CENSORED
CAN WE NOT THREATEN FAMOUS IDOLS WITH DEATH, PLEASE?
WOBL

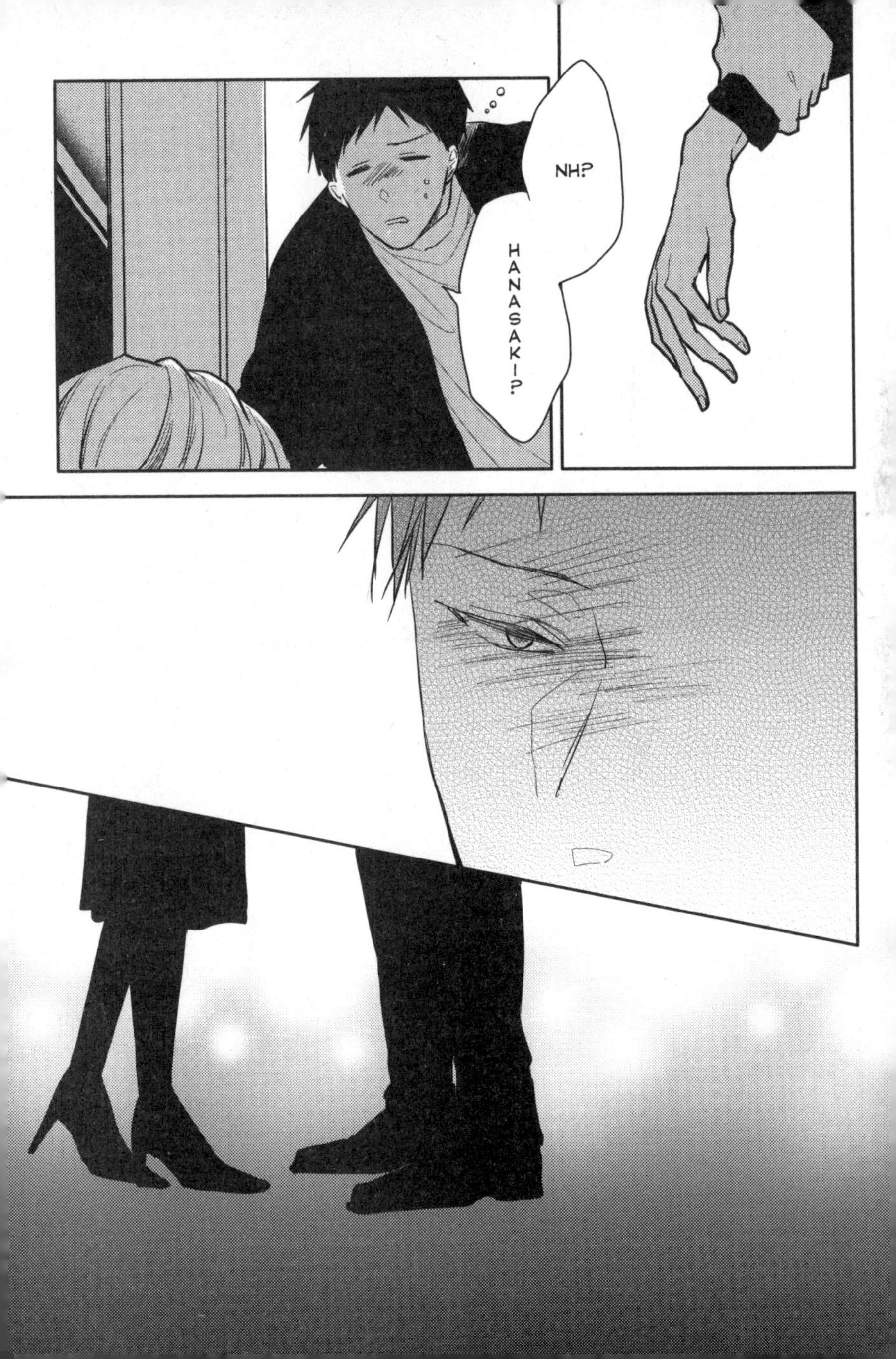
NH?
HANASAKI?

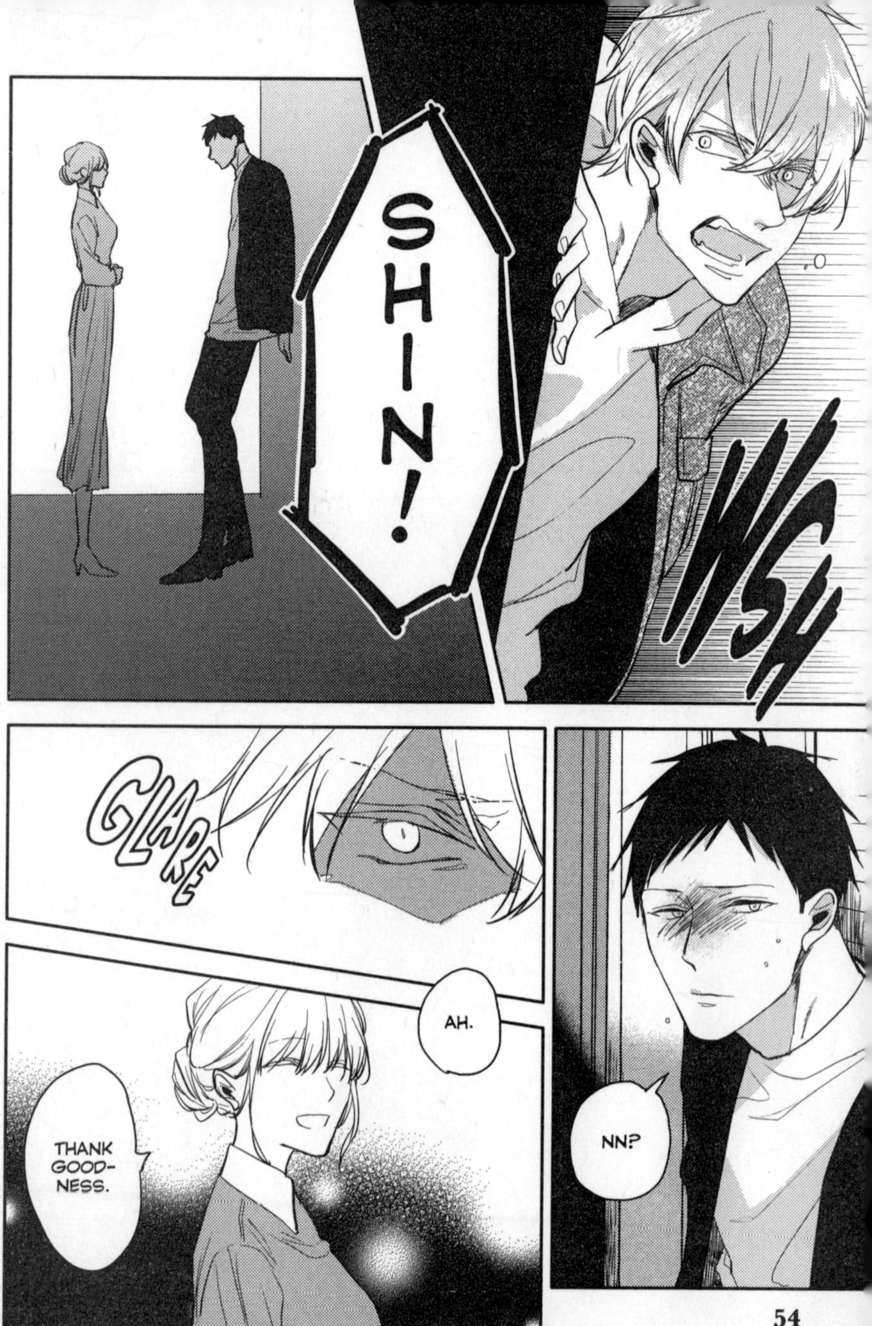

SHIN!
WSH
NN?
GLARE
AH.
THANK GOODNESS.

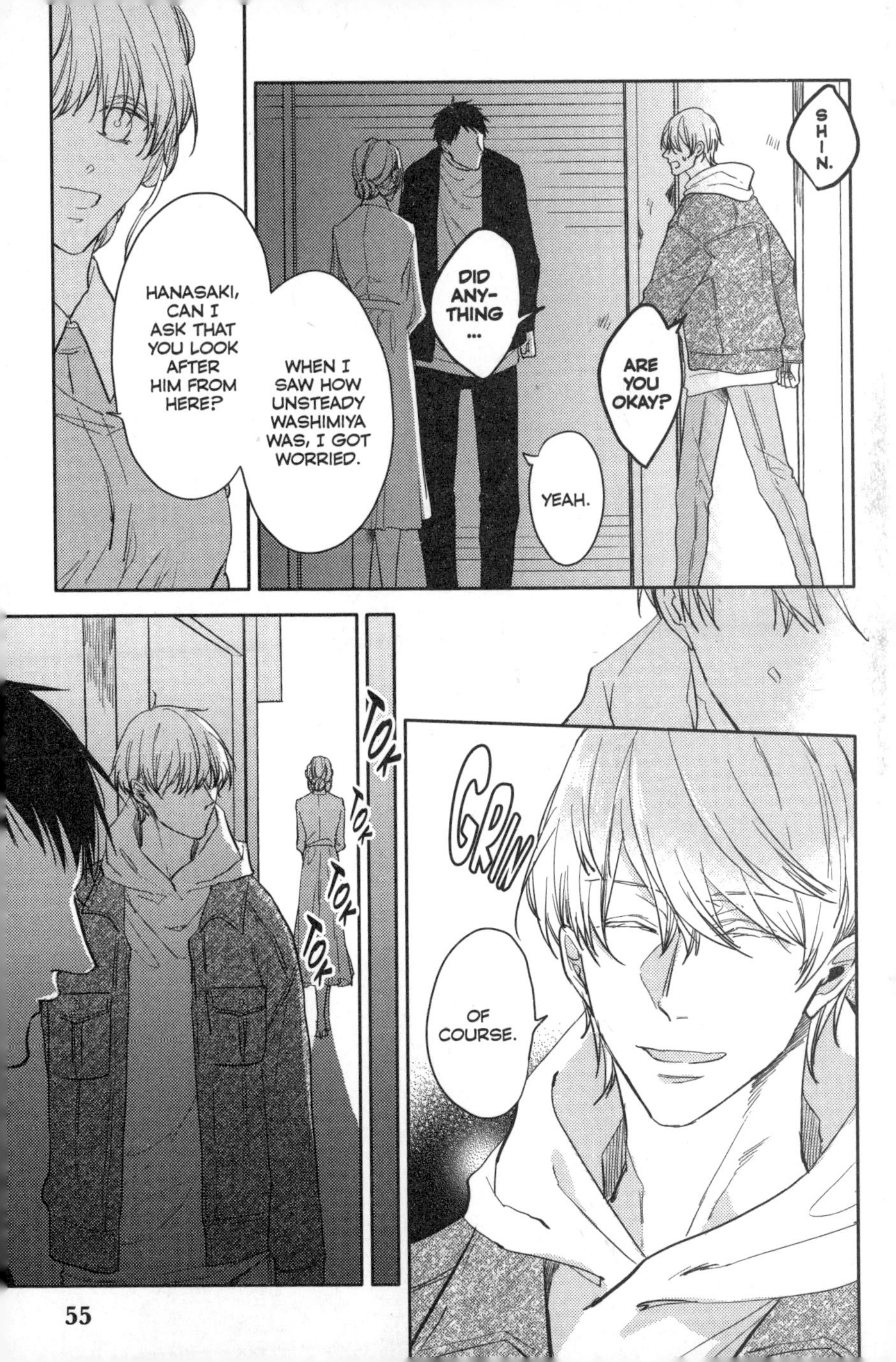
SHIN.
ARE YOU OKAY?
YEAH.
DID ANYTHING...
WHEN I SAW HOW UNSTEADY WASHIMIYA WAS, I GOT WORRIED.
HANASAKI, CAN I ASK THAT YOU LOOK AFTER HIM FROM HERE?
GRIN
OF COURSE.
TOK TOK TOK TOK

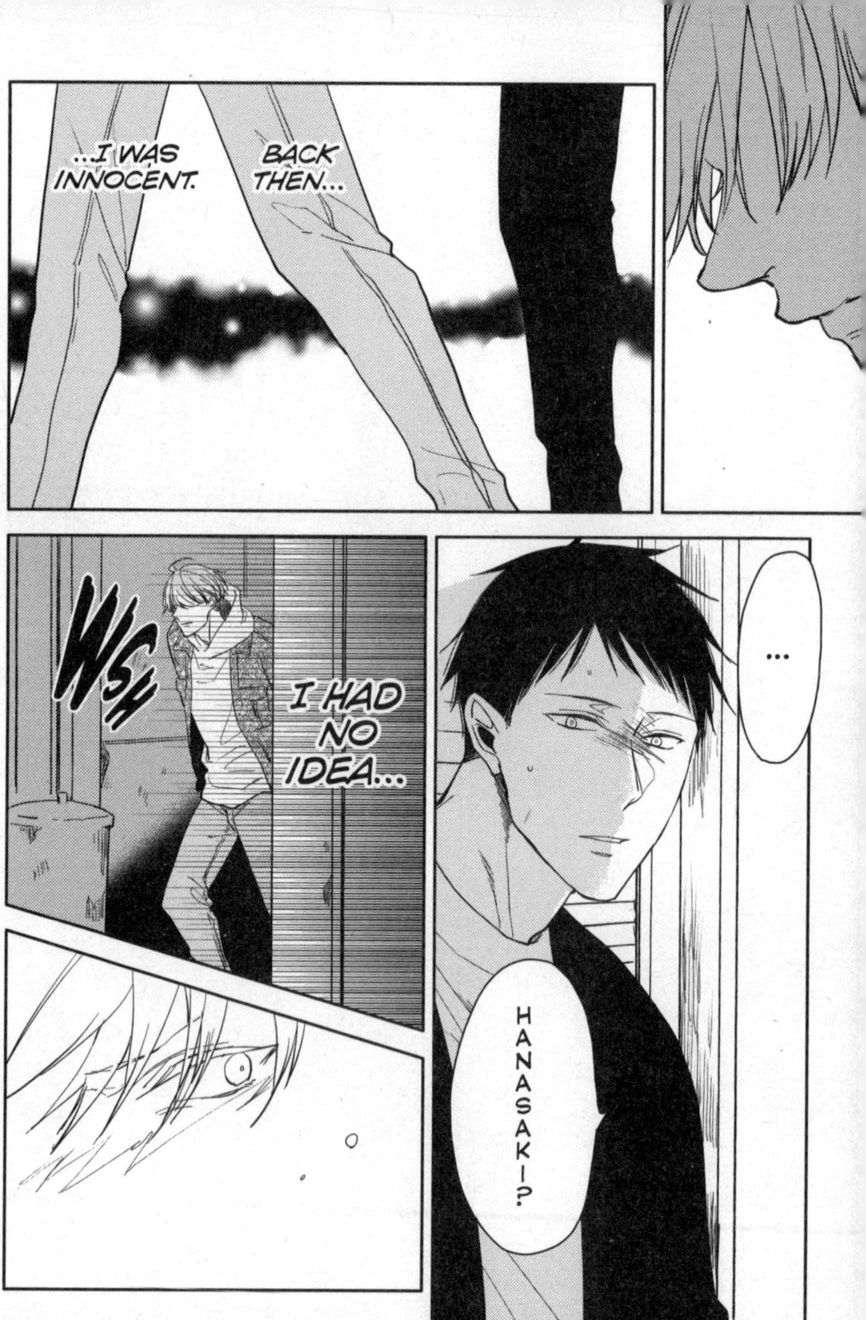
BACK THEN...
...I WAS INNOCENT.
...
HANASAKI!?
I HAD NO IDEA...
WSH

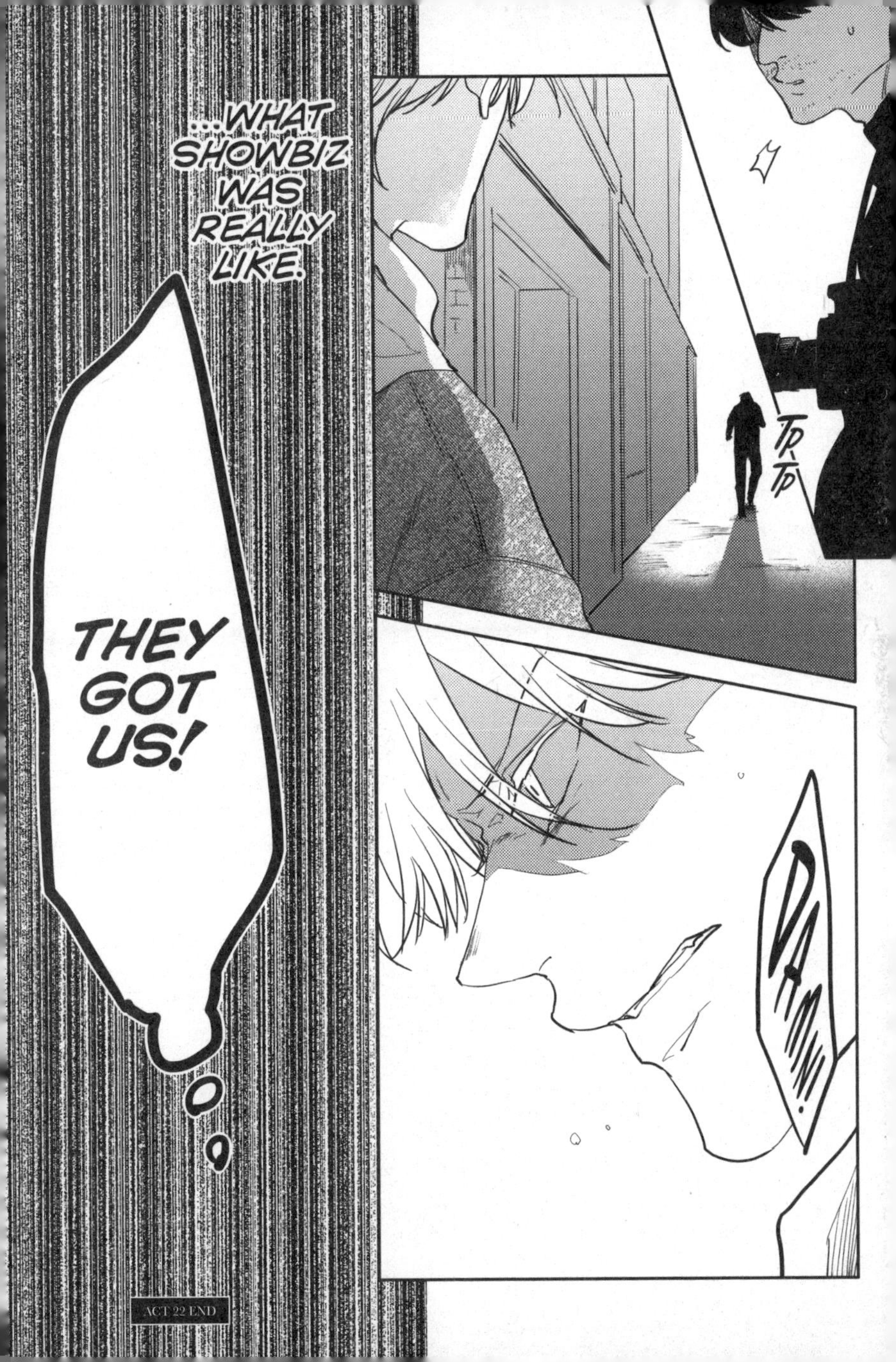
TP TP
DAMN!!
...WHAT SHOWBIZ WAS REALLY LIKE.
THEY GOT US!
ACT 22 END

Black
or White

Black or White

or White

ACT 23

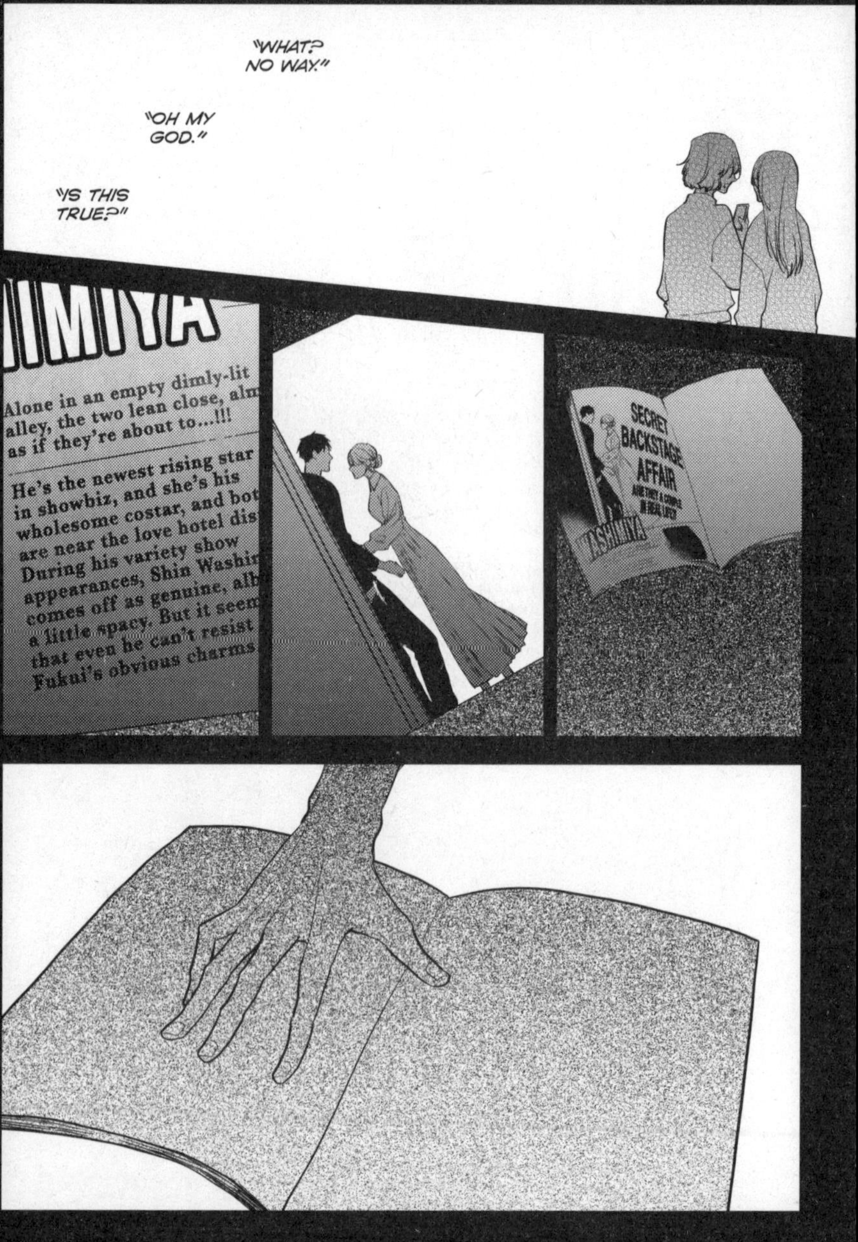
"WHAT? NO WAY."
"OH MY GOD."
"IS THIS TRUE?"
SECRET BACKSTAGE AFFAIR
IMIYA
Alone in an empty dimly-lit alley, the two lean close, alm as if they're about to...!!!
He's the newest rising star in showbiz, and she's his wholesome costar, and bot are near the love hotel dis During his variety show appearances, Shin Washi comes off as genuine, alb a little spacy. But it seem that even he can't resist Fukui's obvious charms

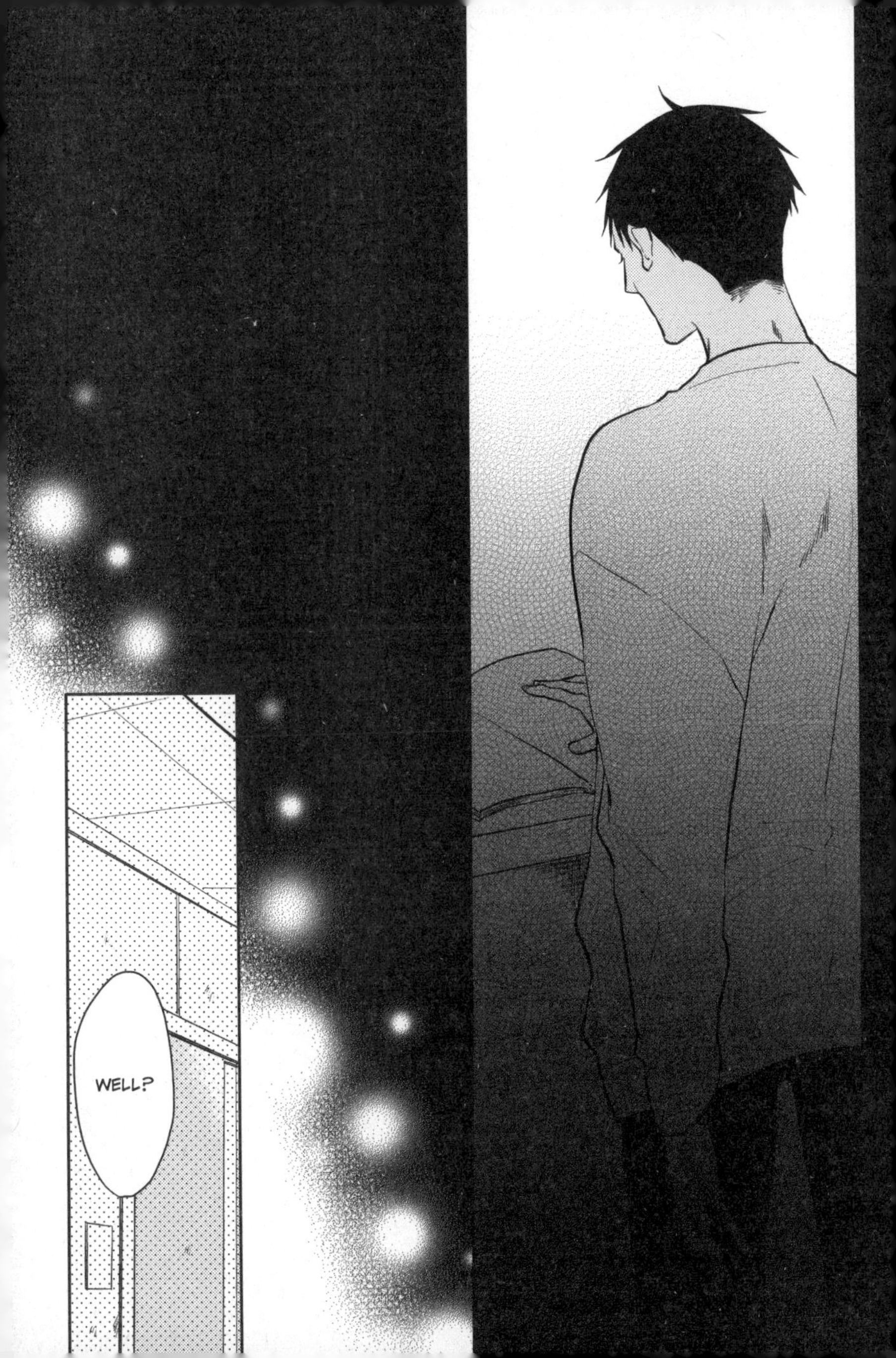
WELL?

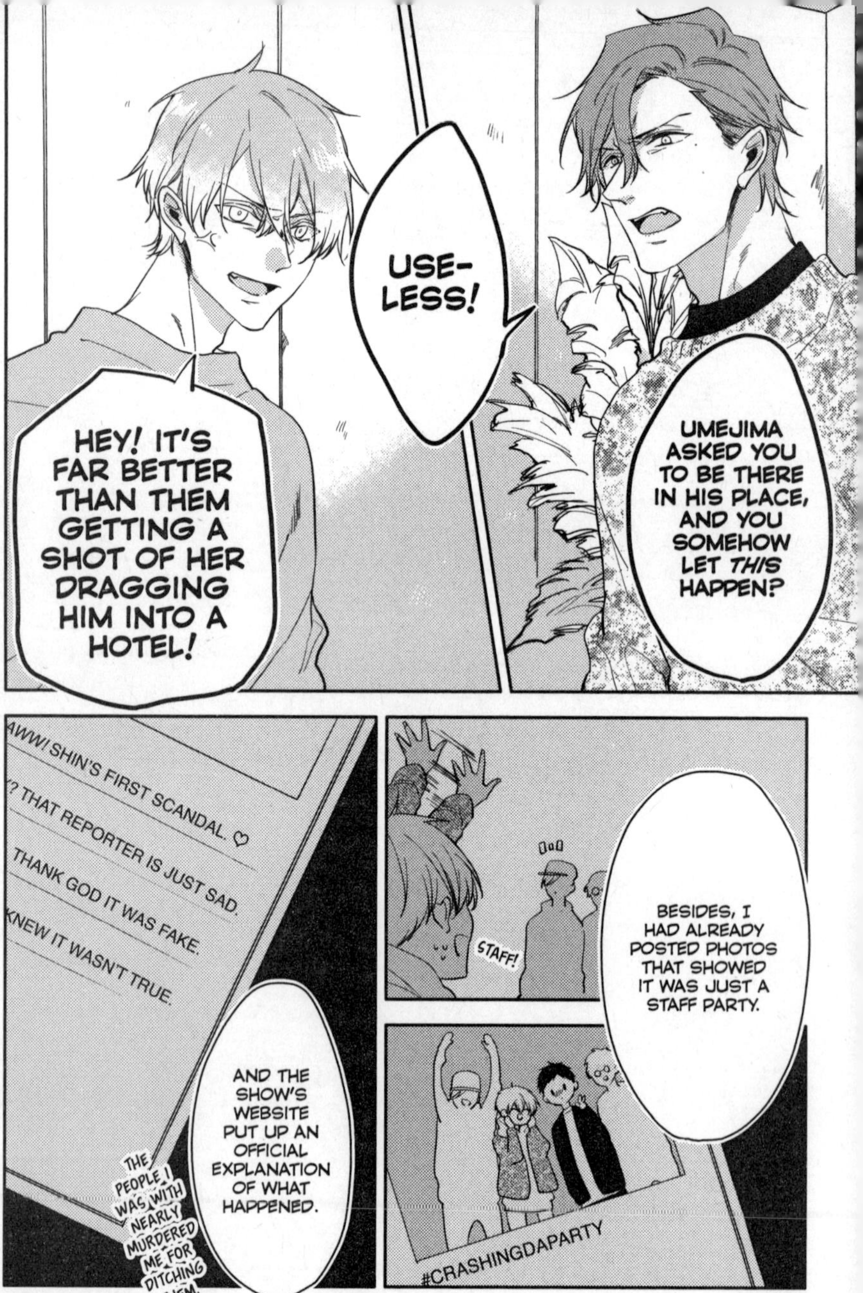
UMEJIMA ASKED YOU TO BE THERE IN HIS PLACE, AND YOU SOMEHOW LET *THIS* HAPPEN?
USE-LESS!
HEY! IT'S FAR BETTER THAN THEM GETTING A SHOT OF HER DRAGGING HIM INTO A HOTEL!
BESIDES, I HAD ALREADY POSTED PHOTOS THAT SHOWED IT WAS JUST A STAFF PARTY.
STAFF!
#CRASHINGDAPARTY
AWW! SHIN'S FIRST SCANDAL. ♡
THAT REPORTER IS JUST SAD.
THANK GOD IT WAS FAKE.
KNEW IT WASN'T TRUE.
AND THE SHOW'S WEBSITE PUT UP AN OFFICIAL EXPLANATION OF WHAT HAPPENED.
THE PEOPLE I WAS WITH NEARLY MURDERED ME FOR DITCHING THEM, Y'KNOW.

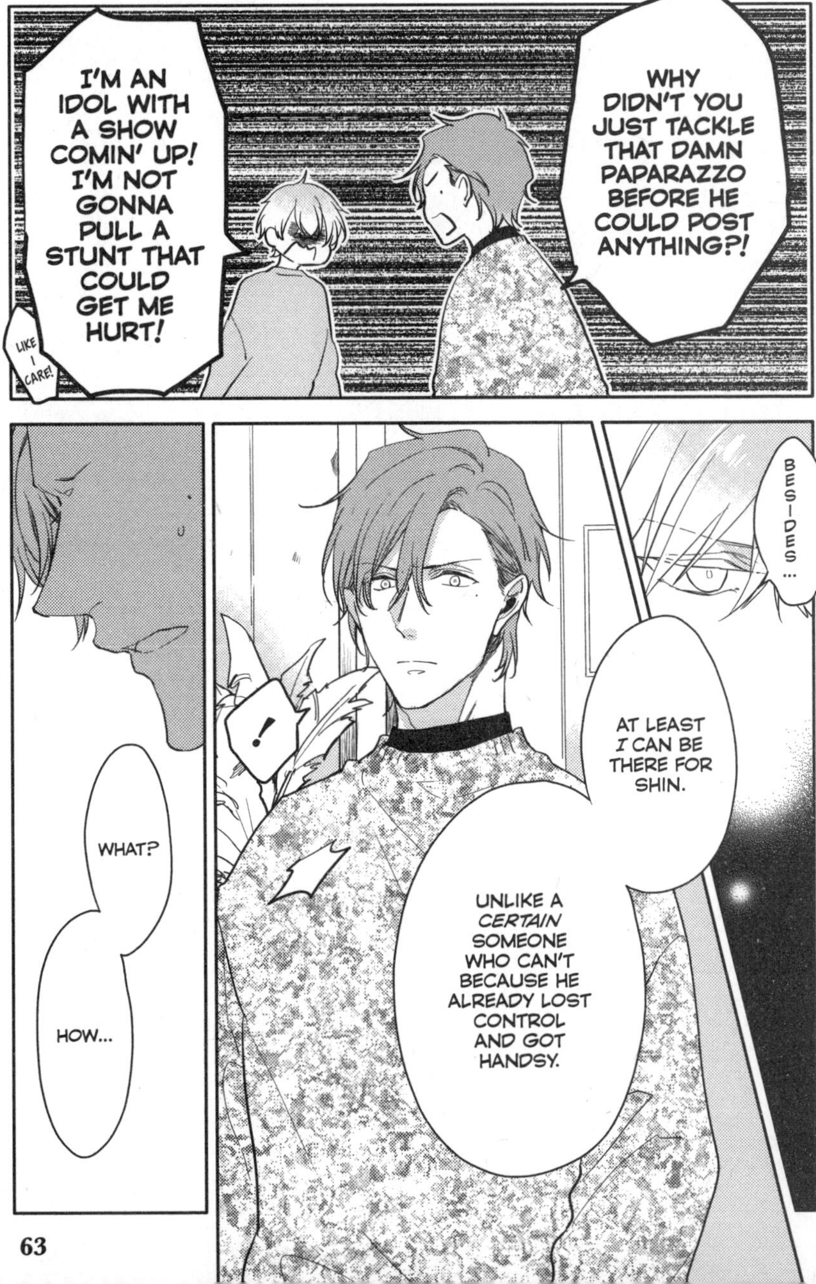
WHY DIDN'T YOU JUST TACKLE THAT DAMN PAPARAZZO BEFORE HE COULD POST ANYTHING?!
I'M AN IDOL WITH A SHOW COMIN' UP! I'M NOT GONNA PULL A STUNT THAT COULD GET ME HURT!
LIKE I CARE!
BESIDES...
AT LEAST *I* CAN BE THERE FOR SHIN.
UNLIKE A *CERTAIN* SOMEONE WHO CAN'T BECAUSE HE ALREADY LOST CONTROL AND GOT HANDSY.
!
WHAT?
HOW...

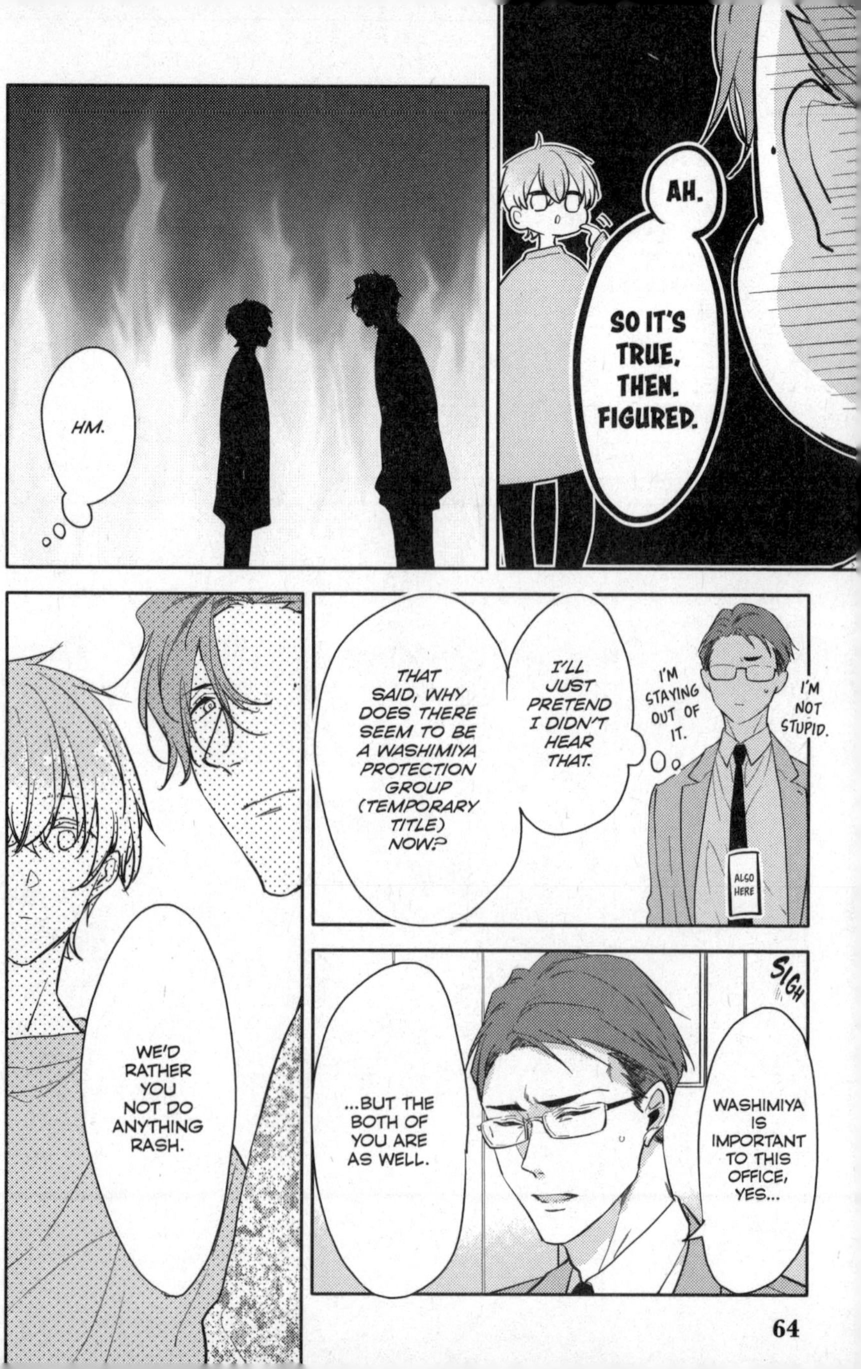
AH.
SO IT'S TRUE, THEN. FIGURED.
HM.
I'M NOT STUPID.
I'M STAYING OUT OF IT.
ALSO HERE
I'LL JUST PRETEND I DIDN'T HEAR THAT.
THAT SAID, WHY DOES THERE SEEM TO BE A WASHIMIYA PROTECTION GROUP (TEMPORARY TITLE) NOW?
SIGH
WASHIMIYA IS IMPORTANT TO THIS OFFICE, YES...
...BUT THE BOTH OF YOU ARE AS WELL.
WE'D RATHER YOU NOT DO ANYTHING RASH.

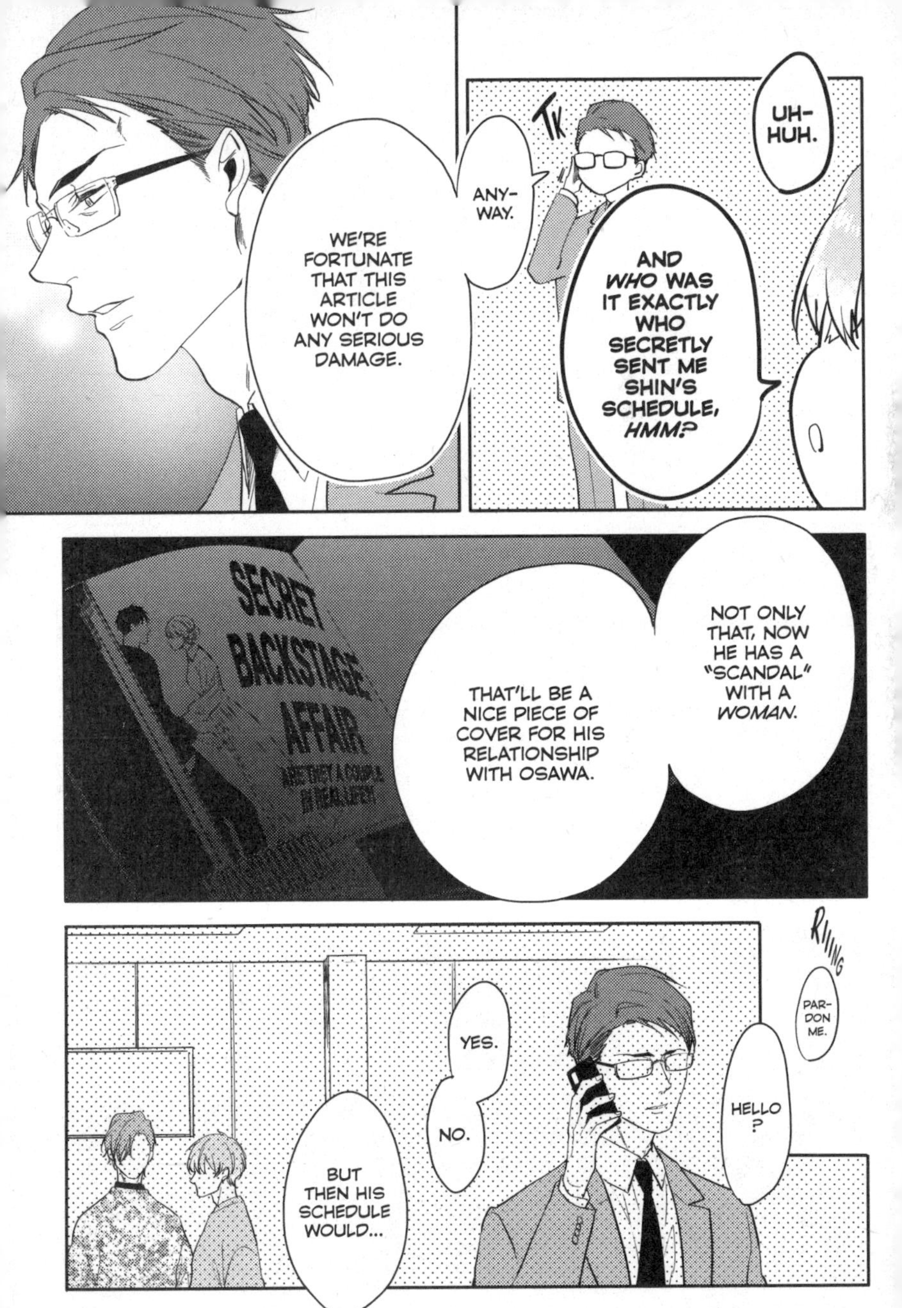
UH-HUH.
AND *WHO* WAS IT EXACTLY WHO SECRETLY SENT ME SHIN'S SCHEDULE, *HMM?*
TK
ANY-WAY.
WE'RE FORTUNATE THAT THIS ARTICLE WON'T DO ANY SERIOUS DAMAGE.
NOT ONLY THAT, NOW HE HAS A "SCANDAL" WITH A *WOMAN*.
THAT'LL BE A NICE PIECE OF COVER FOR HIS RELATIONSHIP WITH OSAWA.
SECRET BACKSTAGE AFFAIR
ARE THEY A COUPLE IN REAL LIFE?!
RIIING
PAR-DON ME.
HELLO?
YES.
NO.
BUT THEN HIS SCHEDULE WOULD...

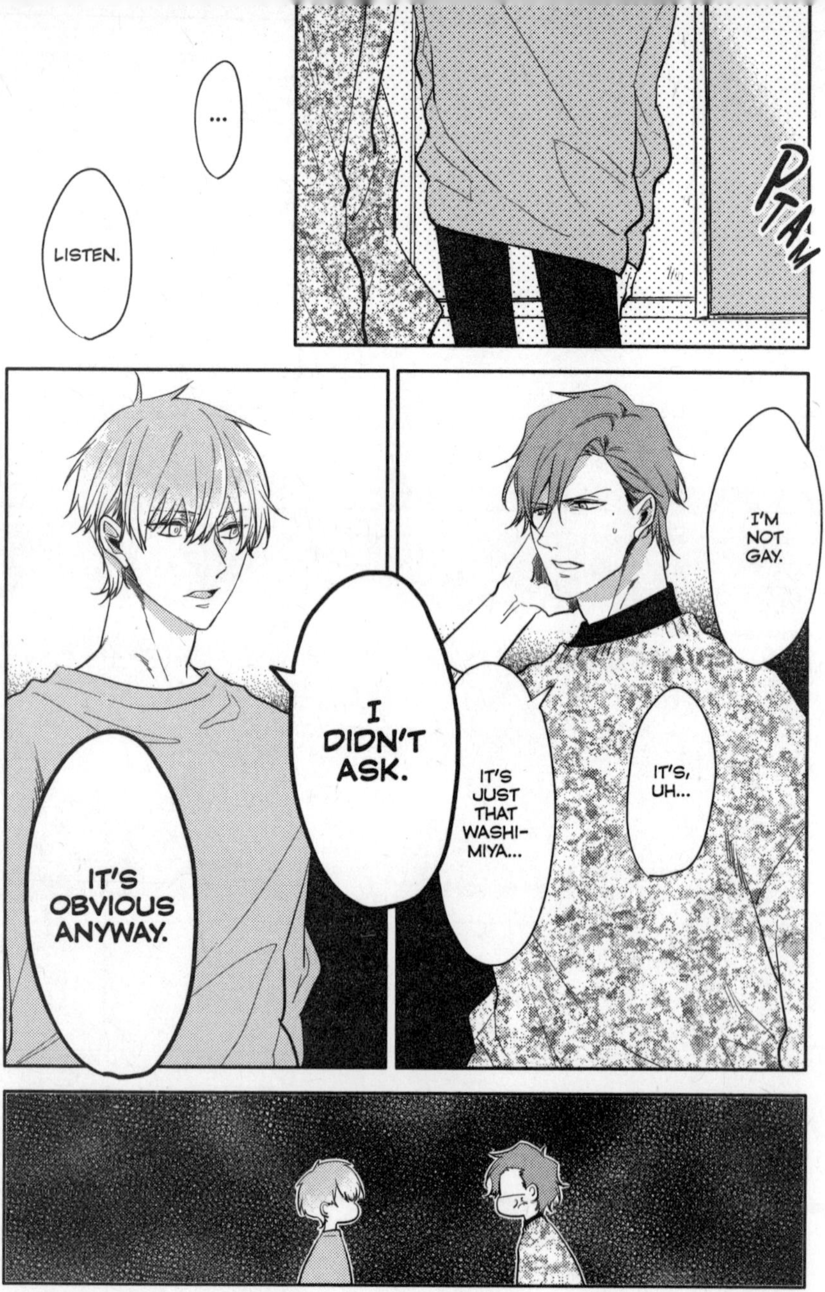
PTAM
...
LISTEN.
I'M NOT GAY.
IT'S, UH...
IT'S JUST THAT WASHIMIYA...
I DIDN'T ASK.
IT'S OBVIOUS ANYWAY.

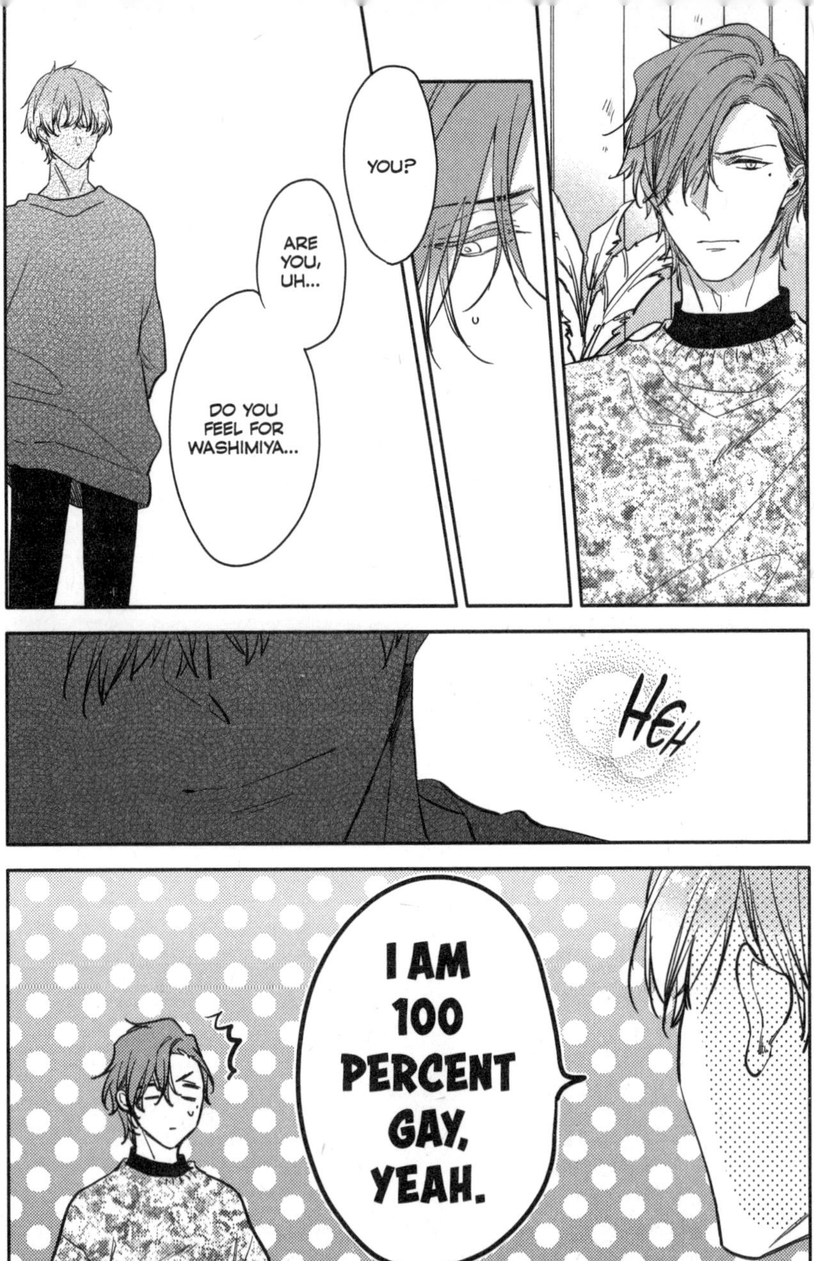
YOU?
ARE YOU, UH...
DO YOU FEEL FOR WASHIMIYA...
HEH
I AM 100 PERCENT GAY, YEAH.

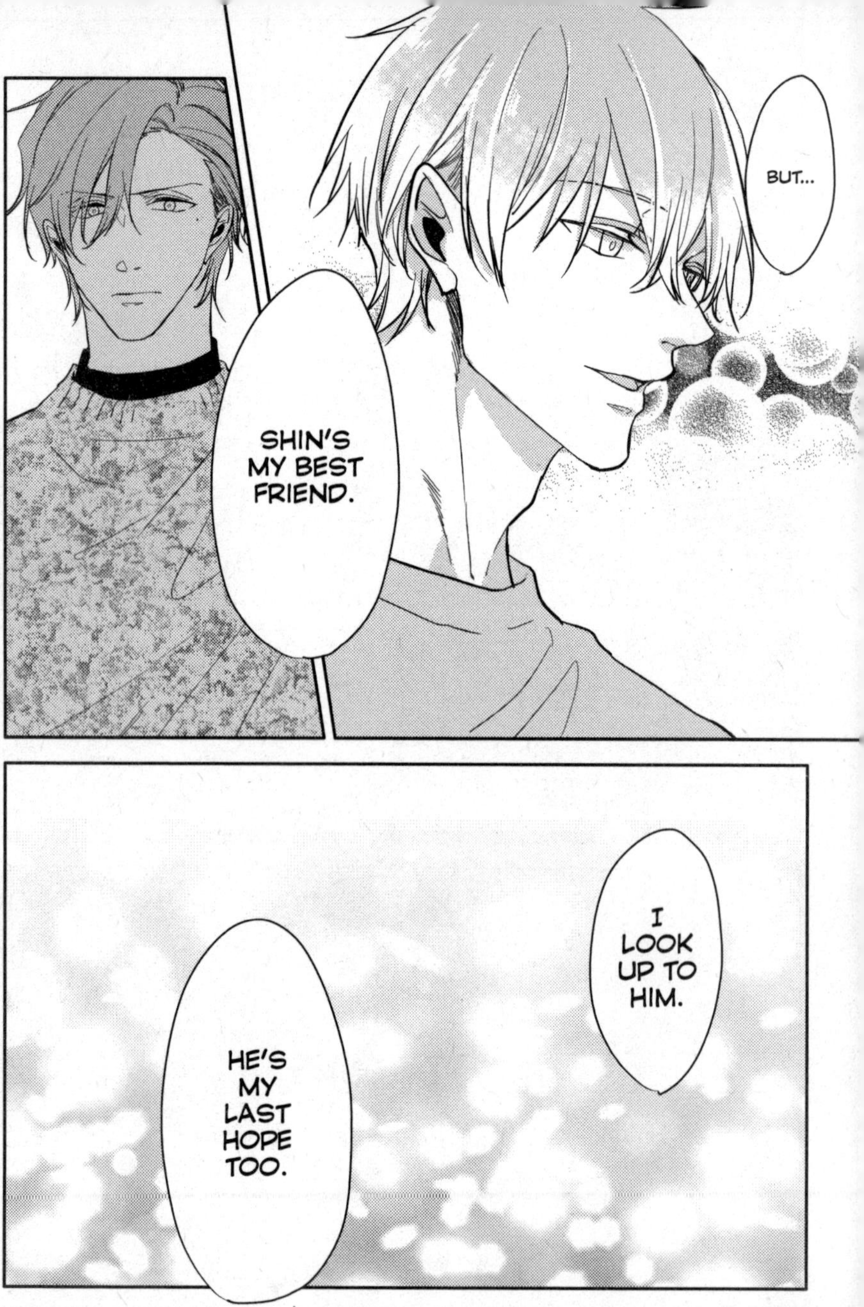
BUT...
SHIN'S MY BEST FRIEND.
I LOOK UP TO HIM.
HE'S MY LAST HOPE TOO.

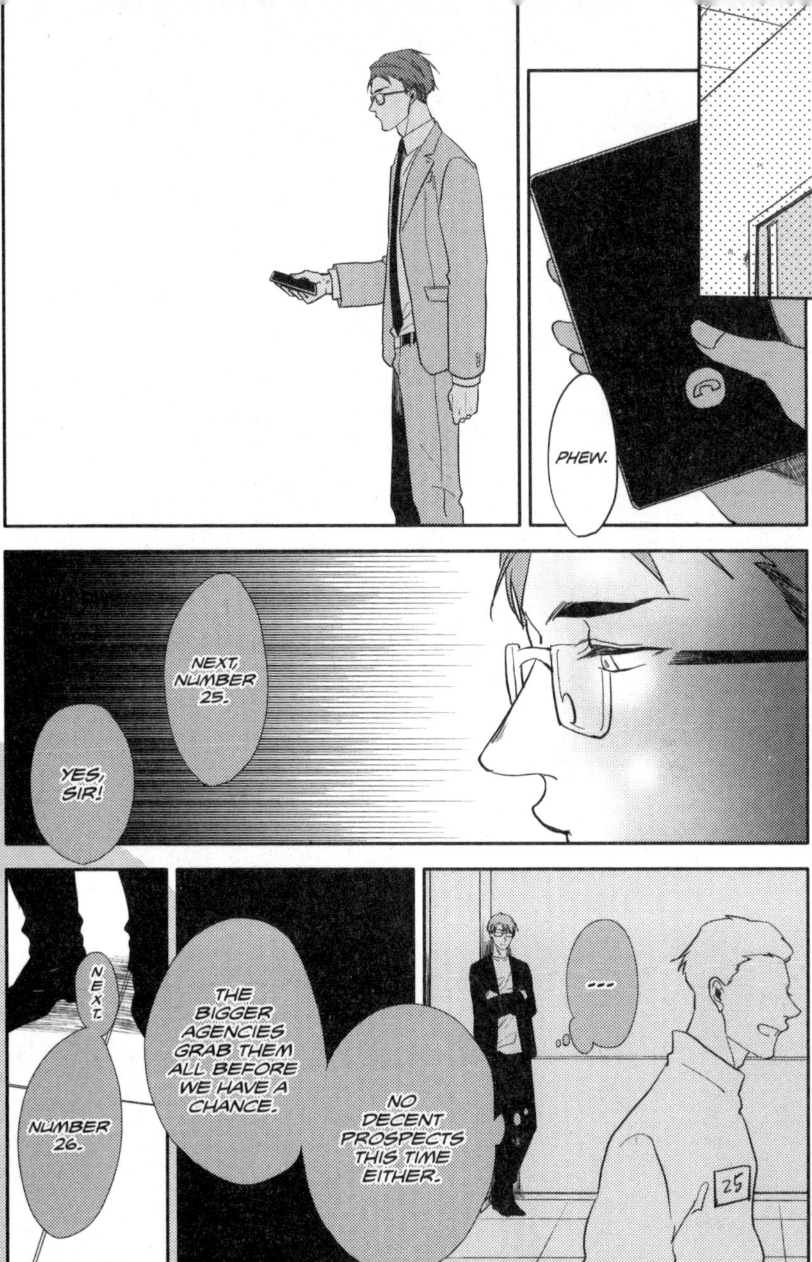
PHEW.
NEXT, NUMBER 25.
YES, SIR!
...
NO DECENT PROSPECTS THIS TIME EITHER.
THE BIGGER AGENCIES GRAB THEM ALL BEFORE WE HAVE A CHANCE.
NEXT.
NUMBER 26.

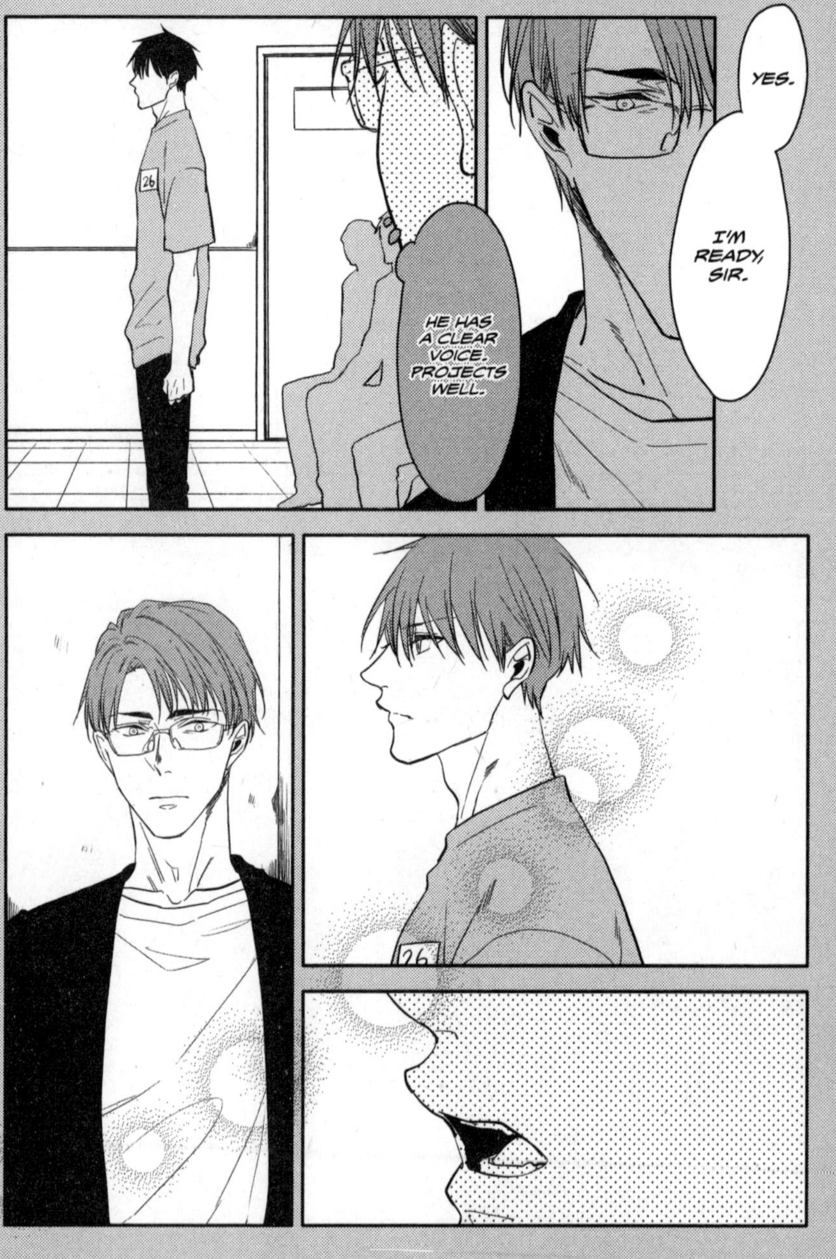
YES.
I'M READY, SIR.
HE HAS A CLEAR VOICE. PROJECTS WELL.

NUMBER 25.

NUMBER 11.

YOU MAY REMAIN.

NUMBER 16.

EXCUSE ME.

ARE YOU A MEMBER OF ANY AGENCY?

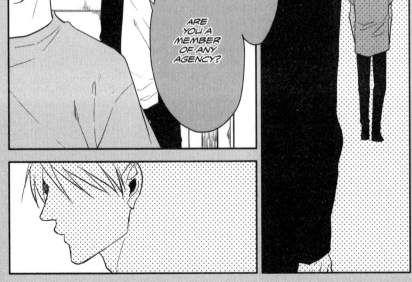

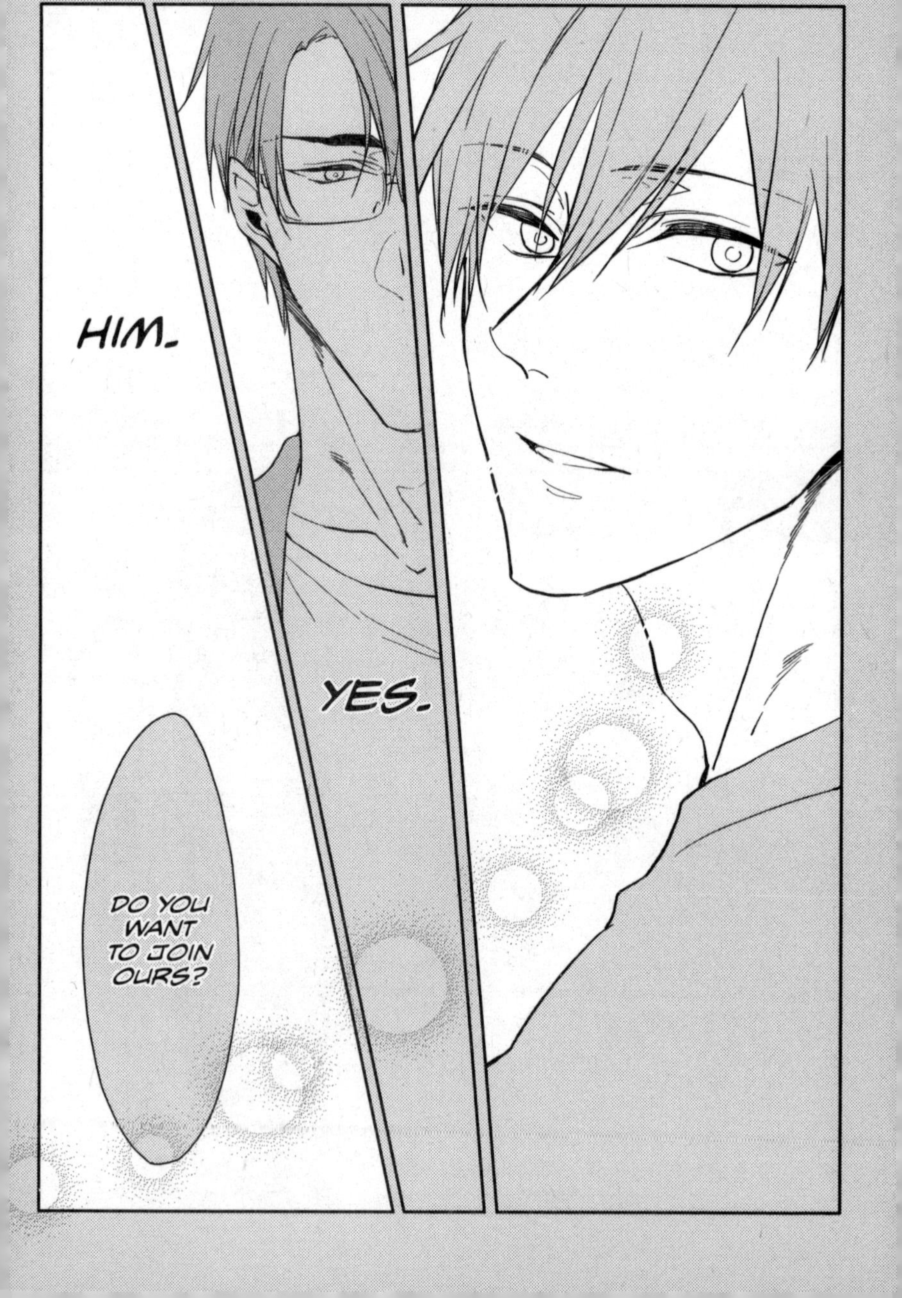
YES_
HIM_
DO YOU WANT TO JOIN OURS?

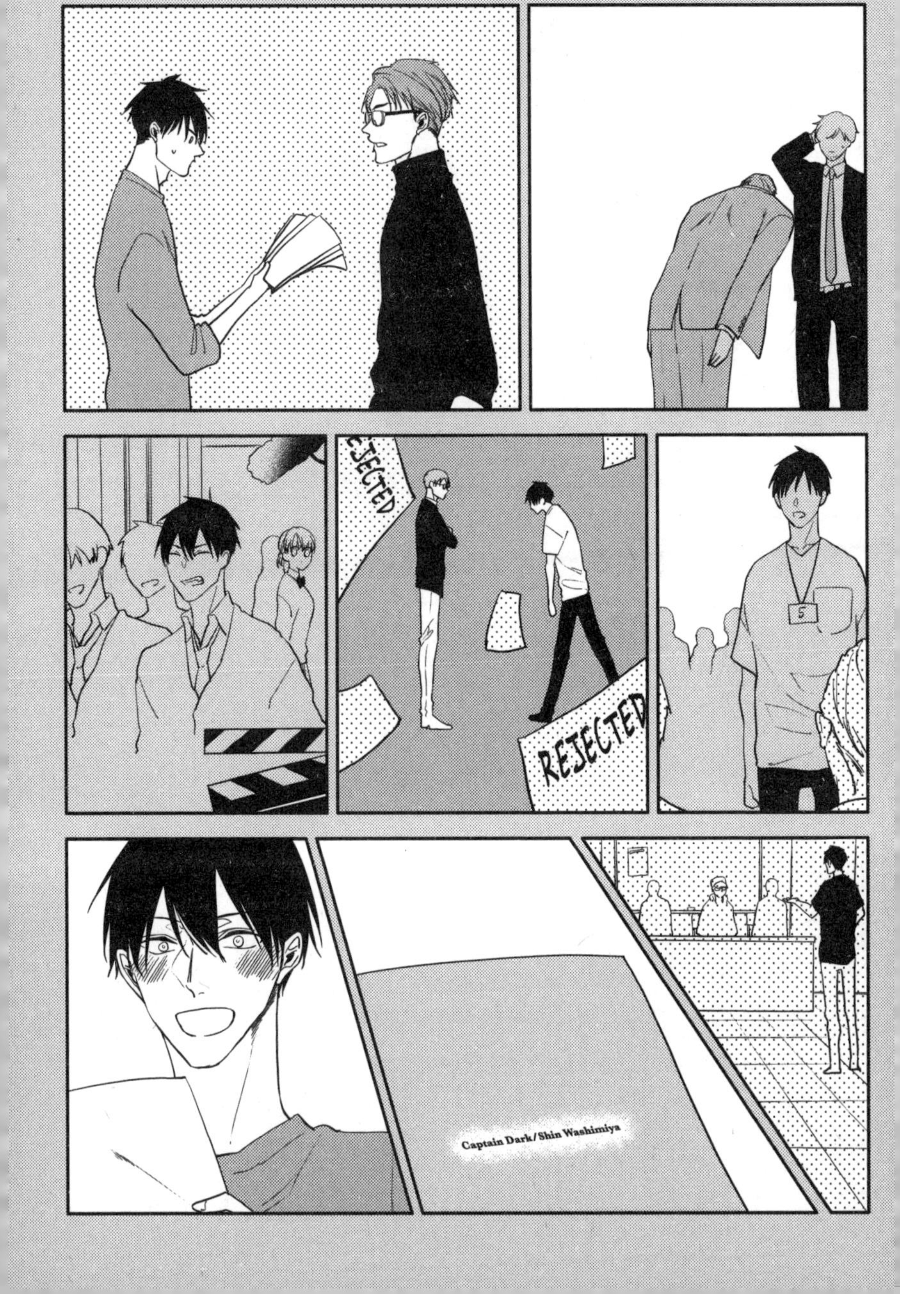
5
REJECTED
REJECTED
Captain Dark/Shin Washimiya

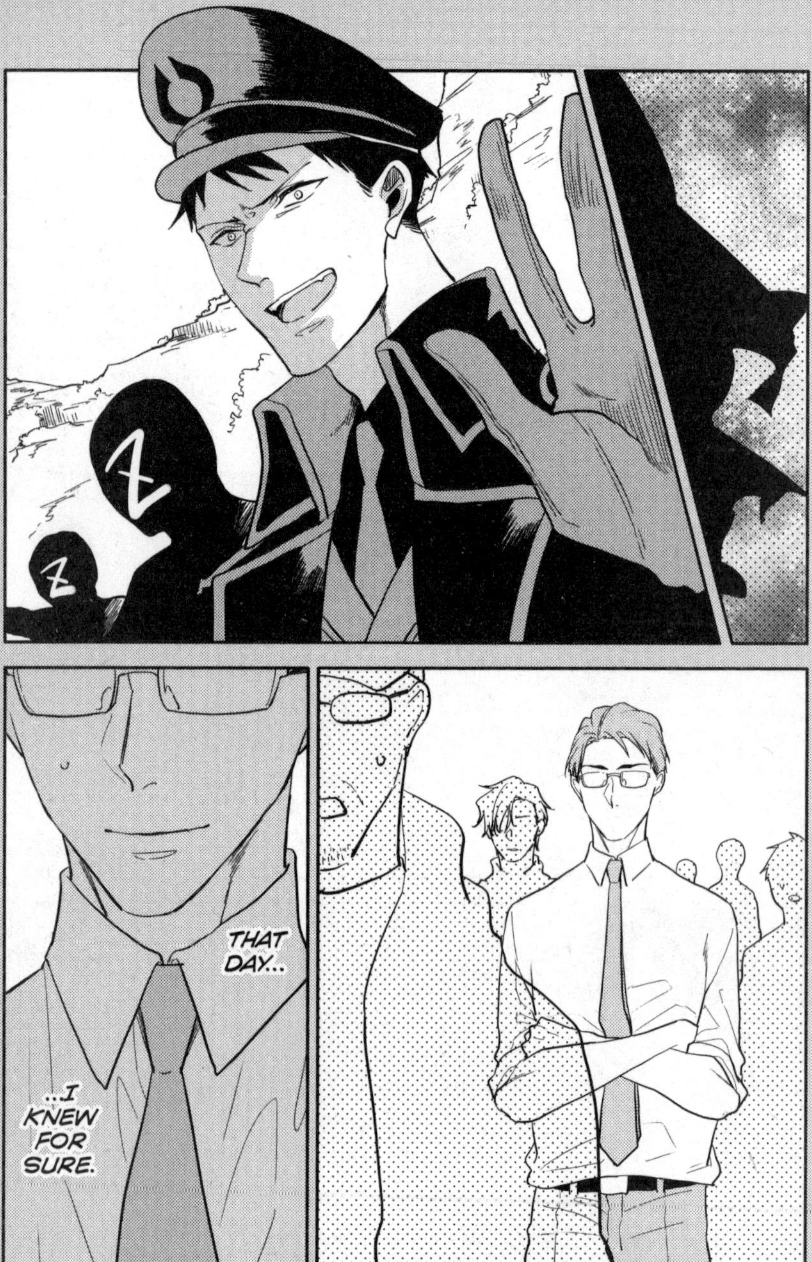
THAT DAY...
...I KNEW FOR SURE.

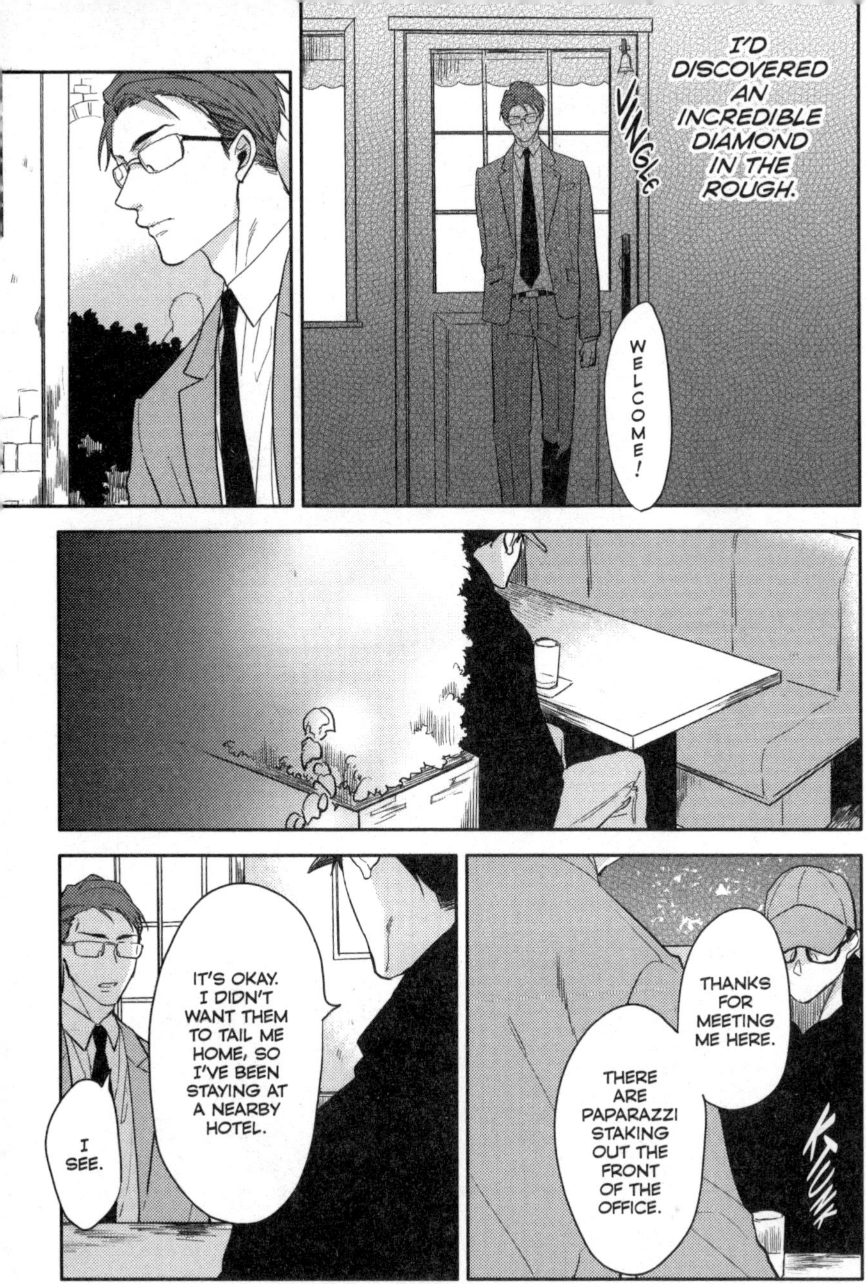
I'D DISCOVERED AN INCREDIBLE DIAMOND IN THE ROUGH.
VINGLE
WELCOME!
THANKS FOR MEETING ME HERE.
THERE ARE PAPARAZZI STAKING OUT THE FRONT OF THE OFFICE.
KTUNK
IT'S OKAY. I DIDN'T WANT THEM TO TAIL ME HOME, SO I'VE BEEN STAYING AT A NEARBY HOTEL.
I SEE.

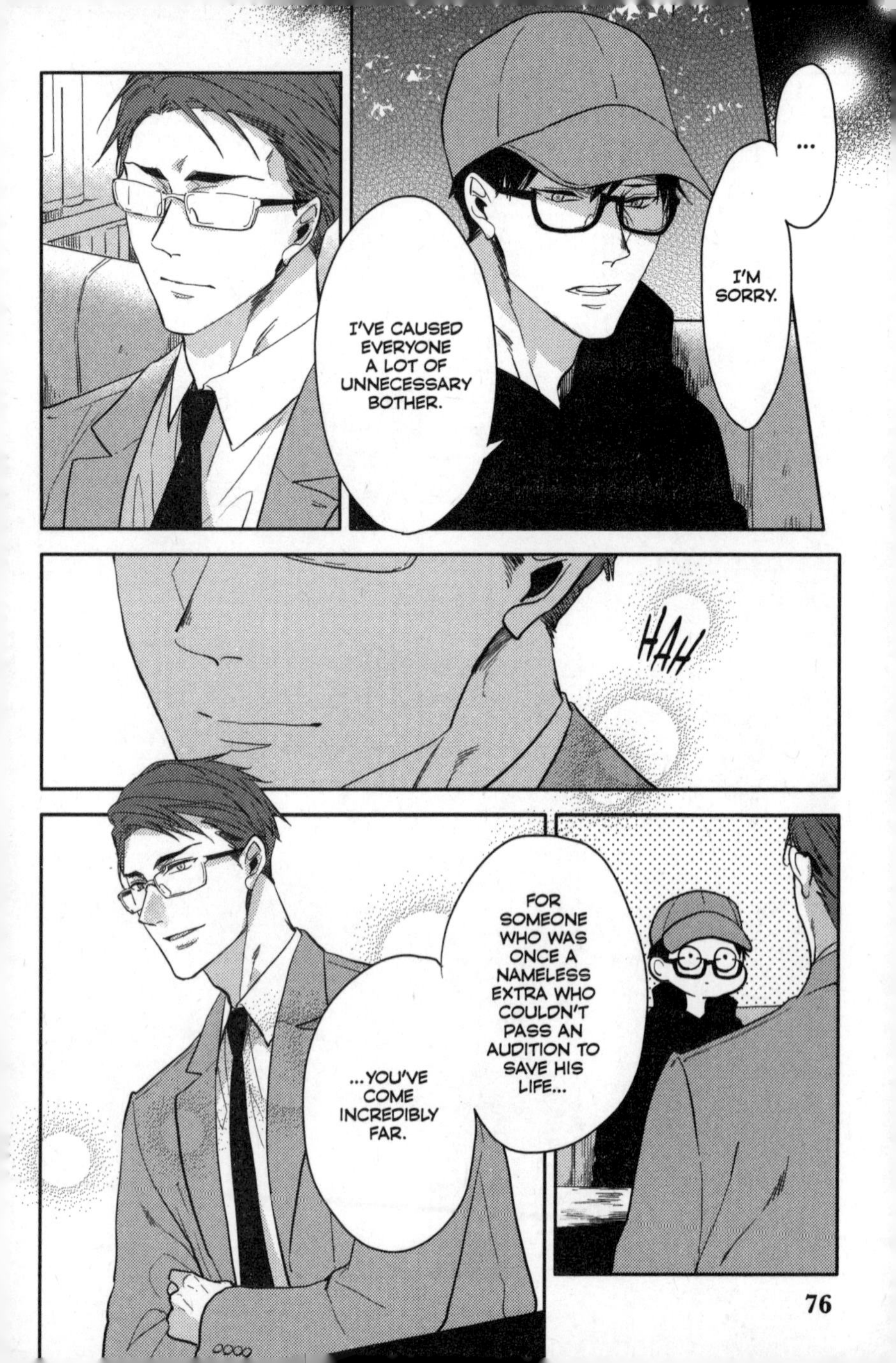
...
I'M SORRY.
I'VE CAUSED EVERYONE A LOT OF UNNECESSARY BOTHER.
HAH
FOR SOMEONE WHO WAS ONCE A NAMELESS EXTRA WHO COULDN'T PASS AN AUDITION TO SAVE HIS LIFE...
...YOU'VE COME INCREDIBLY FAR.

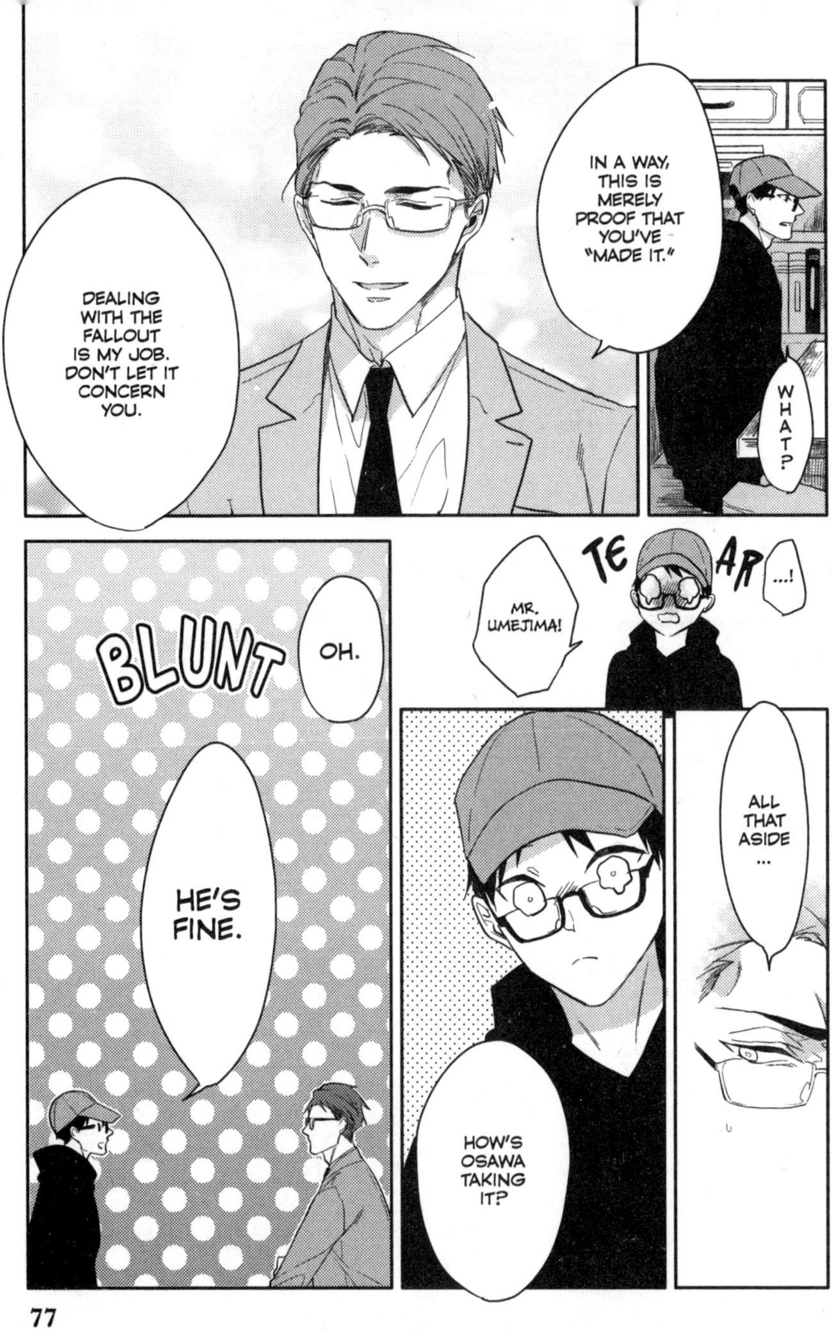
IN A WAY, THIS IS MERELY PROOF THAT YOU'VE "MADE IT."
WHAT?
DEALING WITH THE FALLOUT IS MY JOB. DON'T LET IT CONCERN YOU.
...!
TEAR
MR. UMEJIMA!
ALL THAT ASIDE...
HOW'S OSAWA TAKING IT?
OH.
BLUNT
HE'S FINE.

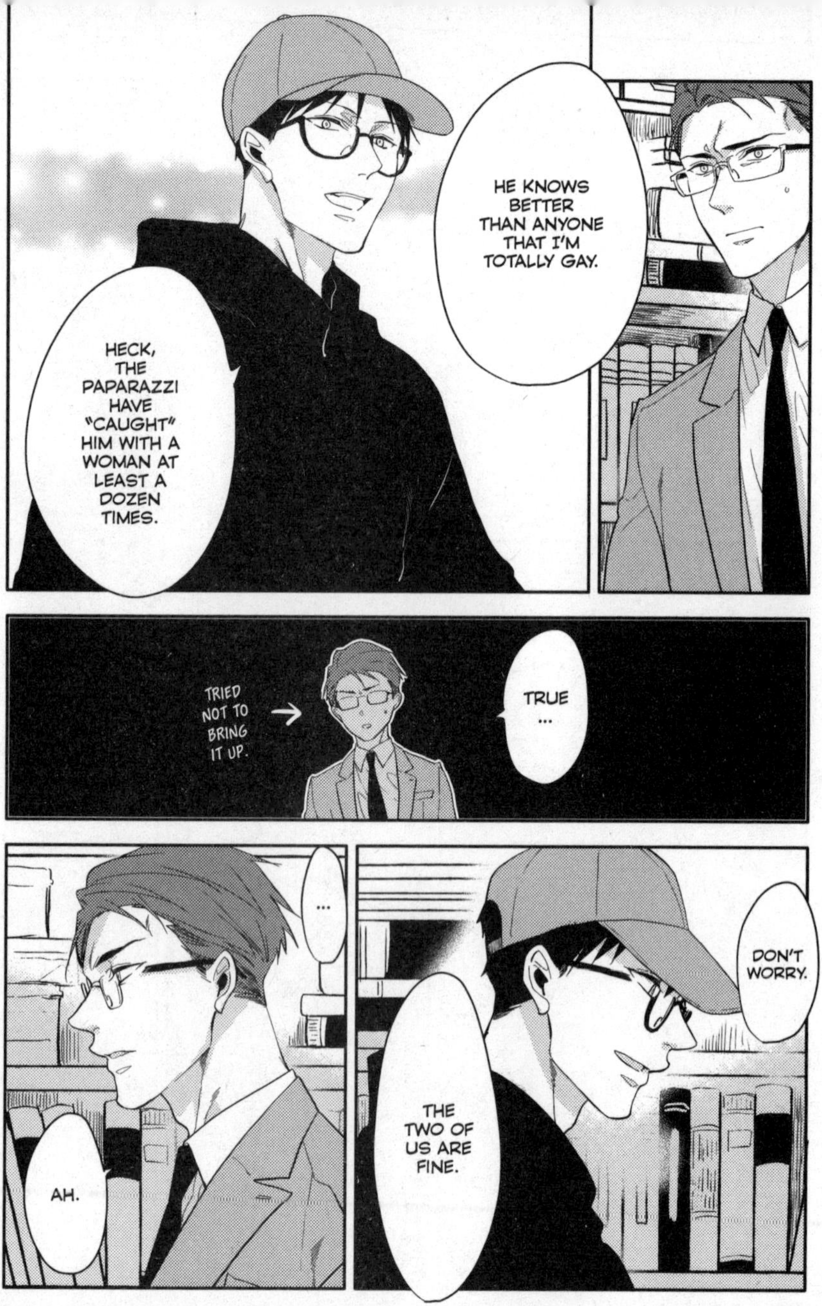
HE KNOWS BETTER THAN ANYONE THAT I'M TOTALLY GAY.
HECK, THE PAPARAZZI HAVE "CAUGHT" HIM WITH A WOMAN AT LEAST A DOZEN TIMES.
TRUE ...
TRIED NOT TO BRING IT UP.
DON'T WORRY.
THE TWO OF US ARE FINE.
...
AH.

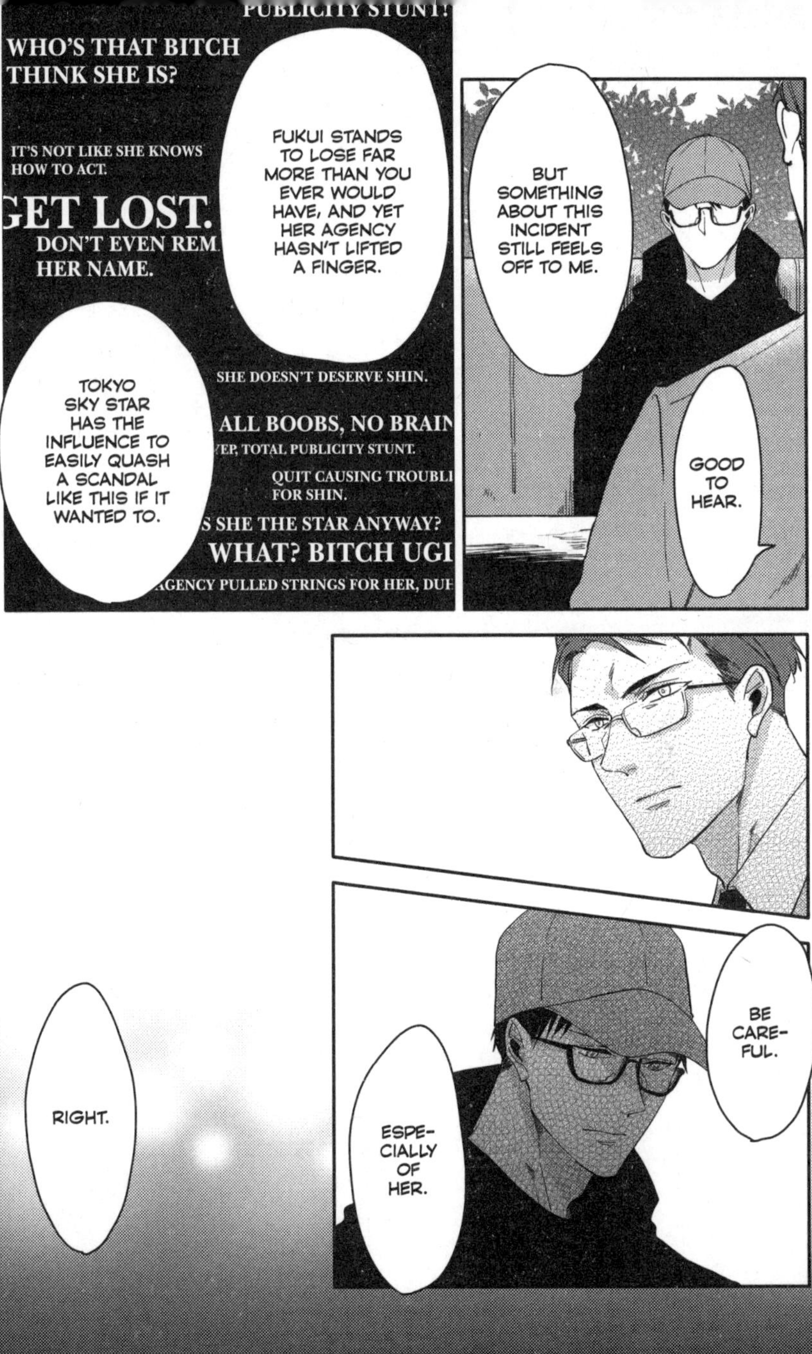
GOOD TO HEAR.
BUT SOMETHING ABOUT THIS INCIDENT STILL FEELS OFF TO ME.
PUBLICITY STUNT!
WHO'S THAT BITCH THINK SHE IS?
IT'S NOT LIKE SHE KNOWS HOW TO ACT.
GET LOST.
DON'T EVEN REM. HER NAME.
FUKUI STANDS TO LOSE FAR MORE THAN YOU EVER WOULD HAVE, AND YET HER AGENCY HASN'T LIFTED A FINGER.
SHE DOESN'T DESERVE SHIN.
ALL BOOBS, NO BRAIN
YEP, TOTAL PUBLICITY STUNT.
QUIT CAUSING TROUBL FOR SHIN.
S SHE THE STAR ANYWAY?
WHAT? BITCH UGI
AGENCY PULLED STRINGS FOR HER, DUH
TOKYO SKY STAR HAS THE INFLUENCE TO EASILY QUASH A SCANDAL LIKE THIS IF IT WANTED TO.
BE CARE-FUL.
ESPE-CIALLY OF HER.
RIGHT.

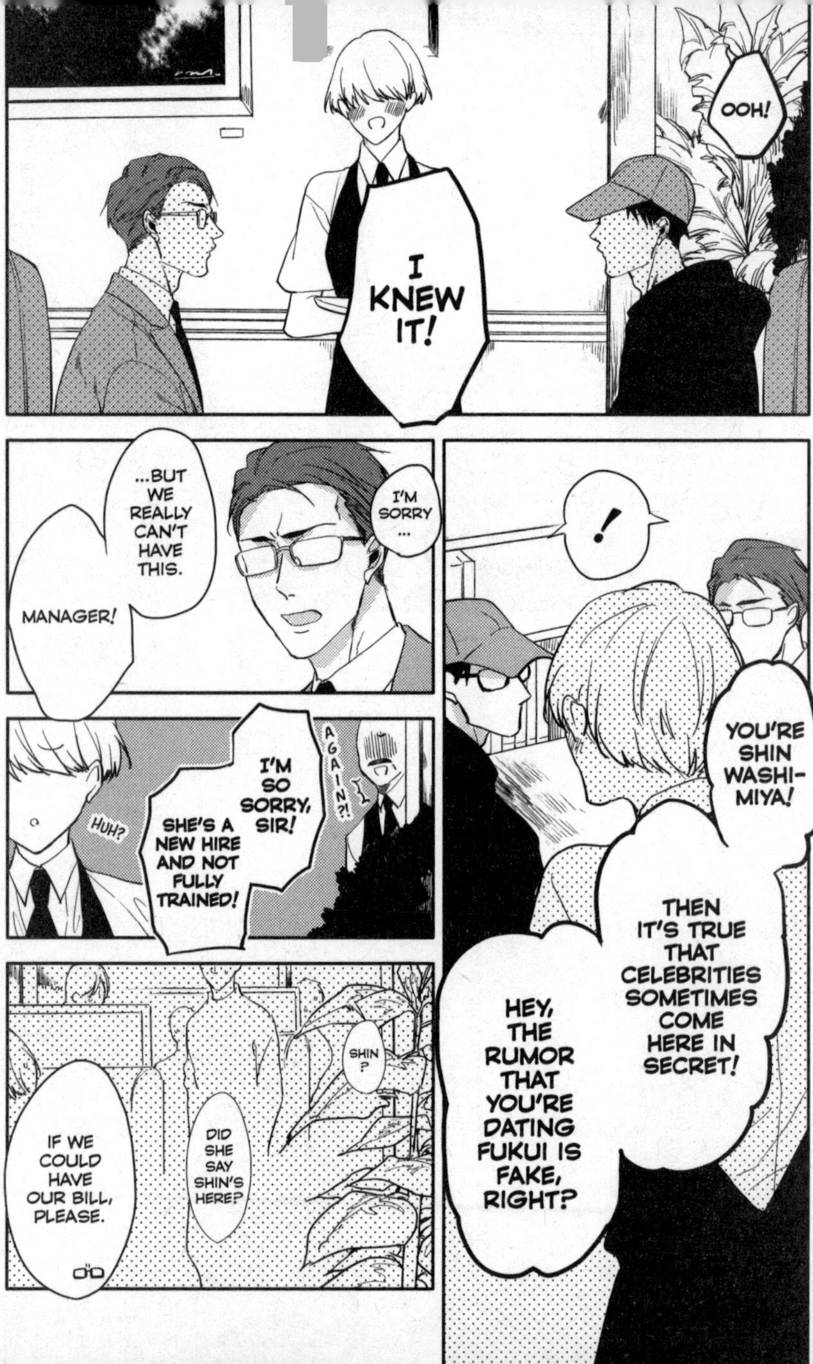

OOH!
I KNEW IT!
!
YOU'RE SHIN WASHIMIYA!
THEN IT'S TRUE THAT CELEBRITIES SOMETIMES COME HERE IN SECRET!
HEY, THE RUMOR THAT YOU'RE DATING FUKUI IS FAKE, RIGHT?
I'M SORRY...
...BUT WE REALLY CAN'T HAVE THIS.
MANAGER!
AGAIN?!
I'M SO SORRY, SIR!
SHE'S A NEW HIRE AND NOT FULLY TRAINED!
HUH?
SHIN?
DID SHE SAY SHIN'S HERE?
IF WE COULD HAVE OUR BILL, PLEASE.

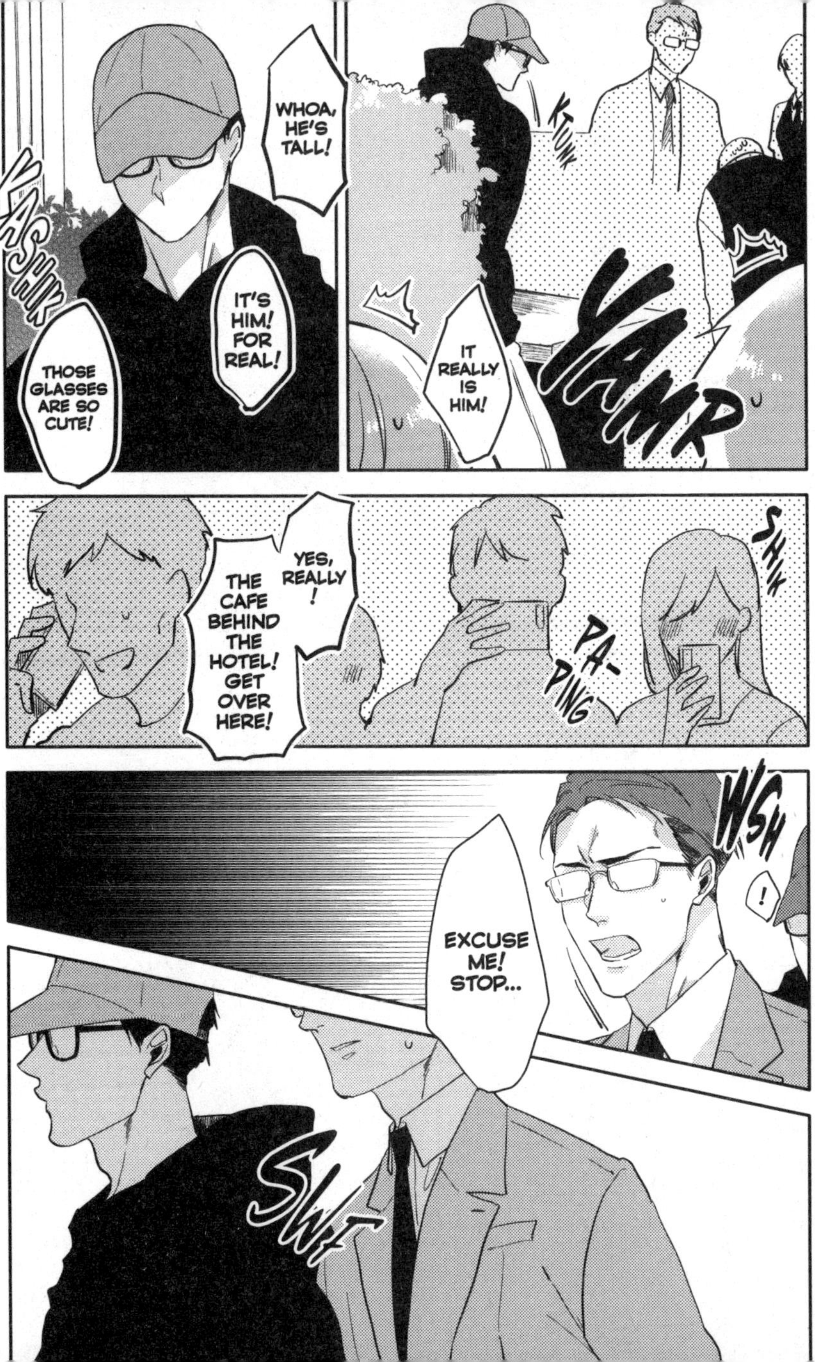
KTUNK
YAMR
IT REALLY IS HIM!
WHOA, HE'S TALL!
IT'S HIM! FOR REAL!
KASHIK
THOSE GLASSES ARE SO CUTE!
SHIK
PA-PING
YES, REALLY!
THE CAFE BEHIND THE HOTEL! GET OVER HERE!
WSH
!
EXCUSE ME! STOP...
SWF

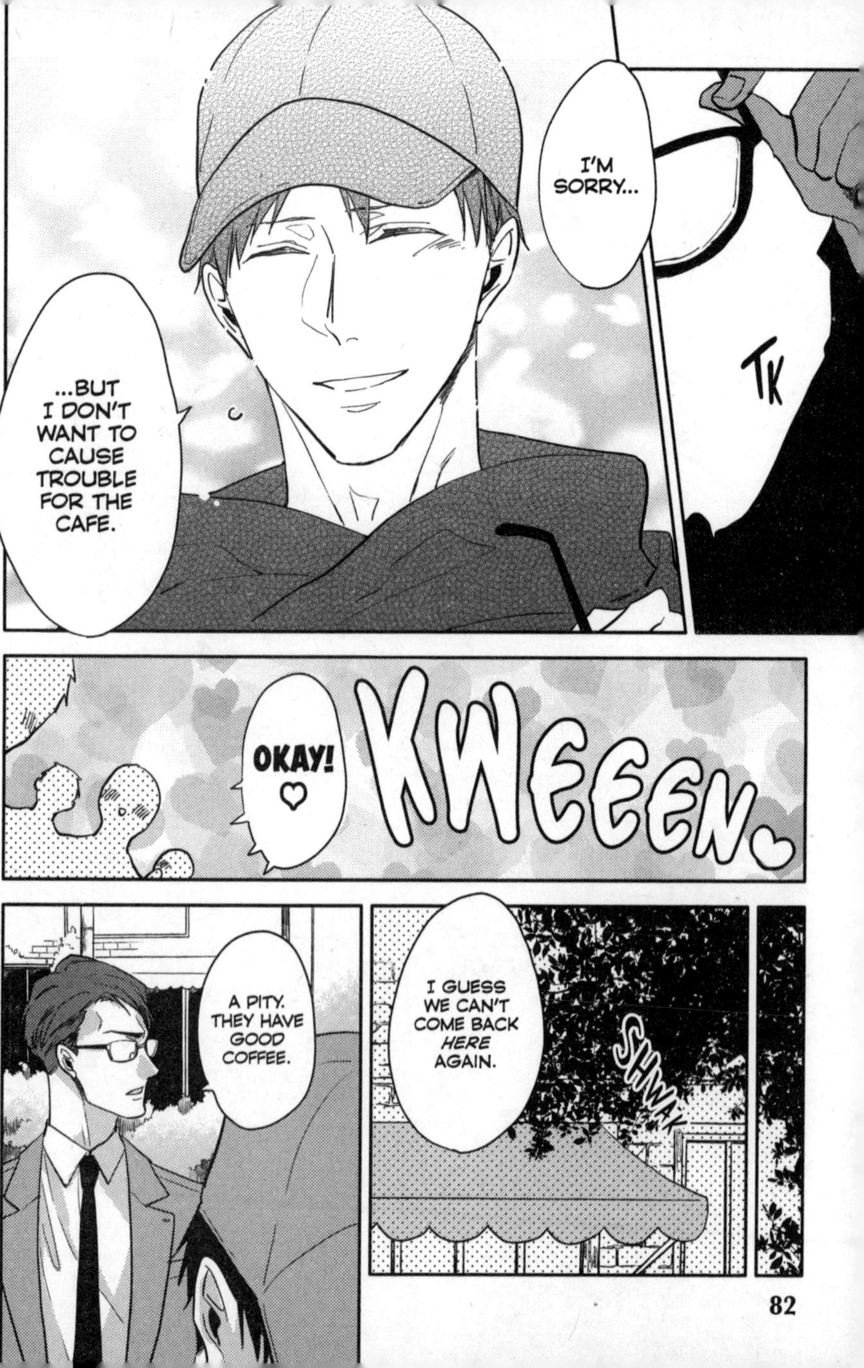
TK
I'M SORRY...
...BUT I DON'T WANT TO CAUSE TROUBLE FOR THE CAFE.
KWEEEN♡
OKAY! ♡
SHWAK
I GUESS WE CAN'T COME BACK *HERE* AGAIN.
A PITY. THEY HAVE GOOD COFFEE.

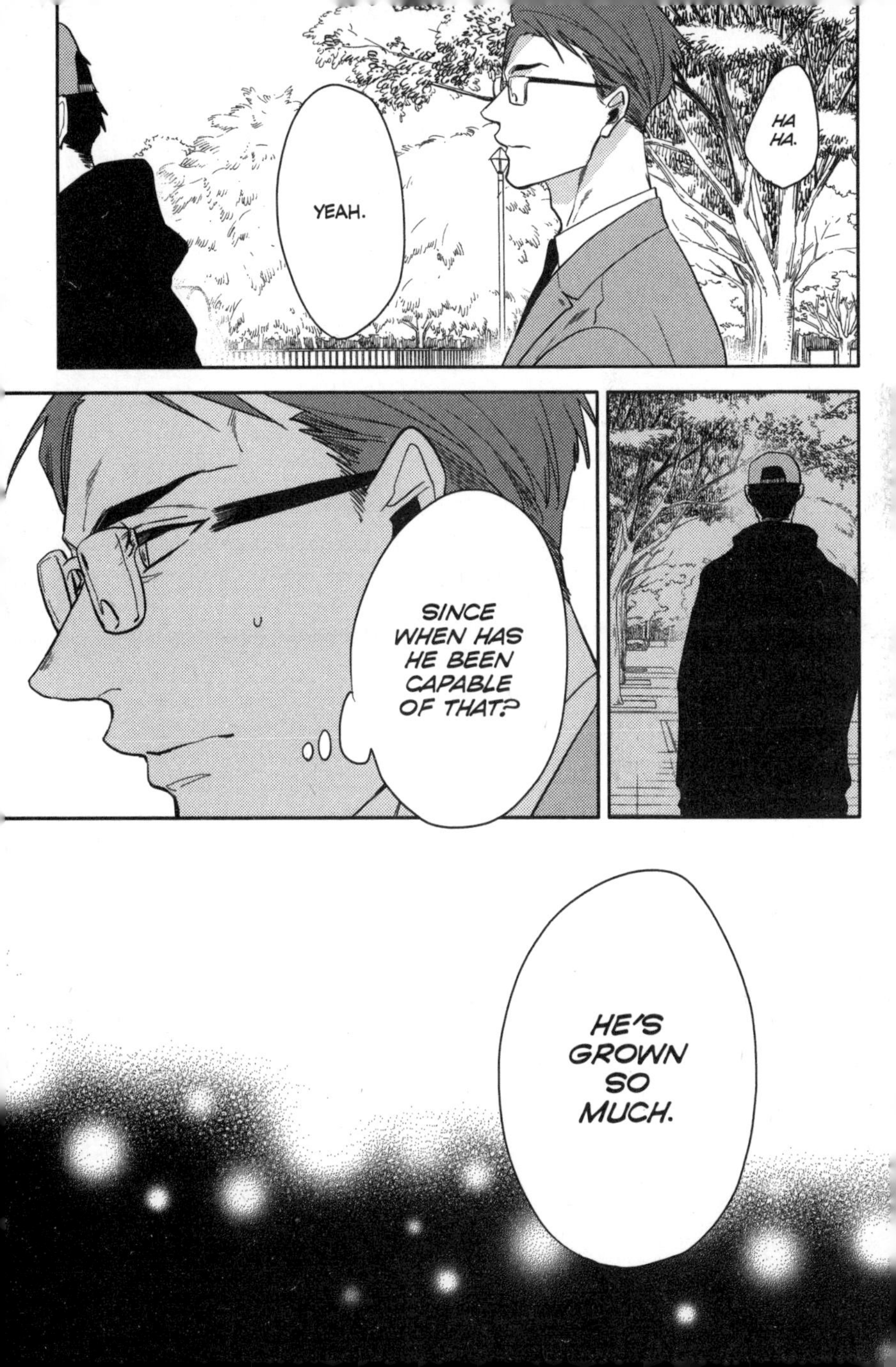
HA HA.
YEAH.
SINCE WHEN HAS HE BEEN CAPABLE OF THAT?
HE'S GROWN SO MUCH.

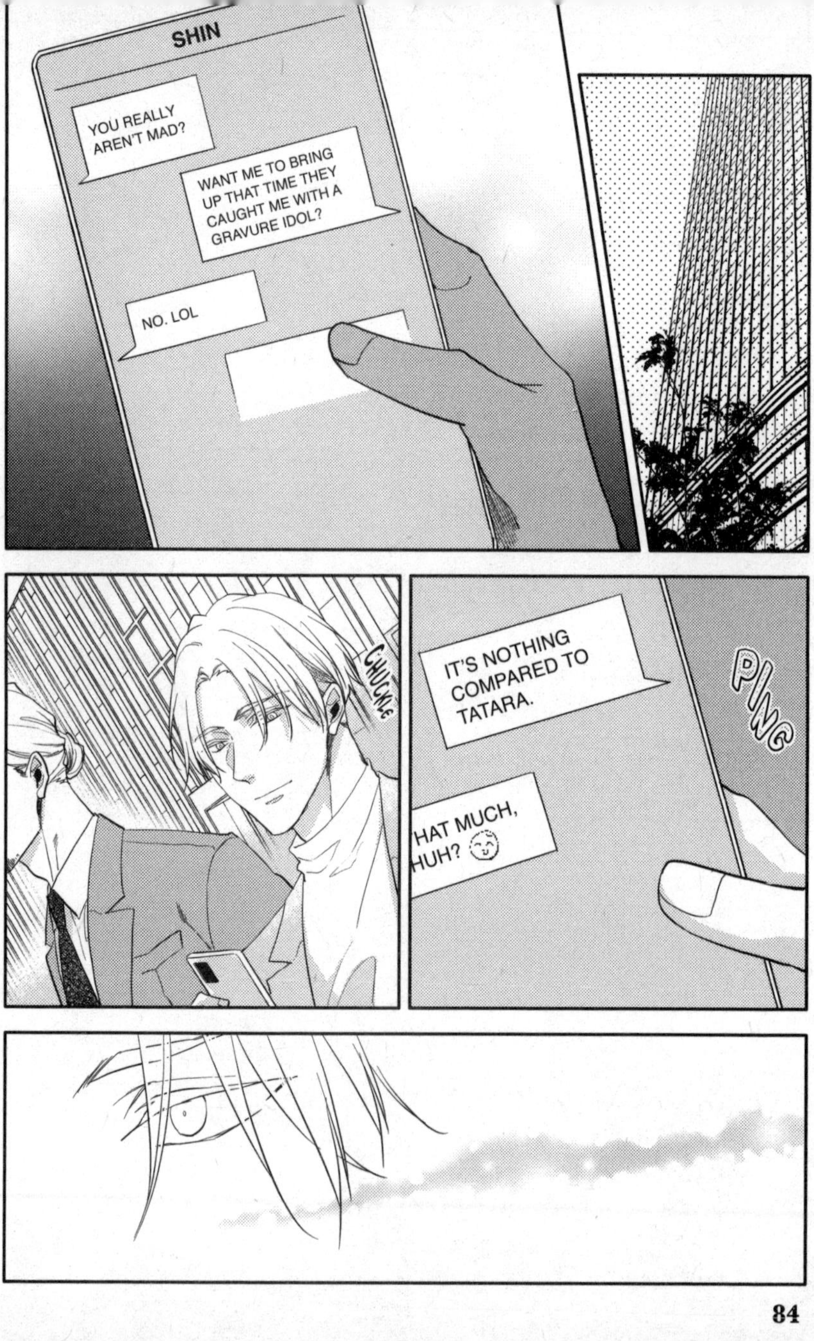
SHIN
YOU REALLY AREN'T MAD?
WANT ME TO BRING UP THAT TIME THEY CAUGHT ME WITH A GRAVURE IDOL?
NO. LOL
PING
IT'S NOTHING COMPARED TO TATARA.
HAT MUCH, HUH?
CHUCKLE

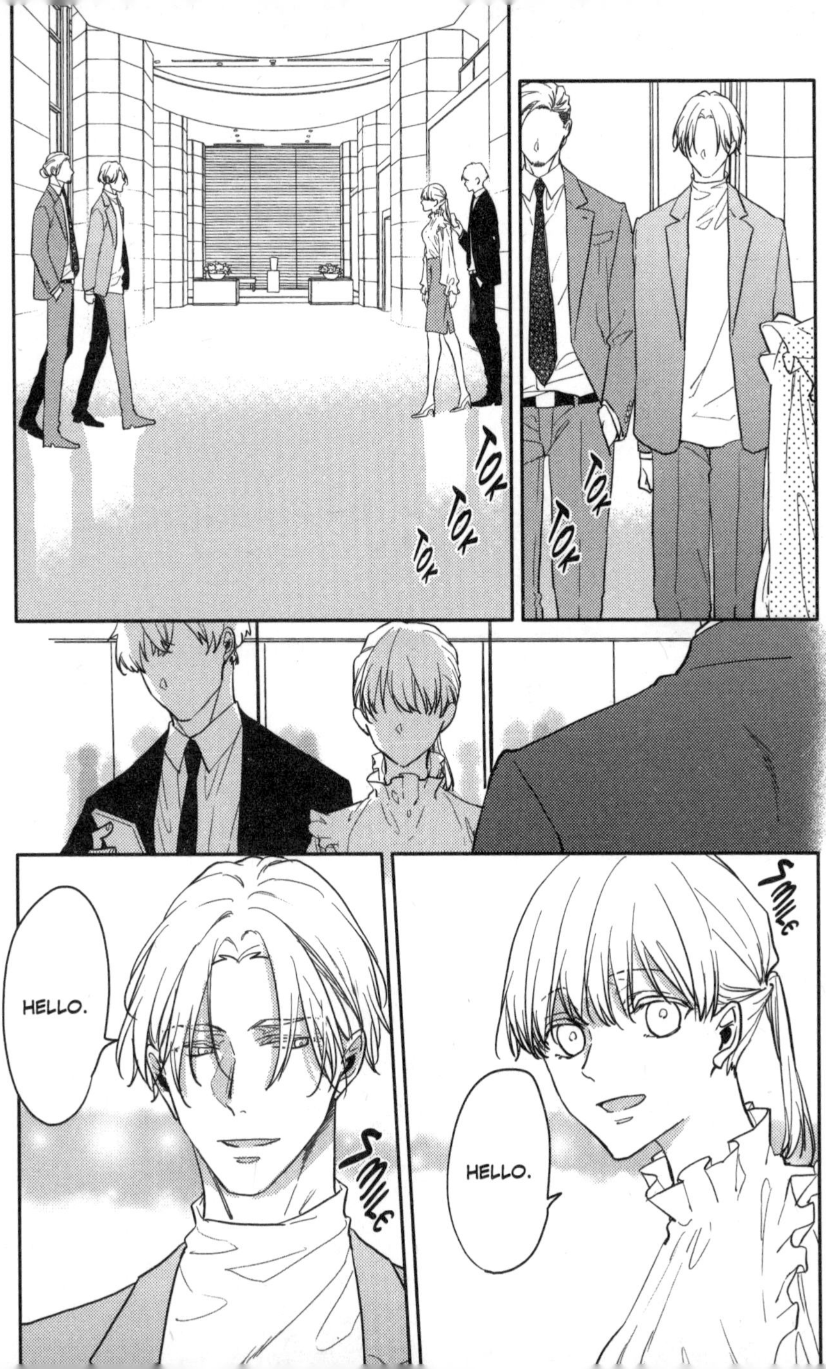
TOK
TOK
TOK
TOK
TOK
SMILE
HELLO.
HELLO.
SMILE

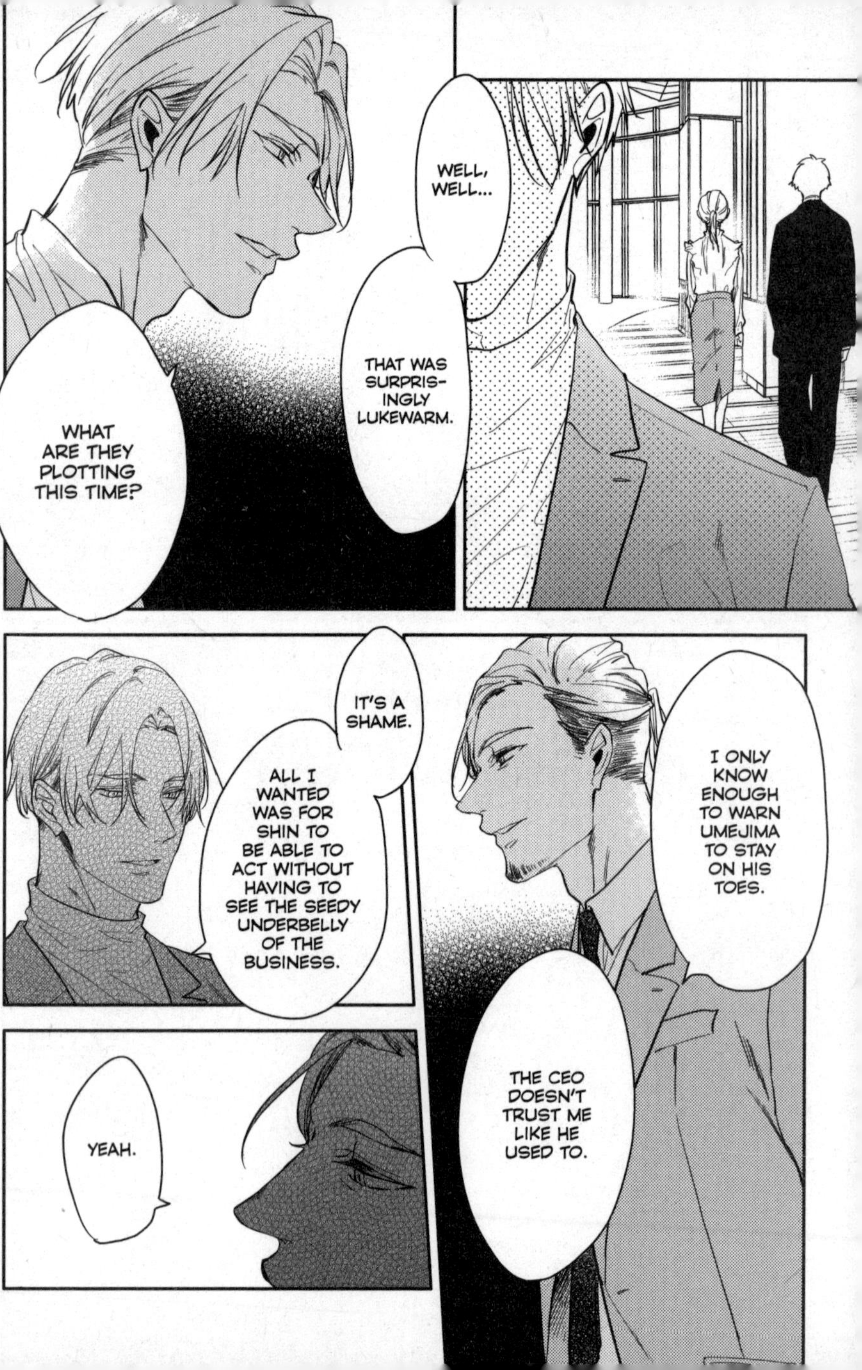
WELL, WELL...
THAT WAS SURPRISINGLY LUKEWARM.
WHAT ARE THEY PLOTTING THIS TIME?
I ONLY KNOW ENOUGH TO WARN UMEJIMA TO STAY ON HIS TOES.
THE CEO DOESN'T TRUST ME LIKE HE USED TO.
IT'S A SHAME.
ALL I WANTED WAS FOR SHIN TO BE ABLE TO ACT WITHOUT HAVING TO SEE THE SEEDY UNDERBELLY OF THE BUSINESS.
YEAH.

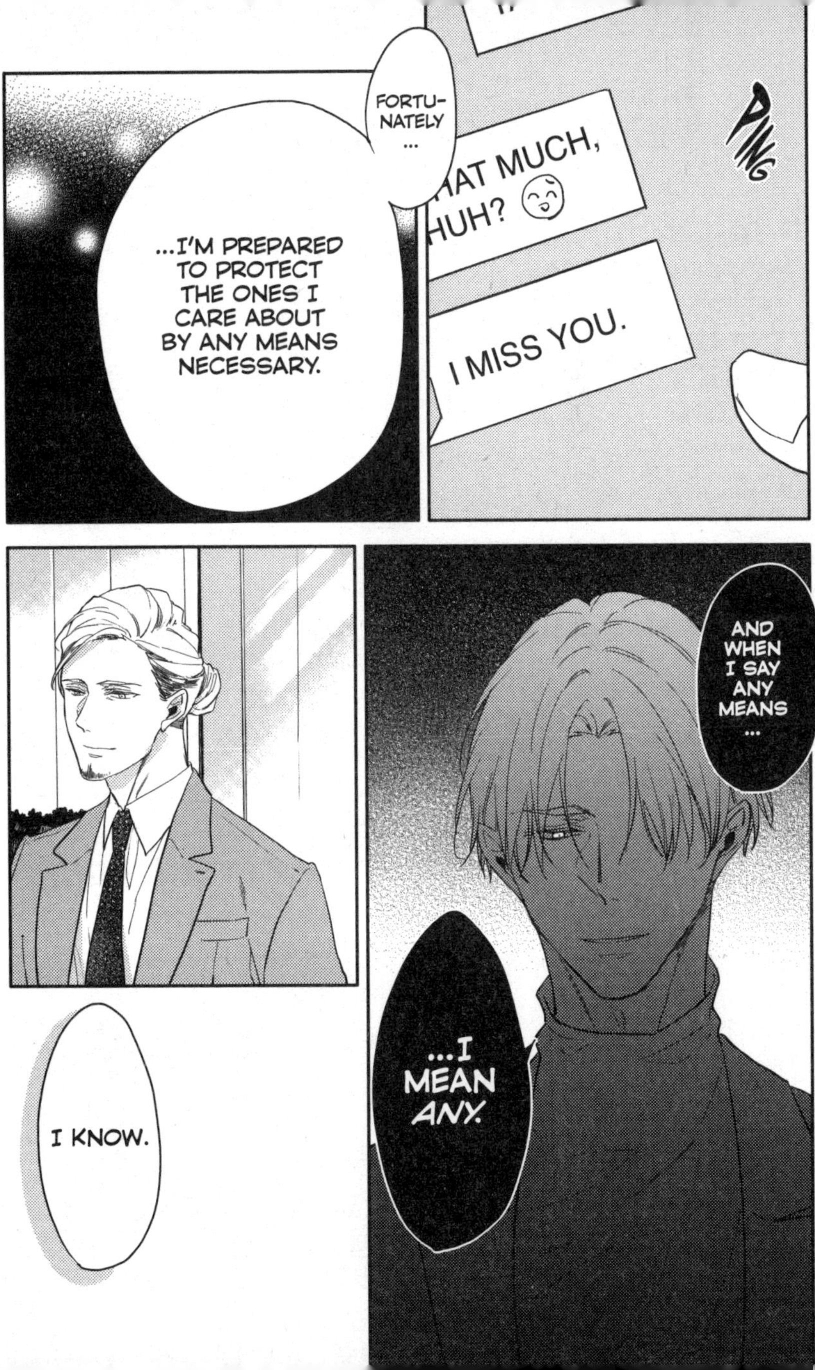
PING
HAT MUCH, HUH?
I MISS YOU.
FORTUNATELY...
...I'M PREPARED TO PROTECT THE ONES I CARE ABOUT BY ANY MEANS NECESSARY.
AND WHEN I SAY ANY MEANS...
...I MEAN ANY.
I KNOW.

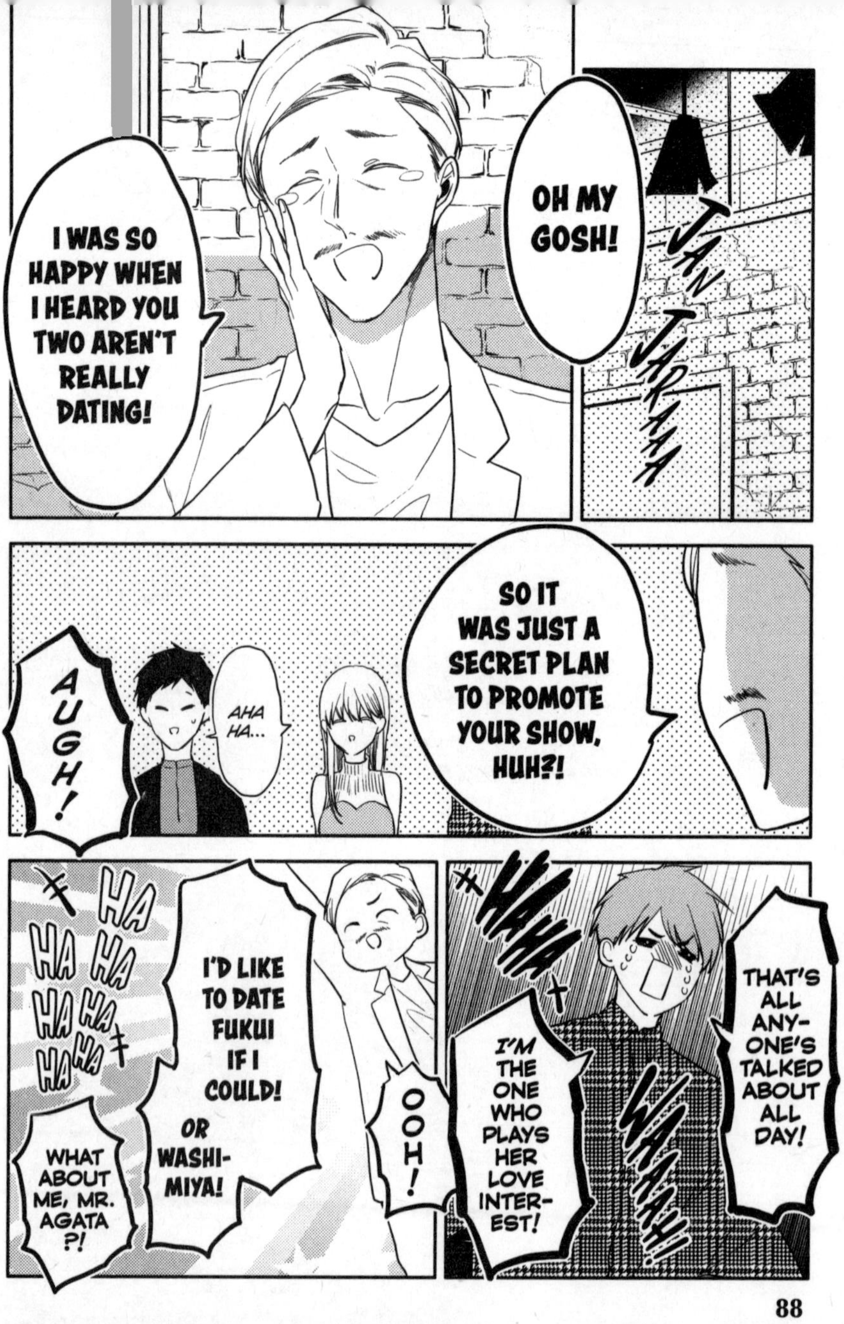
OH MY GOSH!
JAN JARAAAA
I WAS SO HAPPY WHEN I HEARD YOU TWO AREN'T REALLY DATING!
SO IT WAS JUST A SECRET PLAN TO PROMOTE YOUR SHOW, HUH?!
AHA HA...
AUGH!
THAT'S ALL ANY-ONE'S TALKED ABOUT ALL DAY!
WAHAHA
I'M THE ONE WHO PLAYS HER LOVE INTER-EST!
WAAAAH!!
OOH!
I'D LIKE TO DATE FUKUI IF I COULD!
OR WASHI-MIYA!
HA HA HA HA HA HA HA HA
WHAT ABOUT ME, MR. AGATA?!

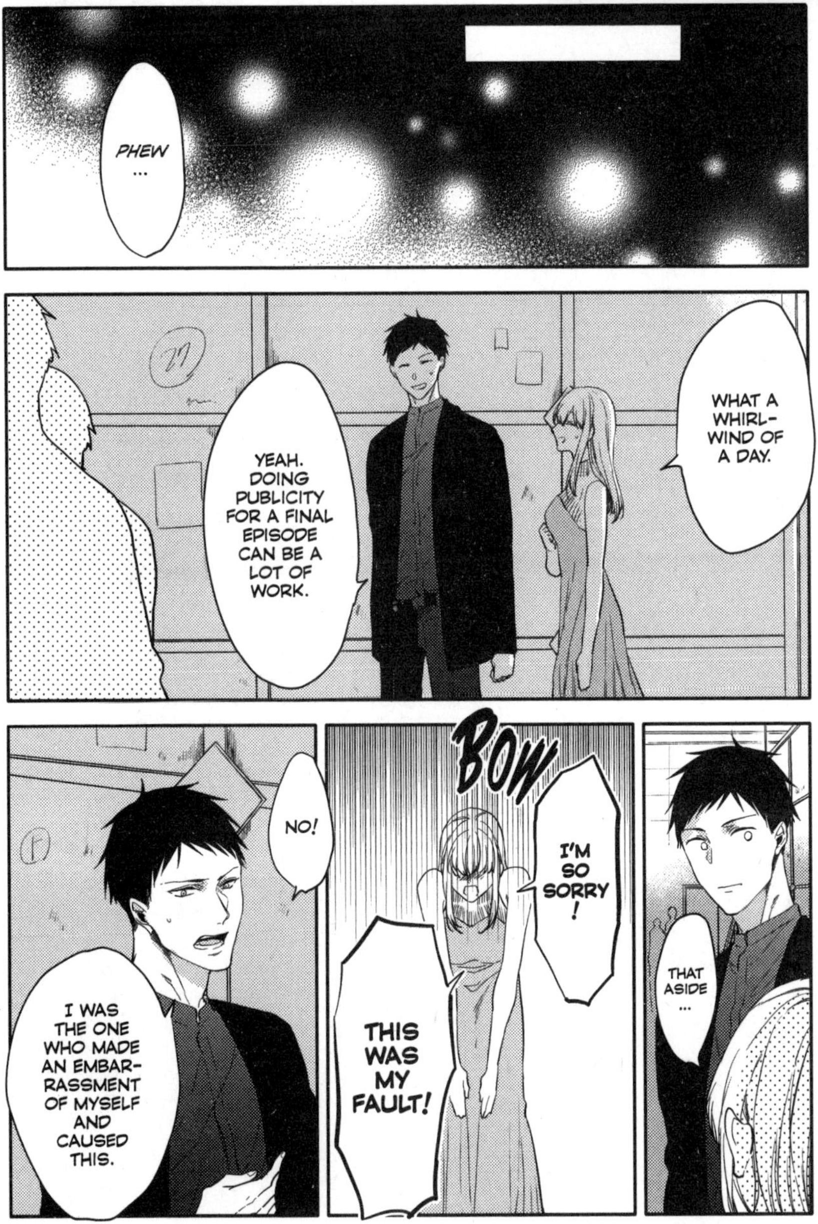
PHEW...
WHAT A WHIRLWIND OF A DAY.
YEAH. DOING PUBLICITY FOR A FINAL EPISODE CAN BE A LOT OF WORK.
THAT ASIDE...
BOW
I'M SO SORRY!
THIS WAS MY FAULT!
NO!
I WAS THE ONE WHO MADE AN EMBARRASSMENT OF MYSELF AND CAUSED THIS.

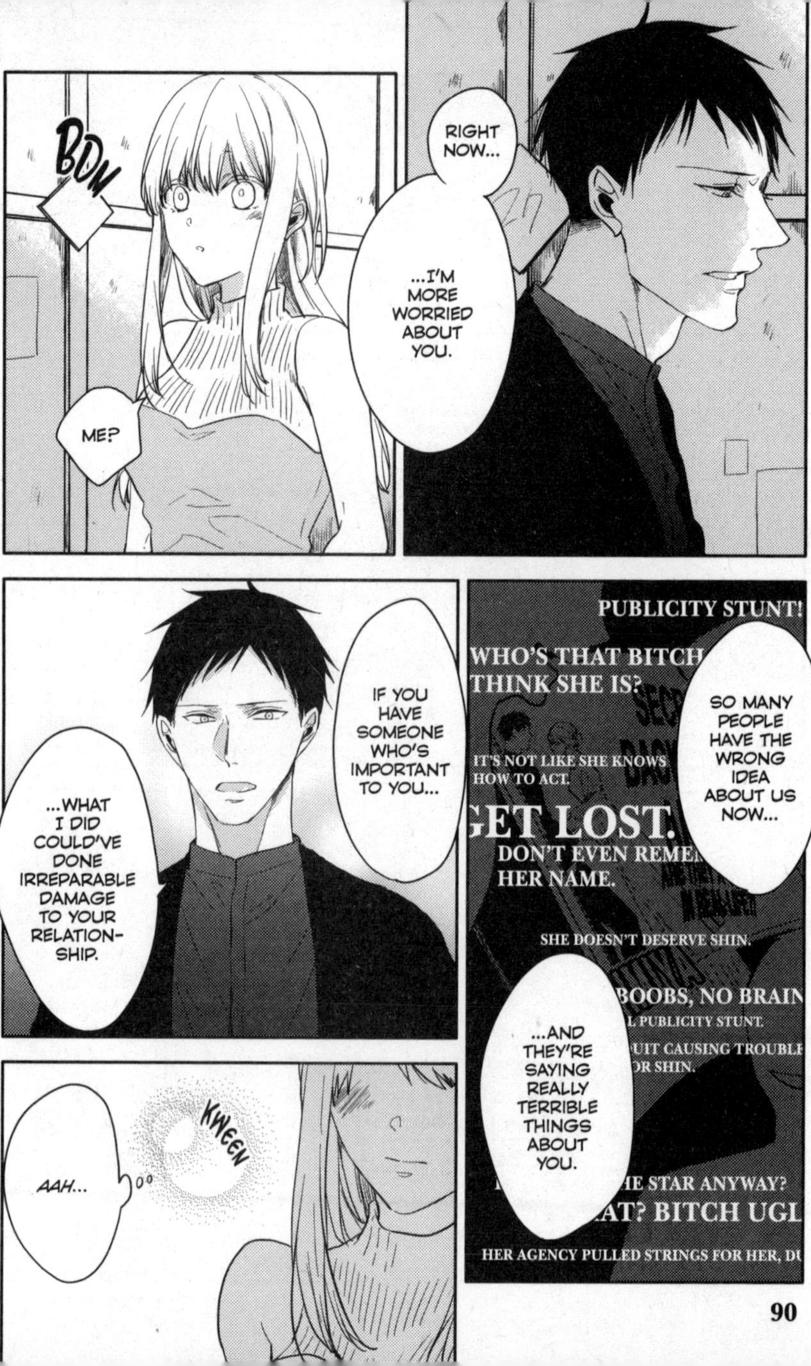
RIGHT NOW...
...I'M MORE WORRIED ABOUT YOU.
BDM
ME?
PUBLICITY STUNT!
WHO'S THAT BITCH
THINK SHE IS?
IT'S NOT LIKE SHE KNOWS
HOW TO ACT.
GET LOST.
HER NAME.
SHE DOESN'T DESERVE SHIN.
BOOBS, NO BRAIN
OR SHIN.
HER AGENCY PULLED STRINGS FOR HER,
SO MANY PEOPLE HAVE THE WRONG IDEA ABOUT US NOW...
...AND THEY'RE SAYING REALLY TERRIBLE THINGS ABOUT YOU.
IF YOU HAVE SOMEONE WHO'S IMPORTANT TO YOU...
...WHAT I DID COULD'VE DONE IRREPARABLE DAMAGE TO YOUR RELATIONSHIP.
KWEEN
AAH...

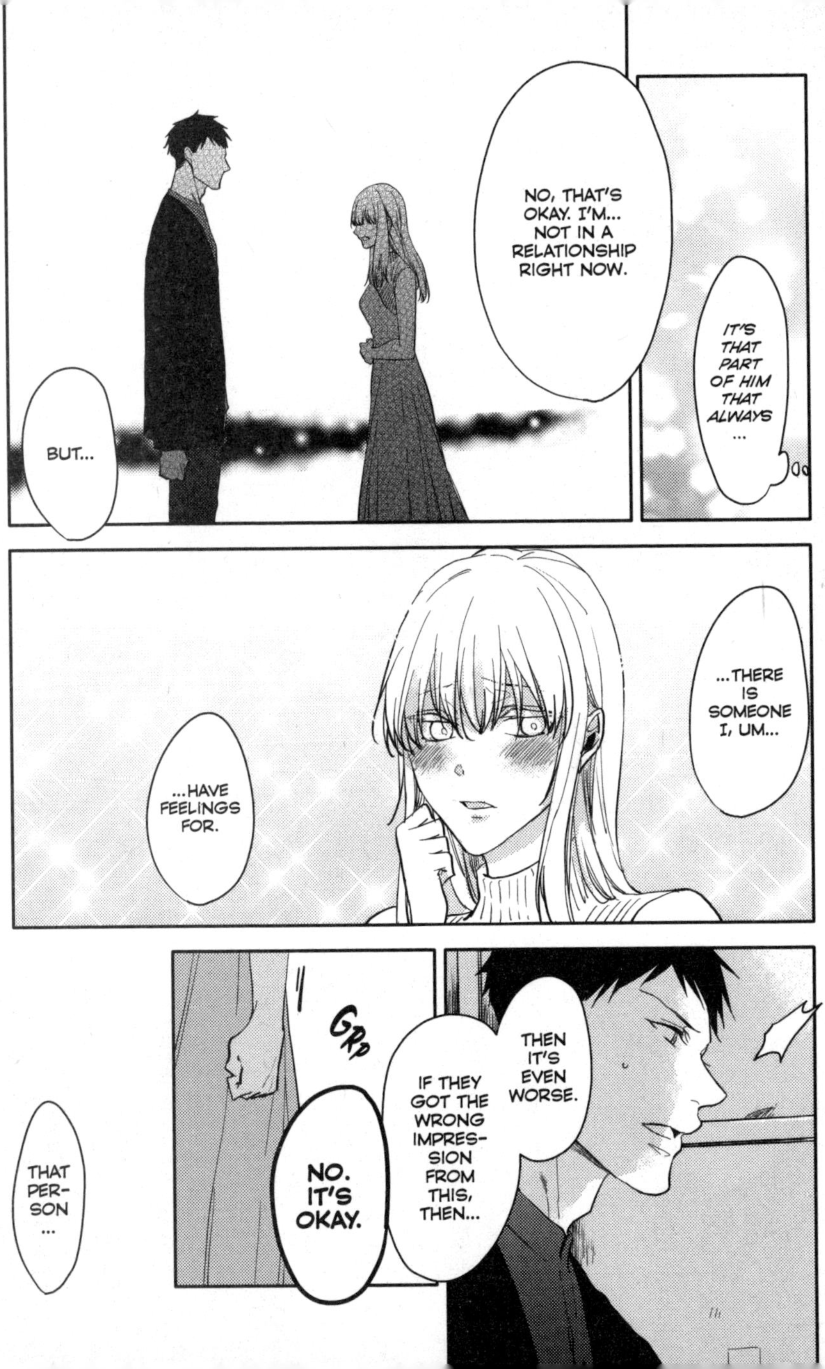
NO, THAT'S OKAY. I'M... NOT IN A RELATIONSHIP RIGHT NOW.
IT'S THAT PART OF HIM THAT ALWAYS ...
BUT...
...THERE IS SOMEONE I, UM...
...HAVE FEELINGS FOR.
THEN IT'S EVEN WORSE.
IF THEY GOT THE WRONG IMPRESSION FROM THIS, THEN...
NO. IT'S OKAY.
GRP
THAT PERSON ...

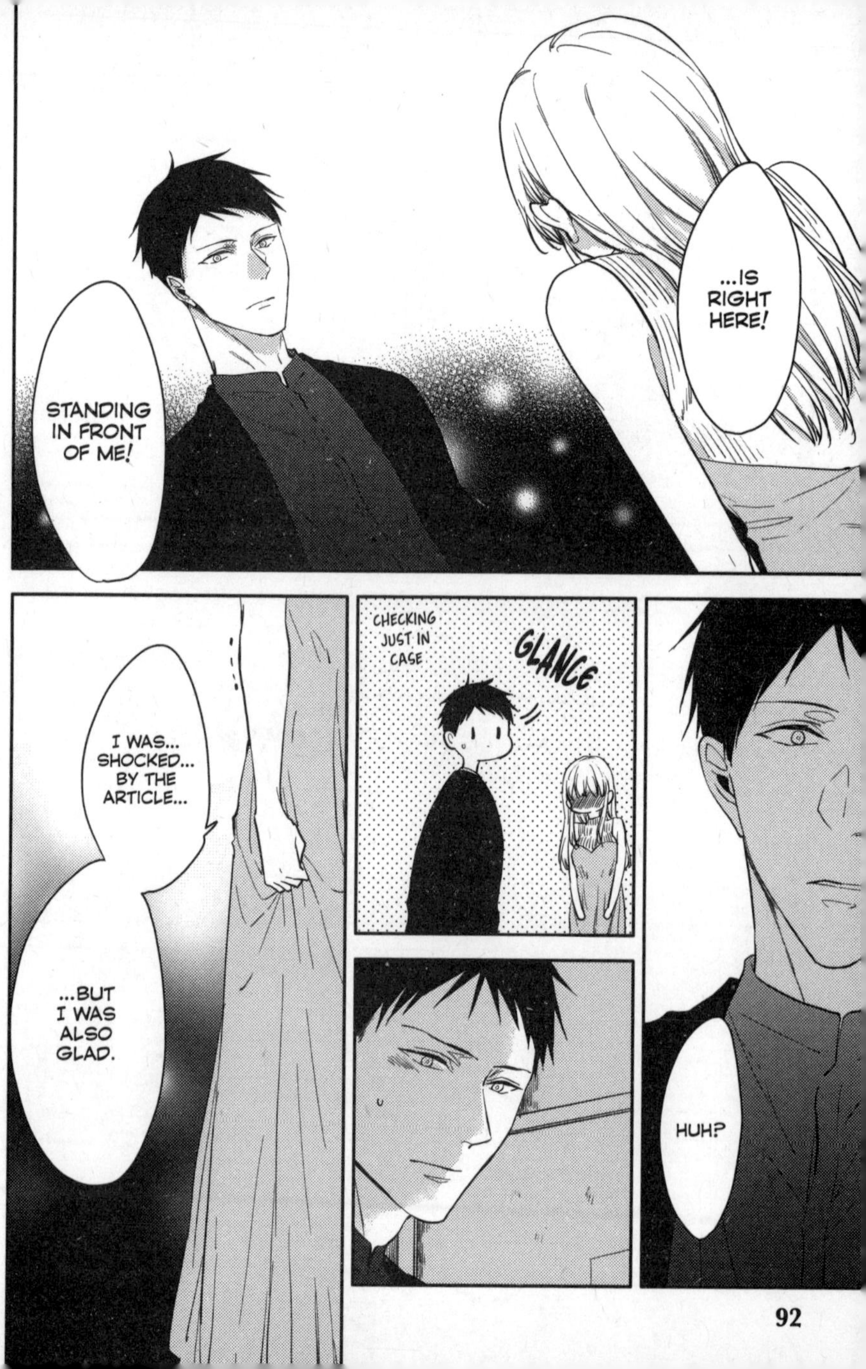
...IS RIGHT HERE!
STANDING IN FRONT OF ME!
HUH?
CHECKING JUST IN CASE
GLANCE
...
I WAS... SHOCKED... BY THE ARTICLE...
...BUT I WAS ALSO GLAD.

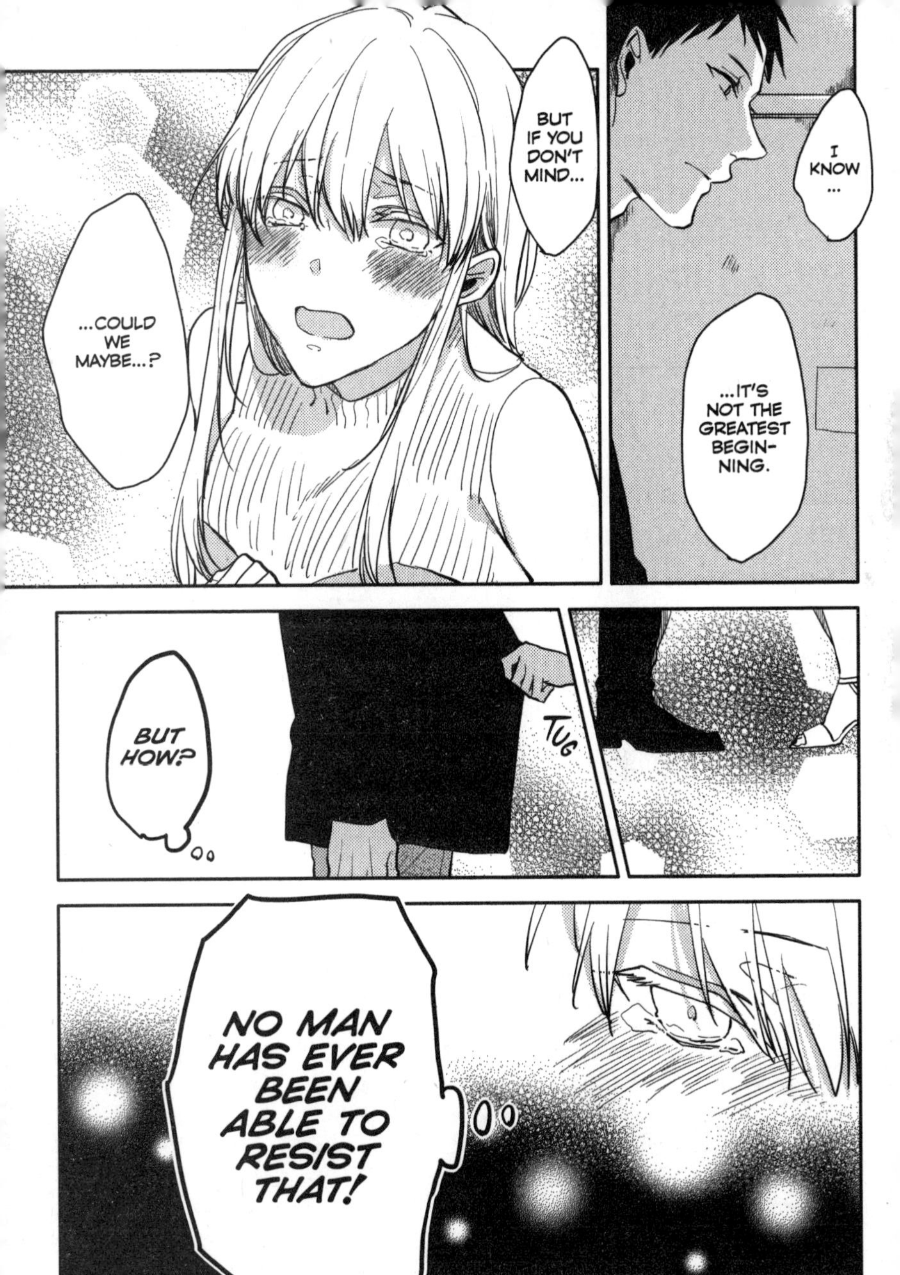
I KNOW...
...IT'S NOT THE GREATEST BEGINNING.
BUT IF YOU DON'T MIND...
...COULD WE MAYBE...?
TUG
BUT HOW?
NO MAN HAS EVER BEEN ABLE TO RESIST THAT!

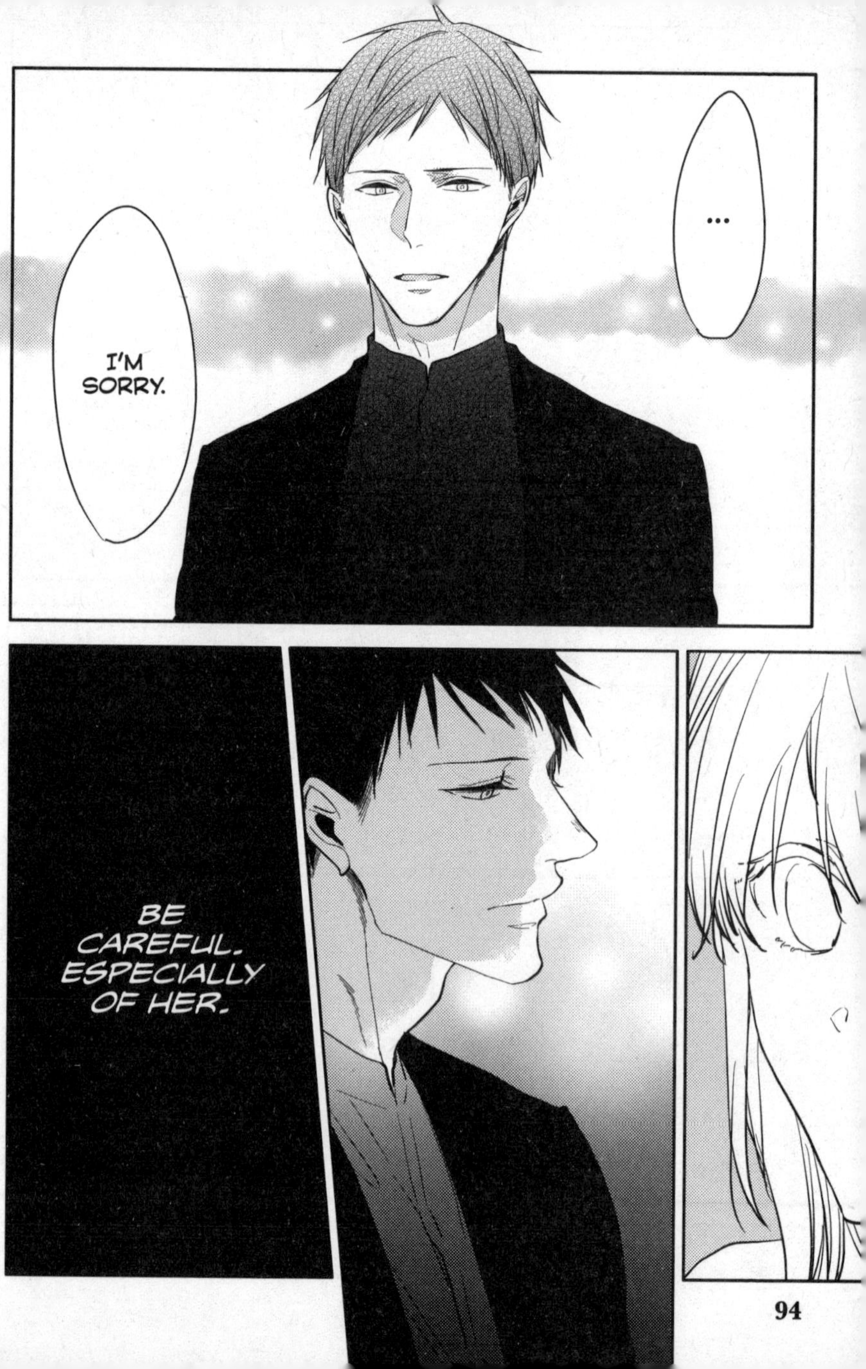
...
I'M SORRY.
BE CAREFUL. ESPECIALLY OF HER.

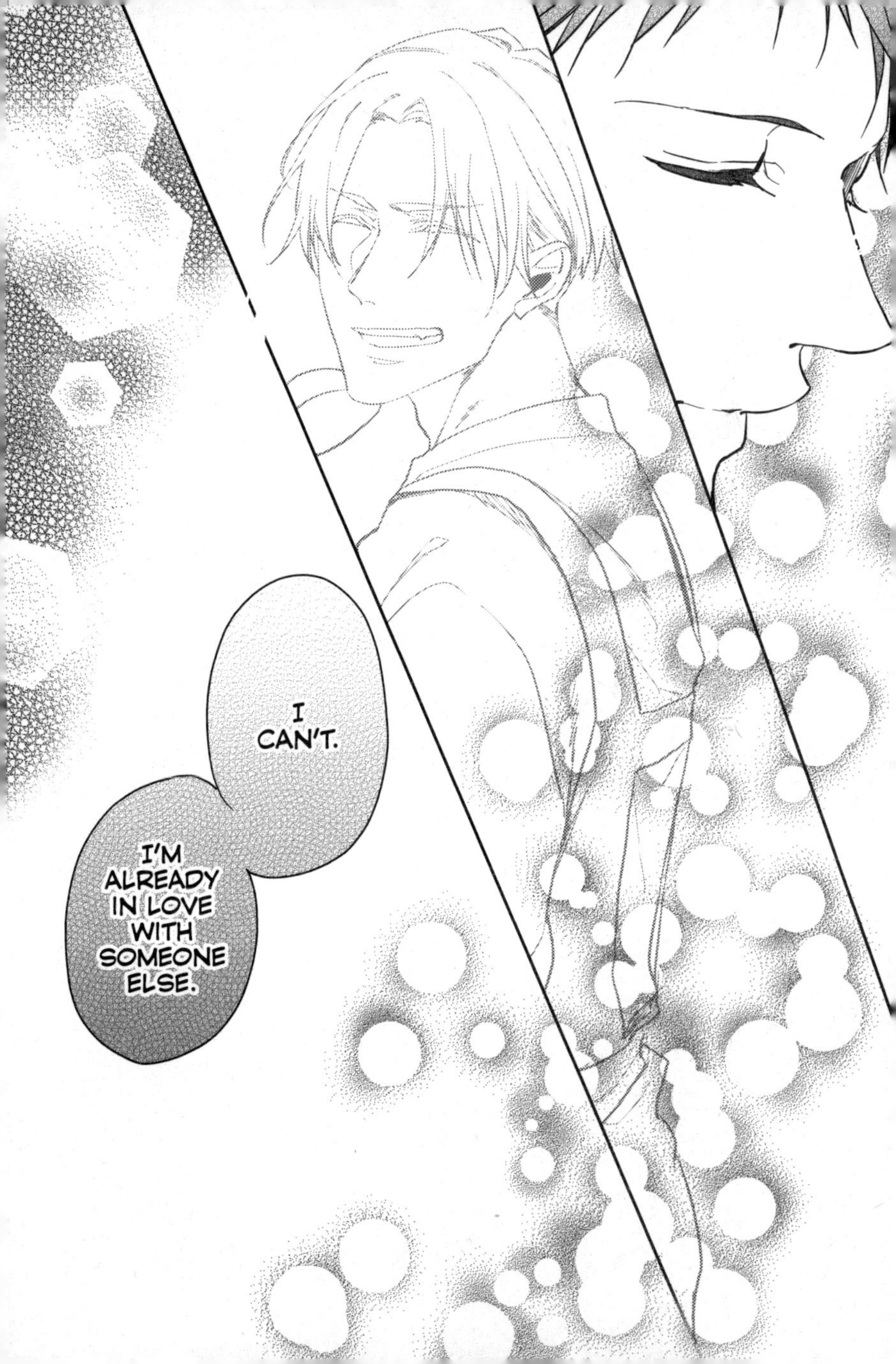
I CAN'T.
I'M ALREADY IN LOVE WITH SOMEONE ELSE.

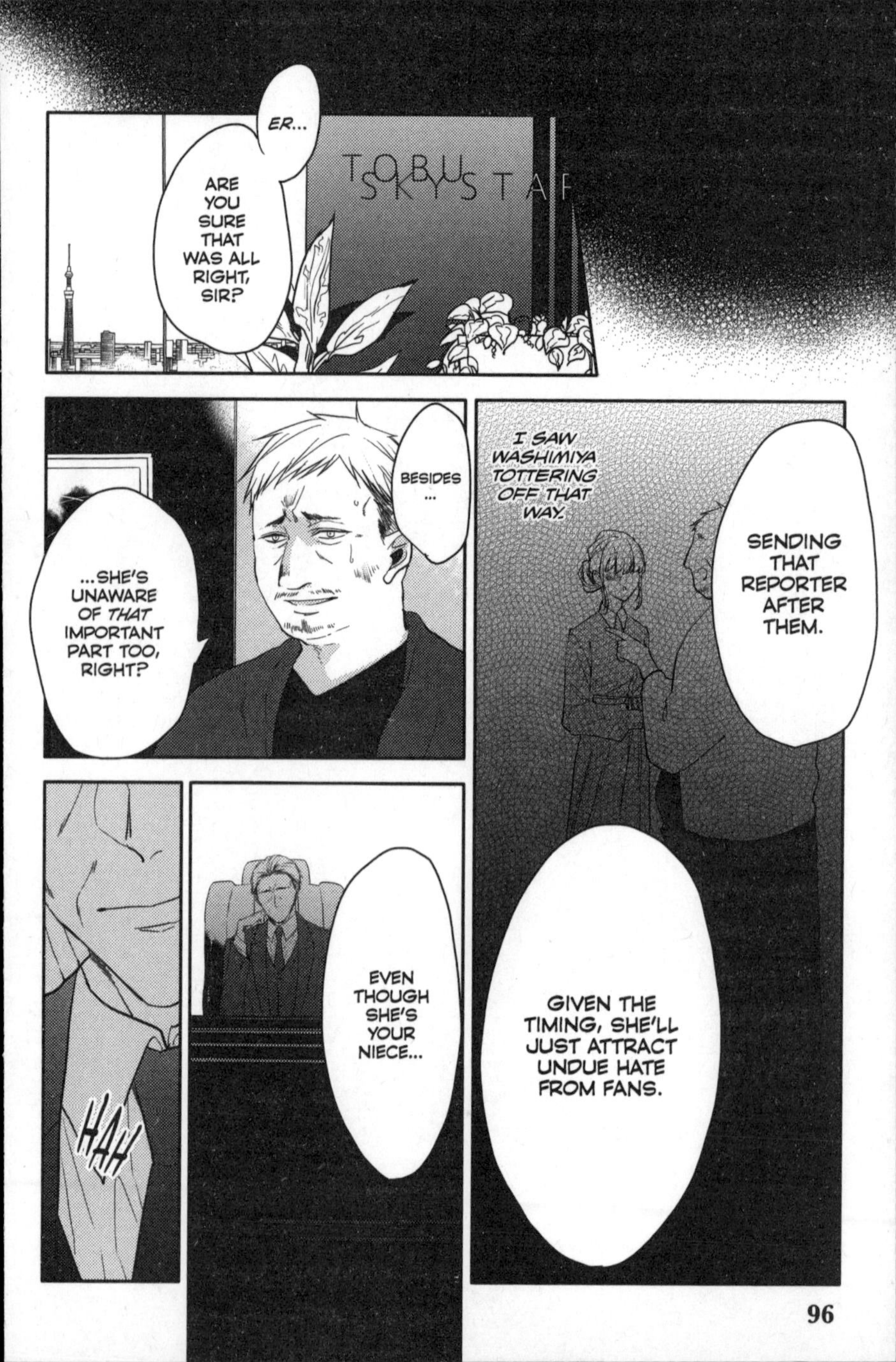
ER...
ARE YOU SURE THAT WAS ALL RIGHT, SIR?
TOBU SKYSTAR
I SAW WASHIMIYA TOTTERING OFF THAT WAY.
SENDING THAT REPORTER AFTER THEM.
GIVEN THE TIMING, SHE'LL JUST ATTRACT UNDUE HATE FROM FANS.
BESIDES...
...SHE'S UNAWARE OF *THAT* IMPORTANT PART TOO, RIGHT?
EVEN THOUGH SHE'S YOUR NIECE...
HAH

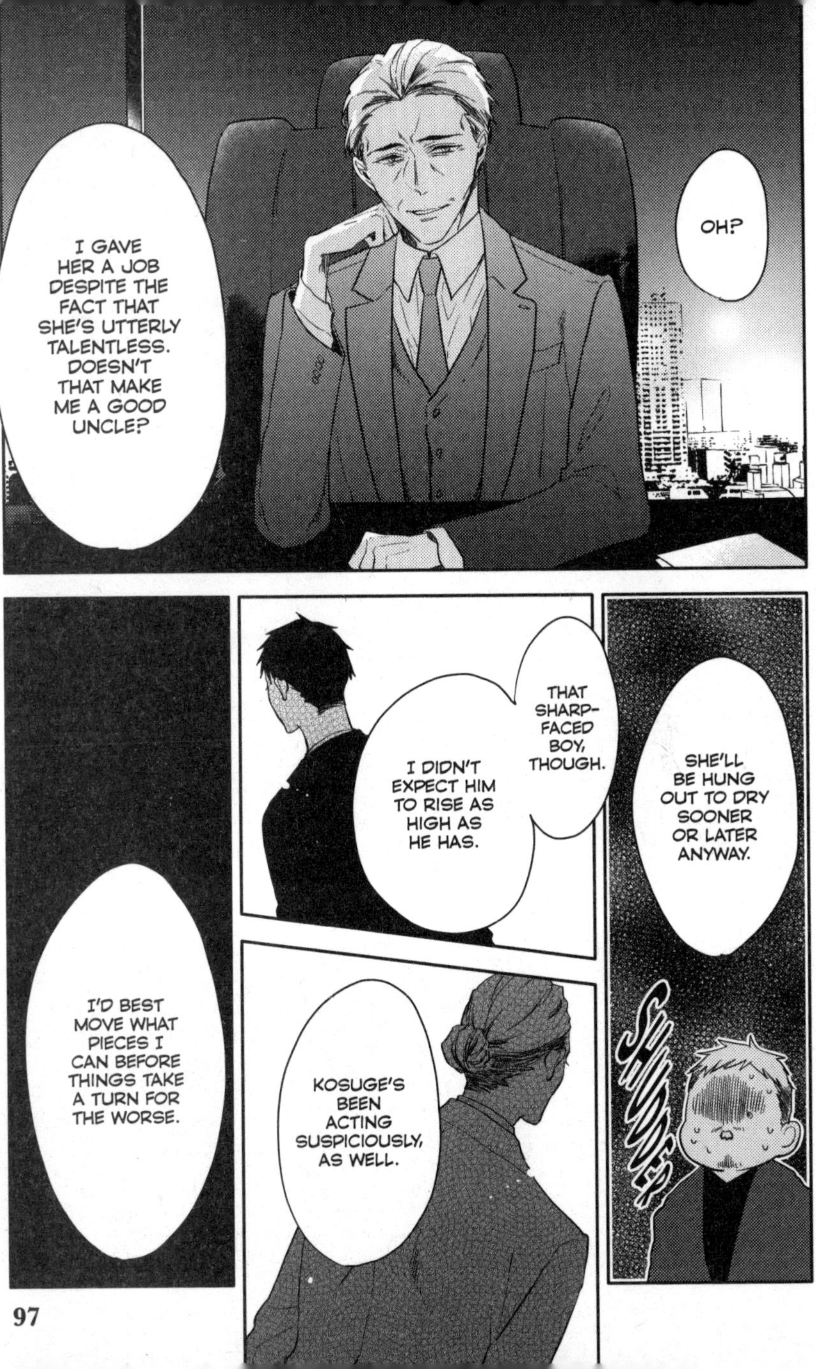
OH?
I GAVE HER A JOB DESPITE THE FACT THAT SHE'S UTTERLY TALENTLESS. DOESN'T THAT MAKE ME A GOOD UNCLE?
SHE'LL BE HUNG OUT TO DRY SOONER OR LATER ANYWAY.
SHUDDER
THAT SHARP-FACED BOY, THOUGH.
I DIDN'T EXPECT HIM TO RISE AS HIGH AS HE HAS.
KOSUGE'S BEEN ACTING SUSPICIOUSLY, AS WELL.
I'D BEST MOVE WHAT PIECES I CAN BEFORE THINGS TAKE A TURN FOR THE WORSE.

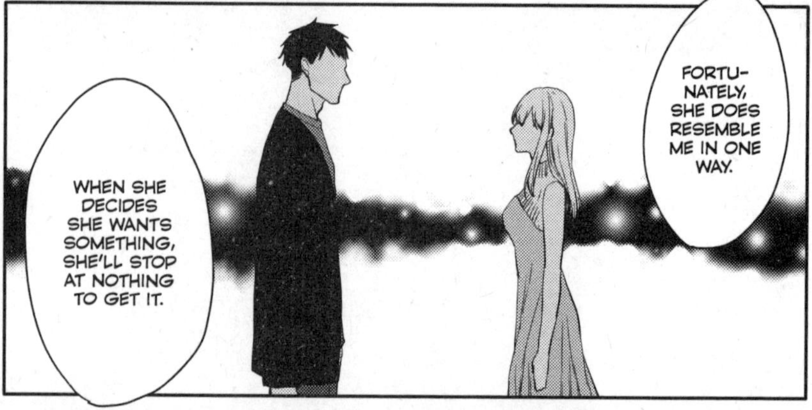
FORTU-NATELY, SHE DOES RESEMBLE ME IN ONE WAY.
WHEN SHE DECIDES SHE WANTS SOMETHING, SHE'LL STOP AT NOTHING TO GET IT.

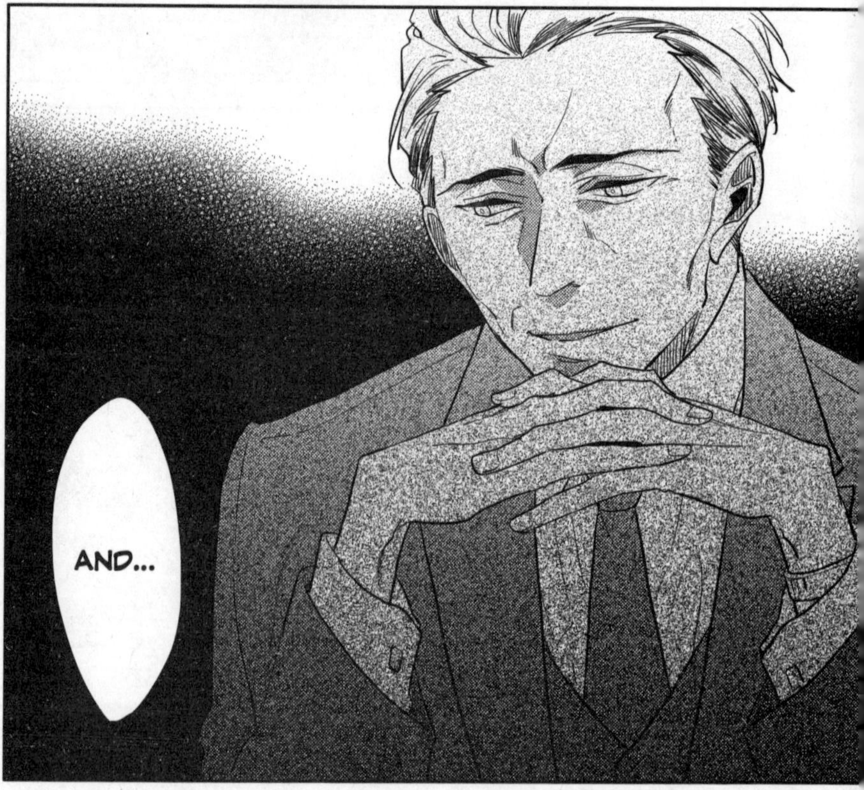
AND...

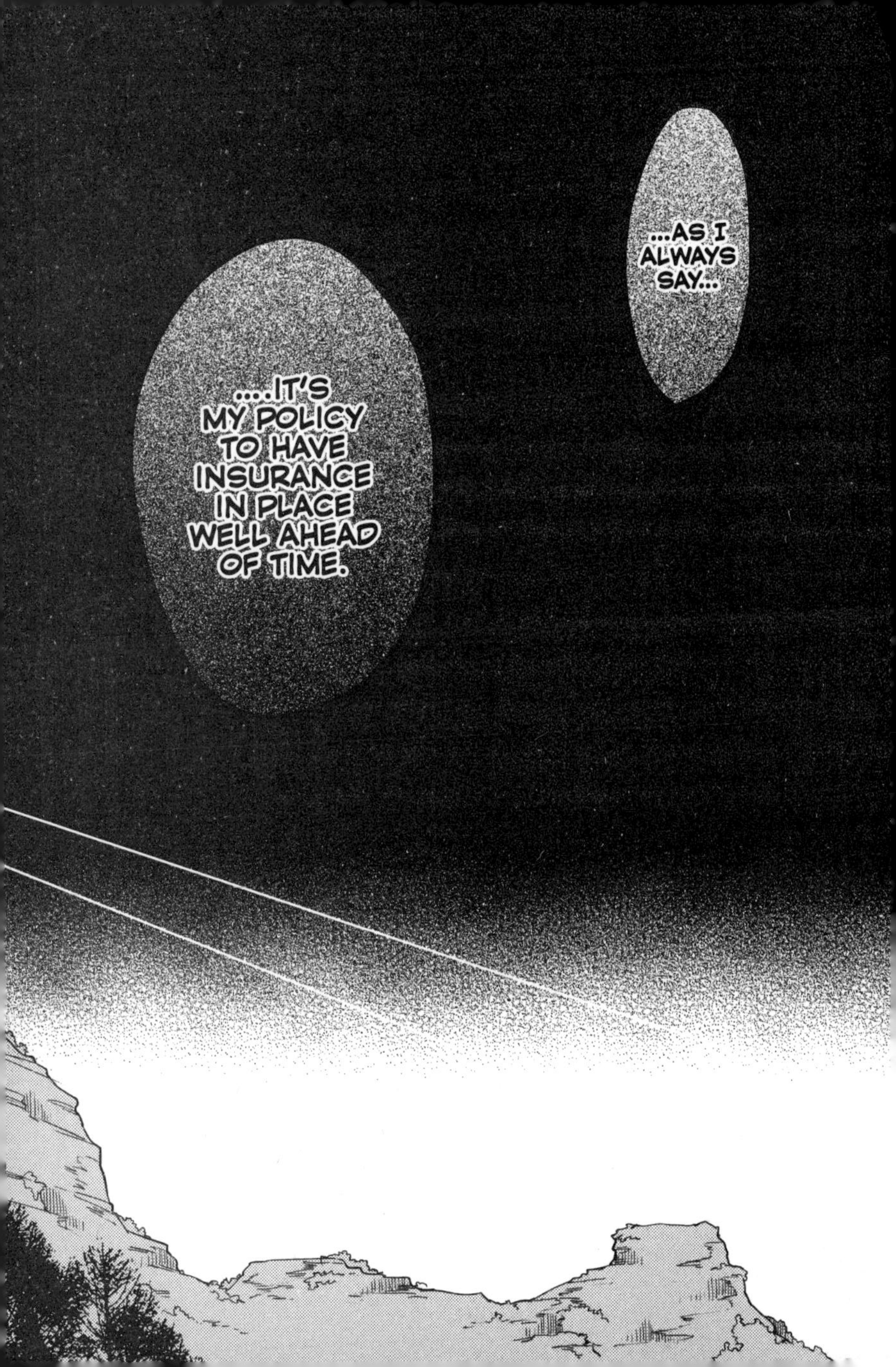
...AS I ALWAYS SAY...
....IT'S MY POLICY TO HAVE INSURANCE IN PLACE WELL AHEAD OF TIME.

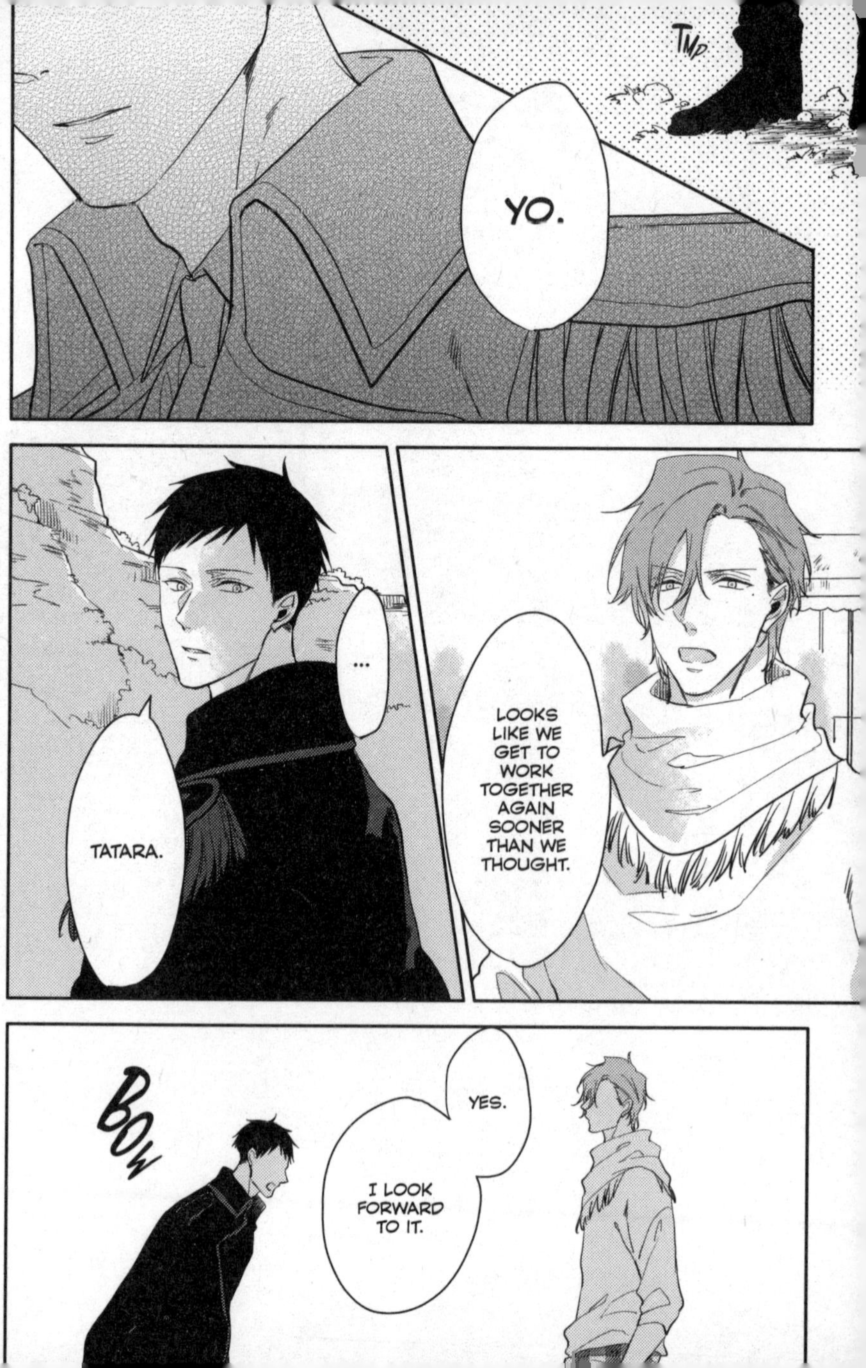
TMP
YO.
LOOKS LIKE WE GET TO WORK TOGETHER AGAIN SOONER THAN WE THOUGHT.
...
TATARA.
YES.
I LOOK FORWARD TO IT.
BOW

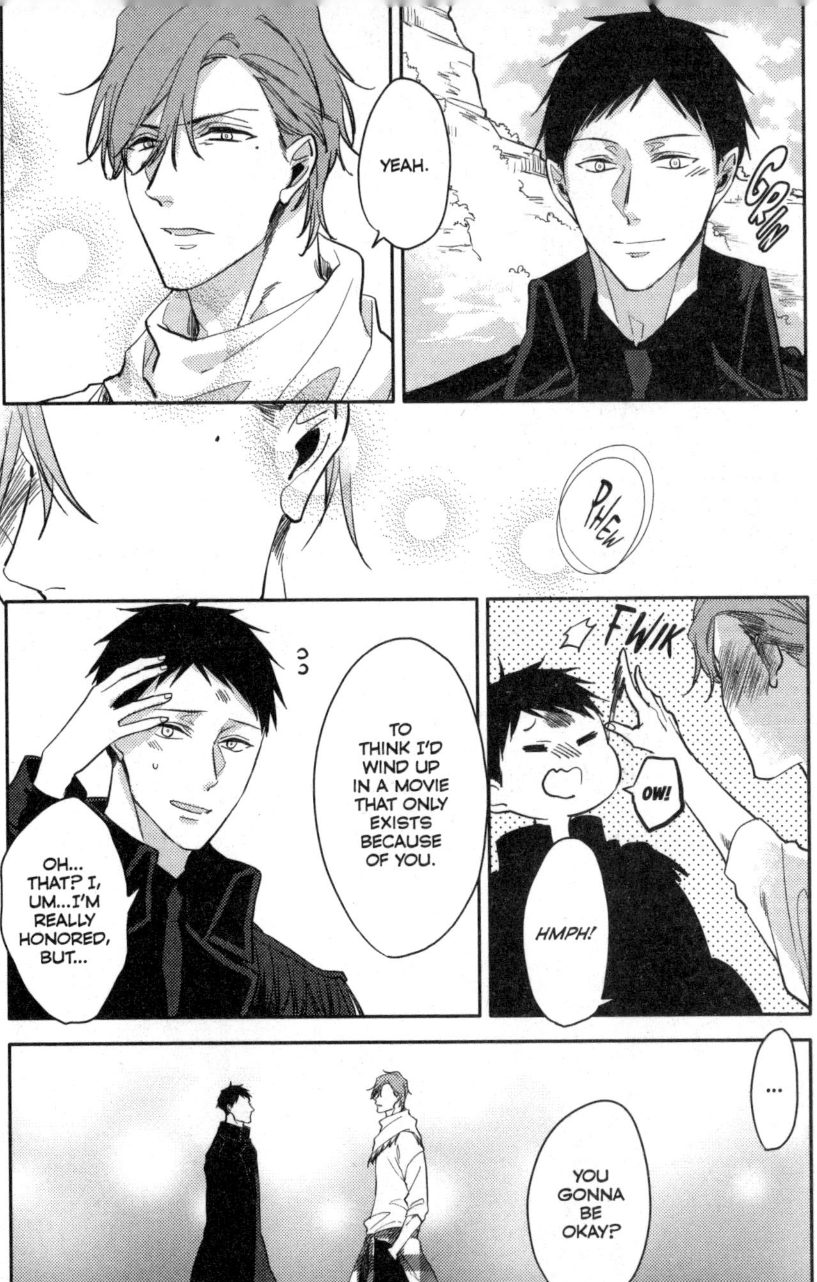
GRIN
YEAH.
PHEW
FWIK
OW!
HMPH!
TO THINK I'D WIND UP IN A MOVIE THAT ONLY EXISTS BECAUSE OF YOU.
OH... THAT? I, UM...I'M REALLY HONORED, BUT...
...
YOU GONNA BE OKAY?

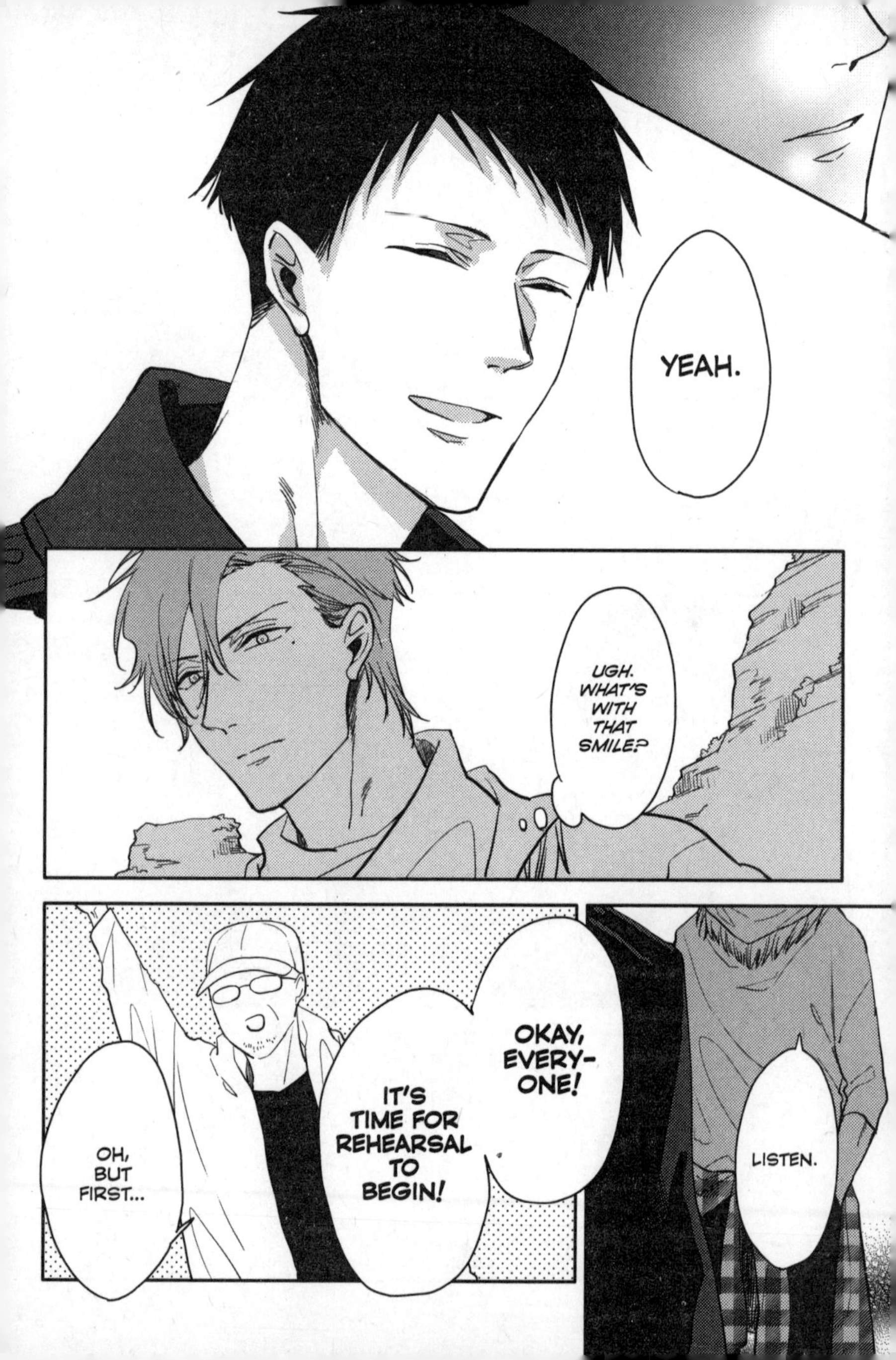
YEAH.
UGH. WHAT'S WITH THAT SMILE?
LISTEN.
OKAY, EVERYONE!
IT'S TIME FOR REHEARSAL TO BEGIN!
OH, BUT FIRST...

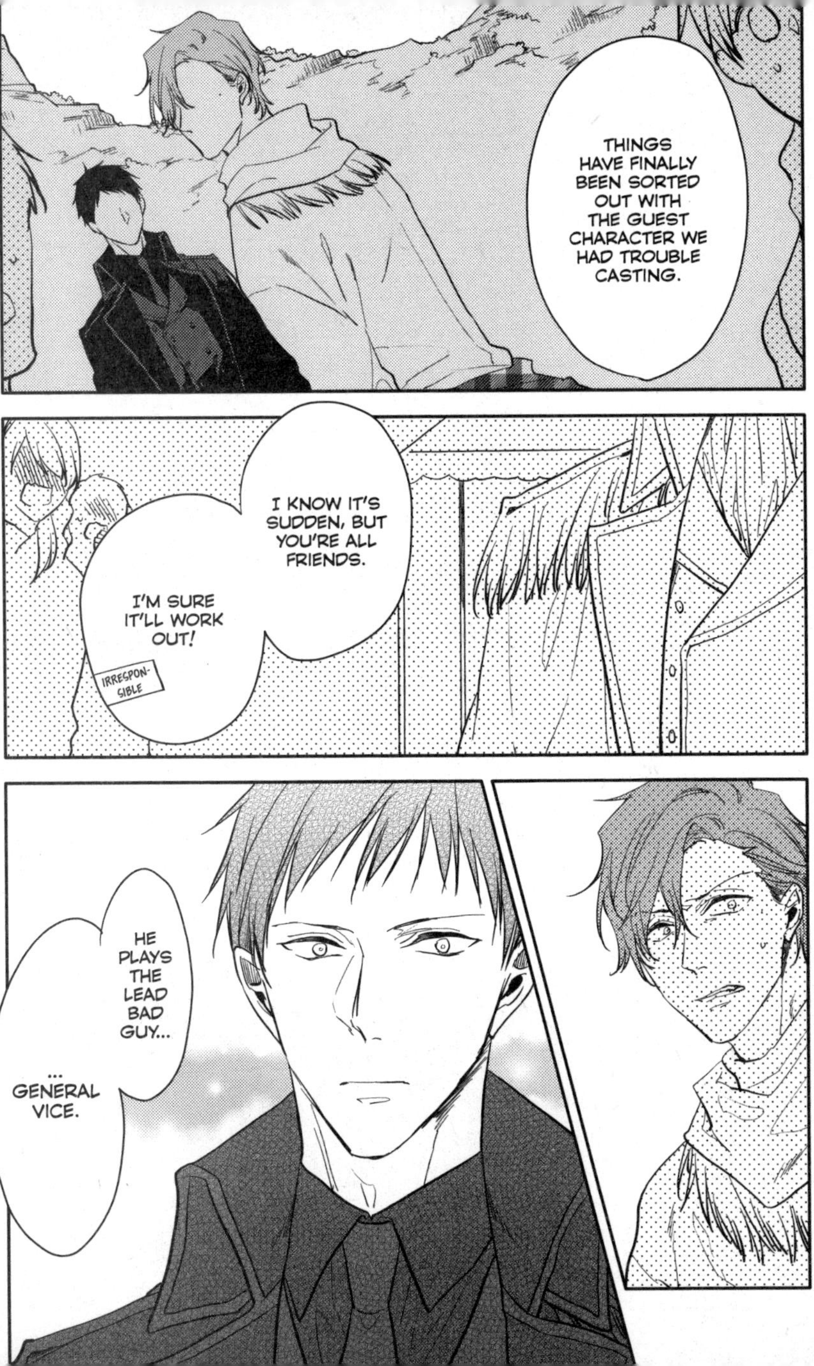
THINGS HAVE FINALLY BEEN SORTED OUT WITH THE GUEST CHARACTER WE HAD TROUBLE CASTING.
I KNOW IT'S SUDDEN, BUT YOU'RE ALL FRIENDS.
I'M SURE IT'LL WORK OUT!
IRRESPONSIBLE
HE PLAYS THE LEAD BAD GUY...
...GENERAL VICE.

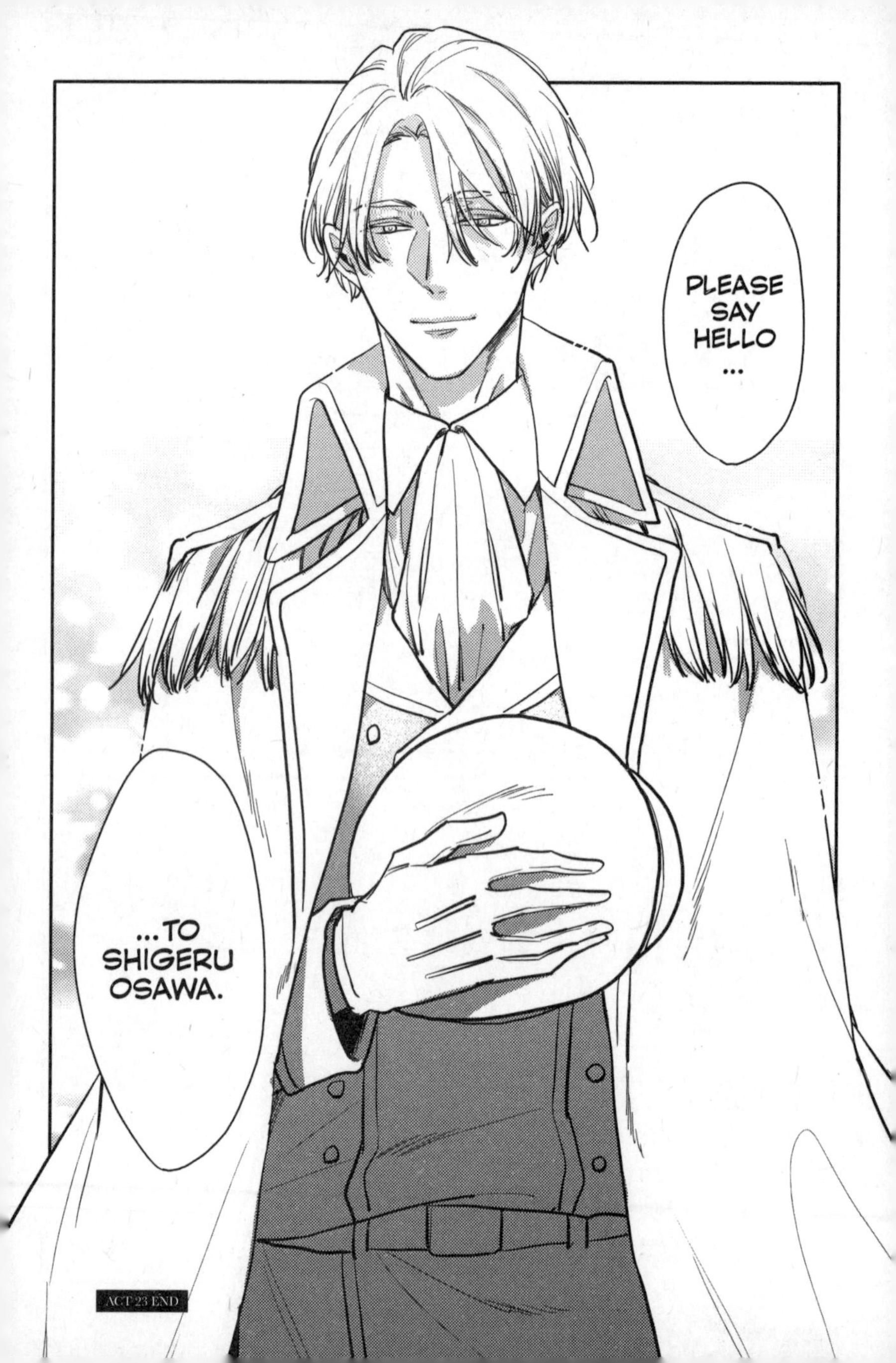
PLEASE SAY HELLO ...
...TO SHIGERU OSAWA.
ACT 23 END

Black
or White

Black or White

ACT 24

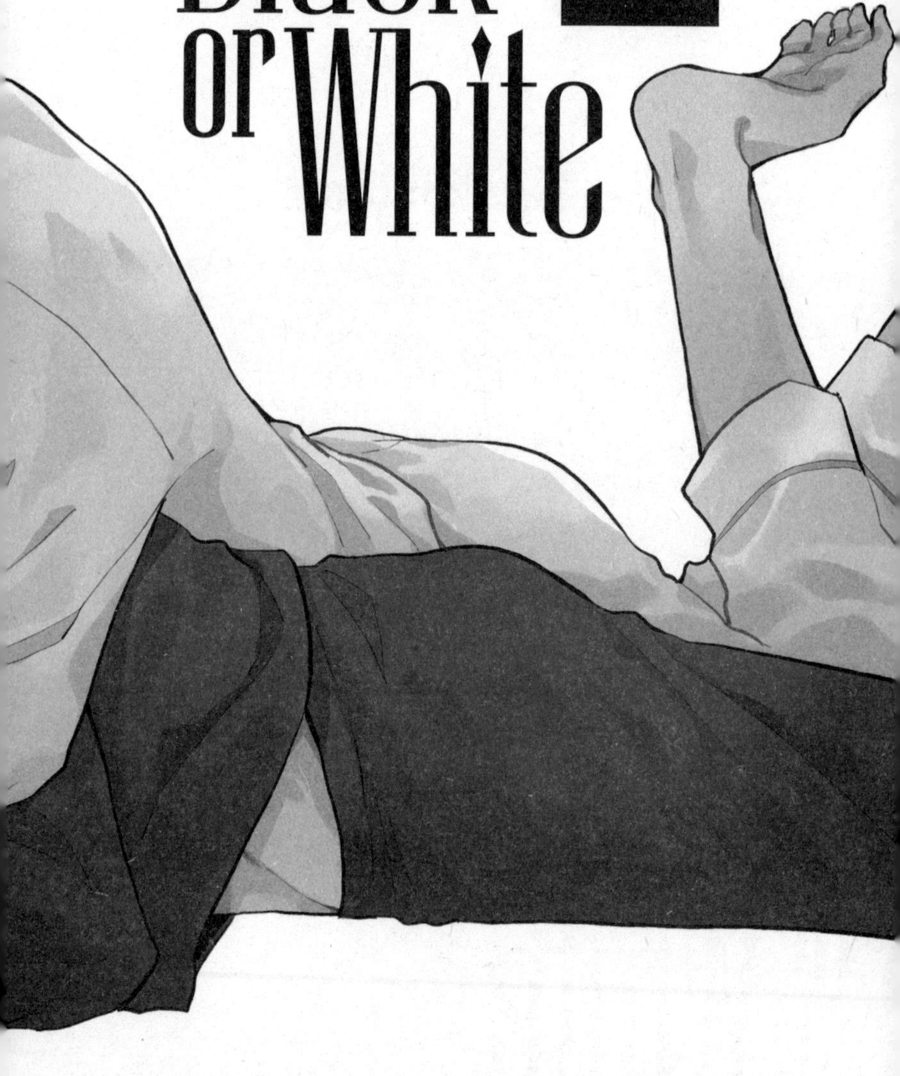

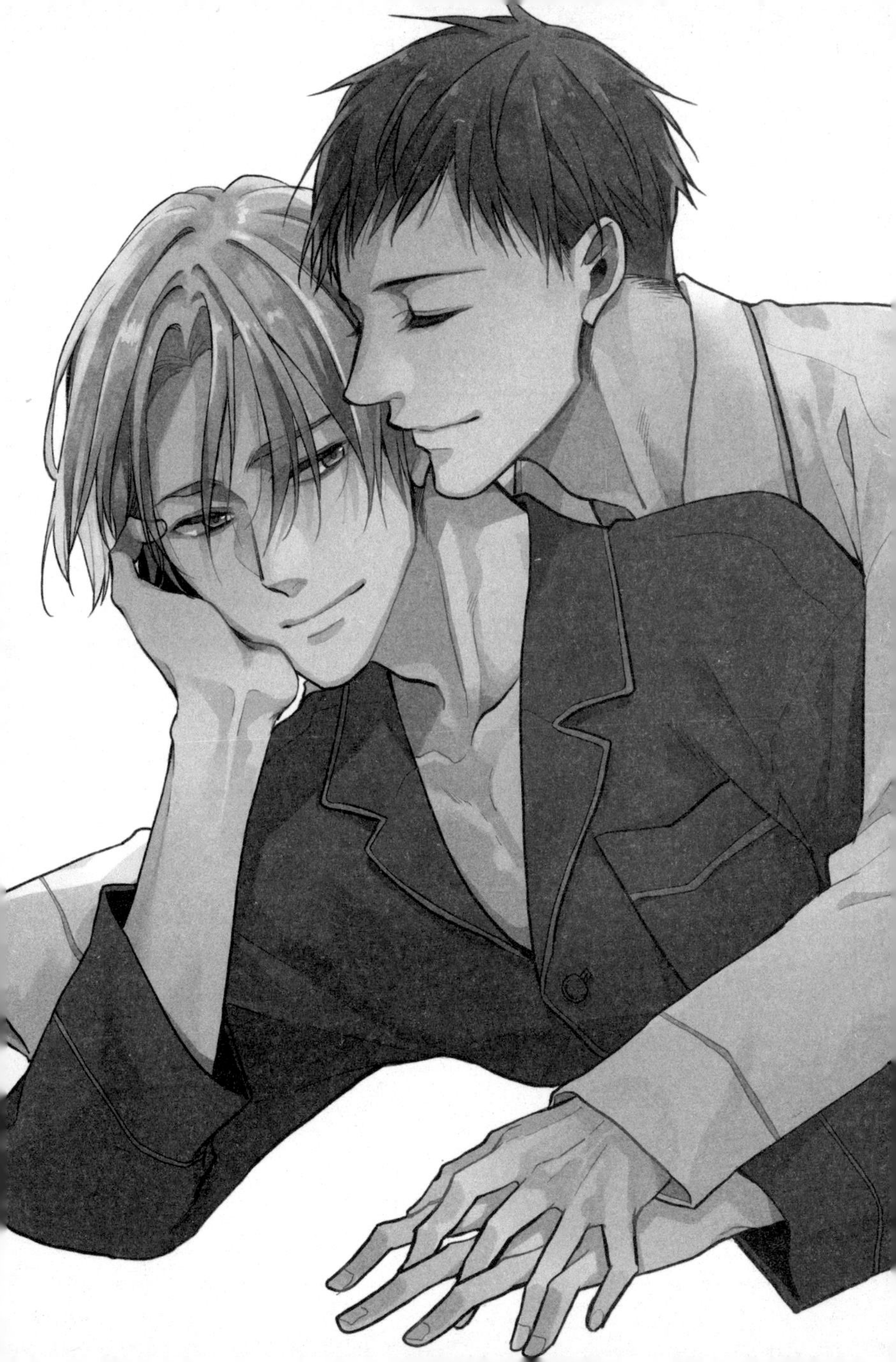

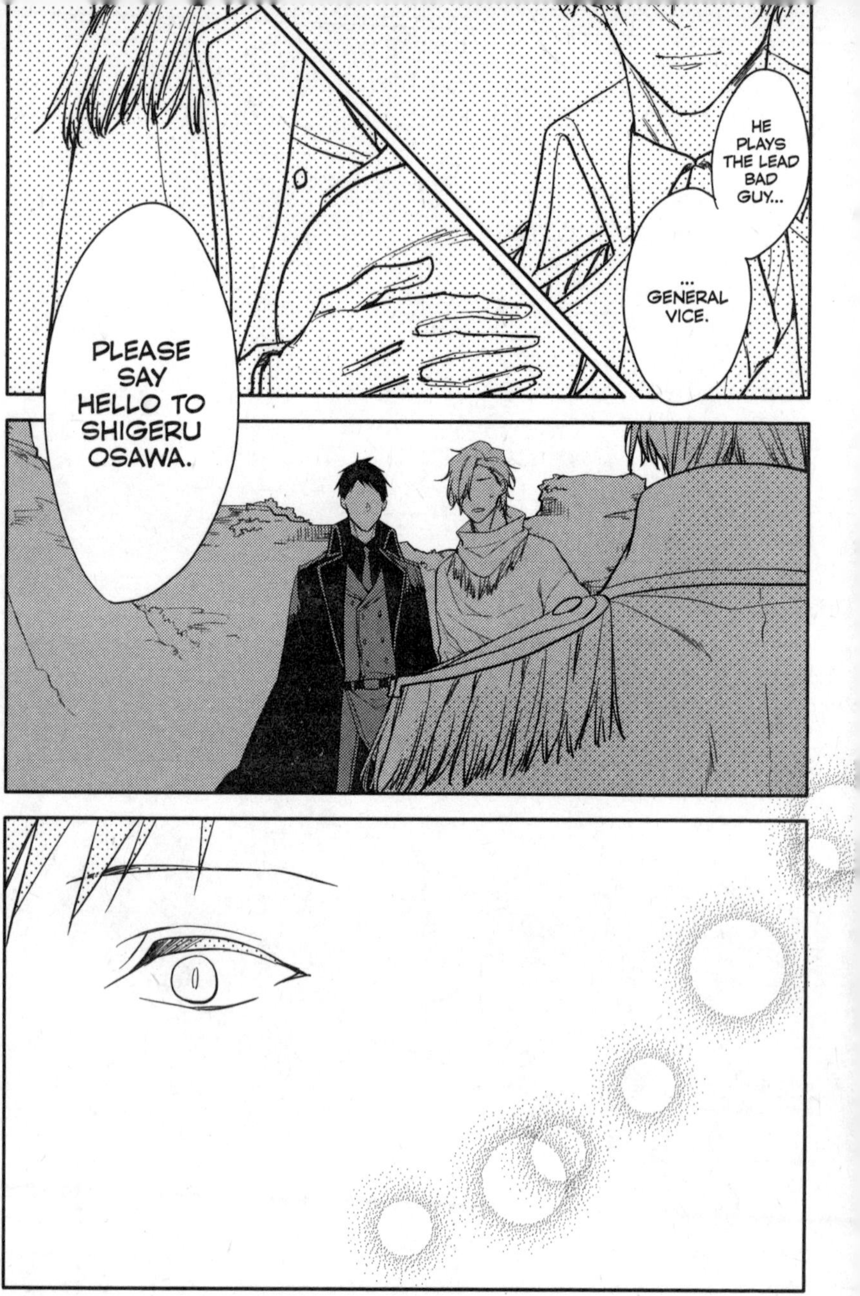
HE PLAYS THE LEAD BAD GUY...
... GENERAL VICE.
PLEASE SAY HELLO TO SHIGERU OSAWA.

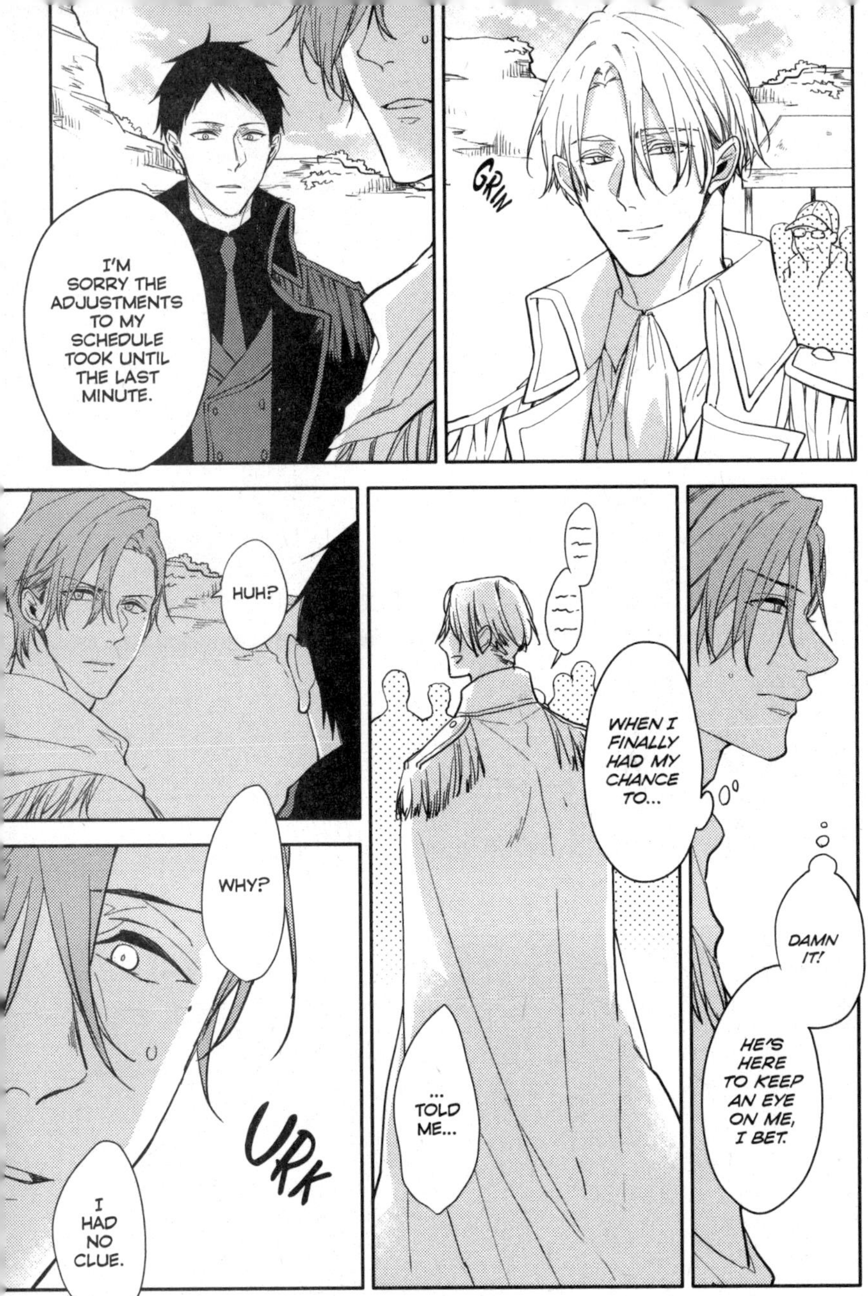
GRIN
I'M SORRY THE ADJUSTMENTS TO MY SCHEDULE TOOK UNTIL THE LAST MINUTE.
DAMN IT!
HE'S HERE TO KEEP AN EYE ON ME, I BET.
WHEN I FINALLY HAD MY CHANCE TO...
...TOLD ME...
HUH?
WHY?
URK
I HAD NO CLUE.

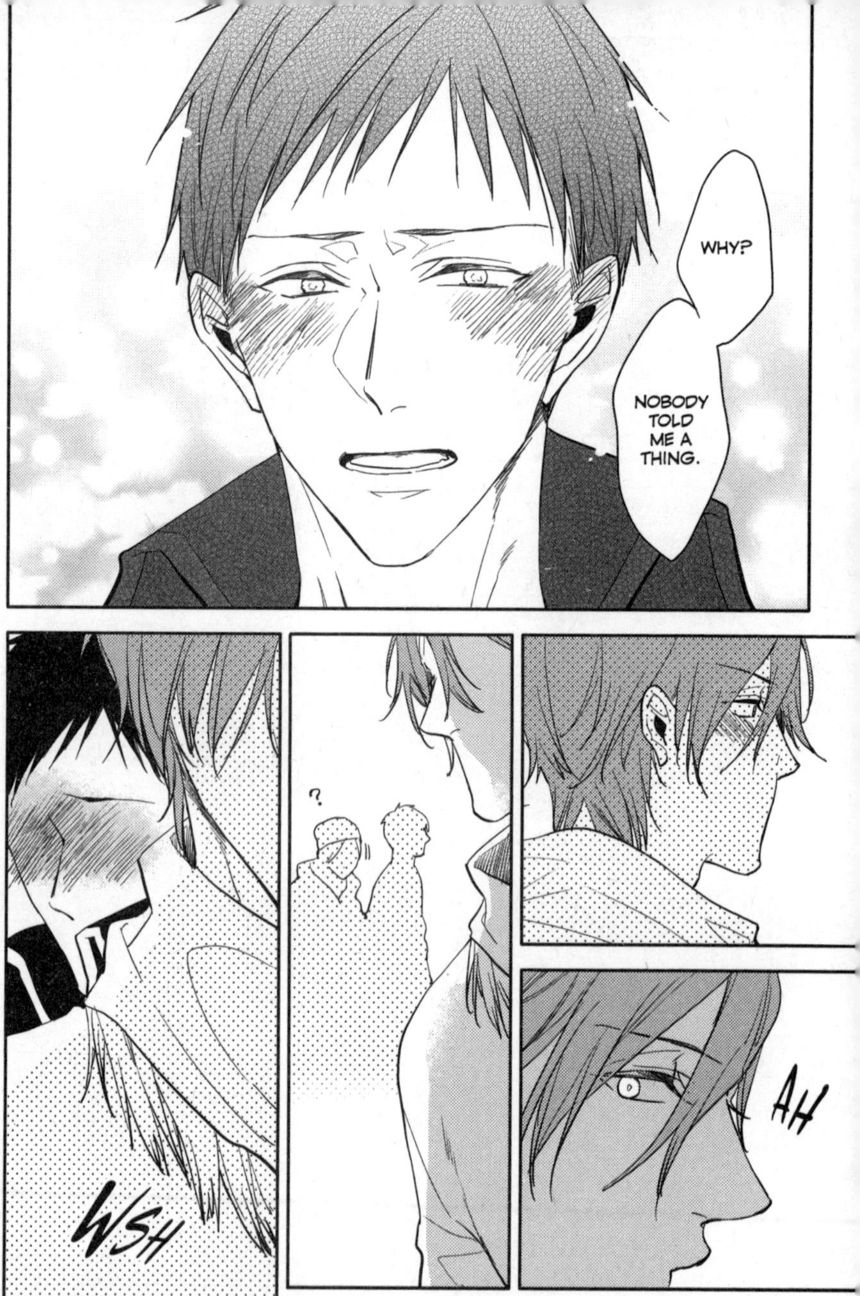
WHY?
NOBODY TOLD ME A THING.
AH
?
WSH

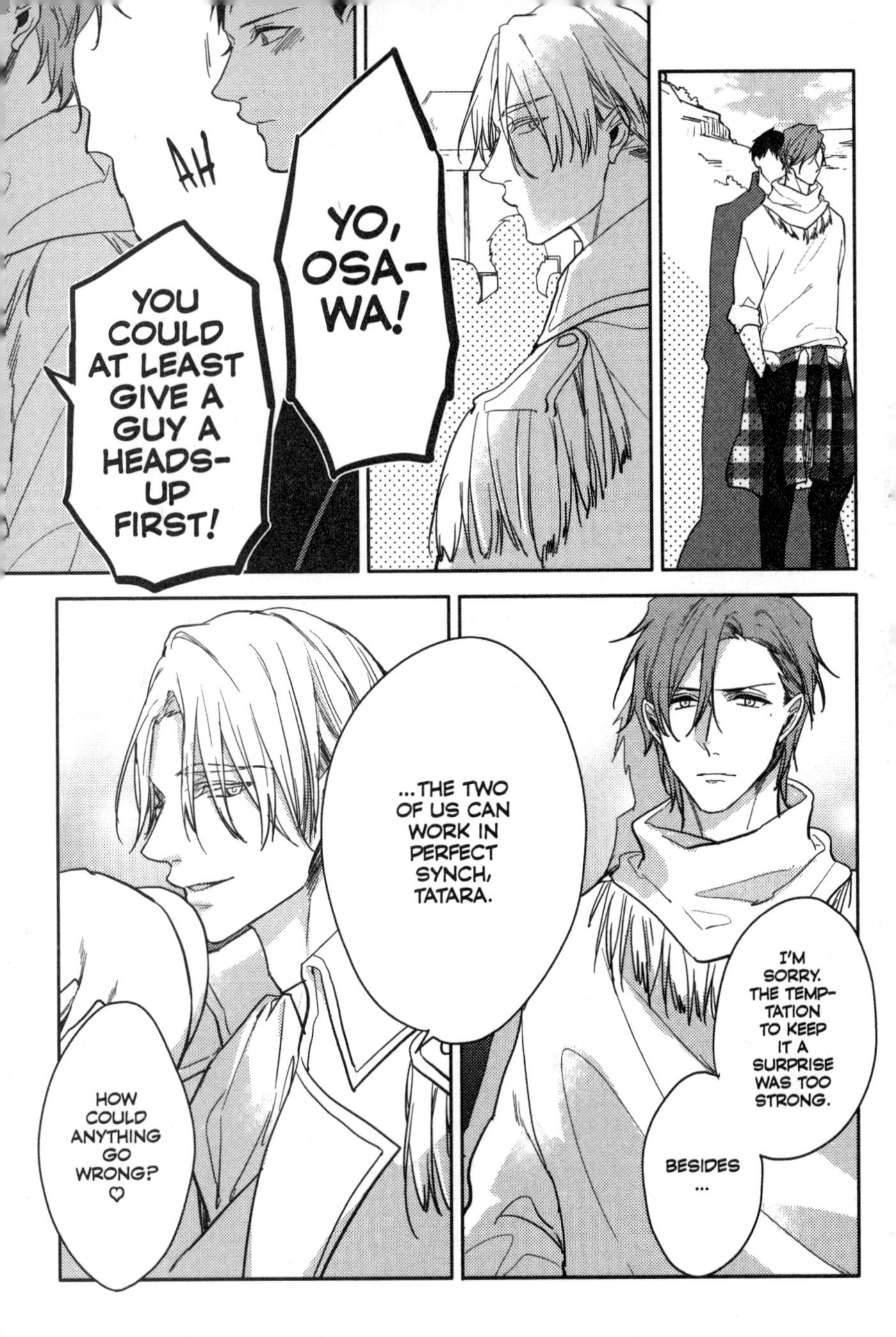
YO, OSA-WA!
AH
YOU COULD AT LEAST GIVE A GUY A HEADS-UP FIRST!
I'M SORRY. THE TEMPTATION TO KEEP IT A SURPRISE WAS TOO STRONG.
BESIDES...
...THE TWO OF US CAN WORK IN PERFECT SYNCH, TATARA.
HOW COULD ANYTHING GO WRONG? ♡

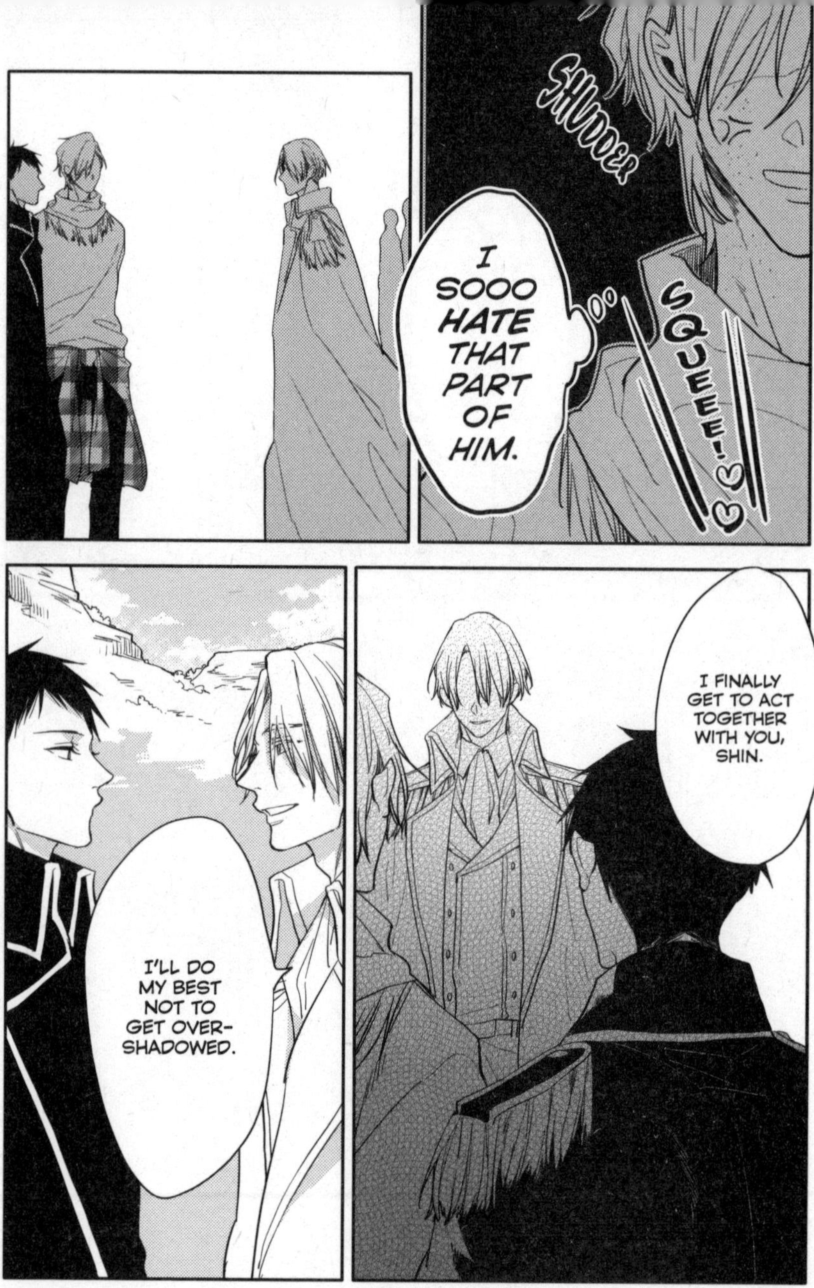
SHUDDER
I SOOO HATE THAT PART OF HIM.
SQUEEE!
I FINALLY GET TO ACT TOGETHER WITH YOU, SHIN.
I'LL DO MY BEST NOT TO GET OVER-SHADOWED.

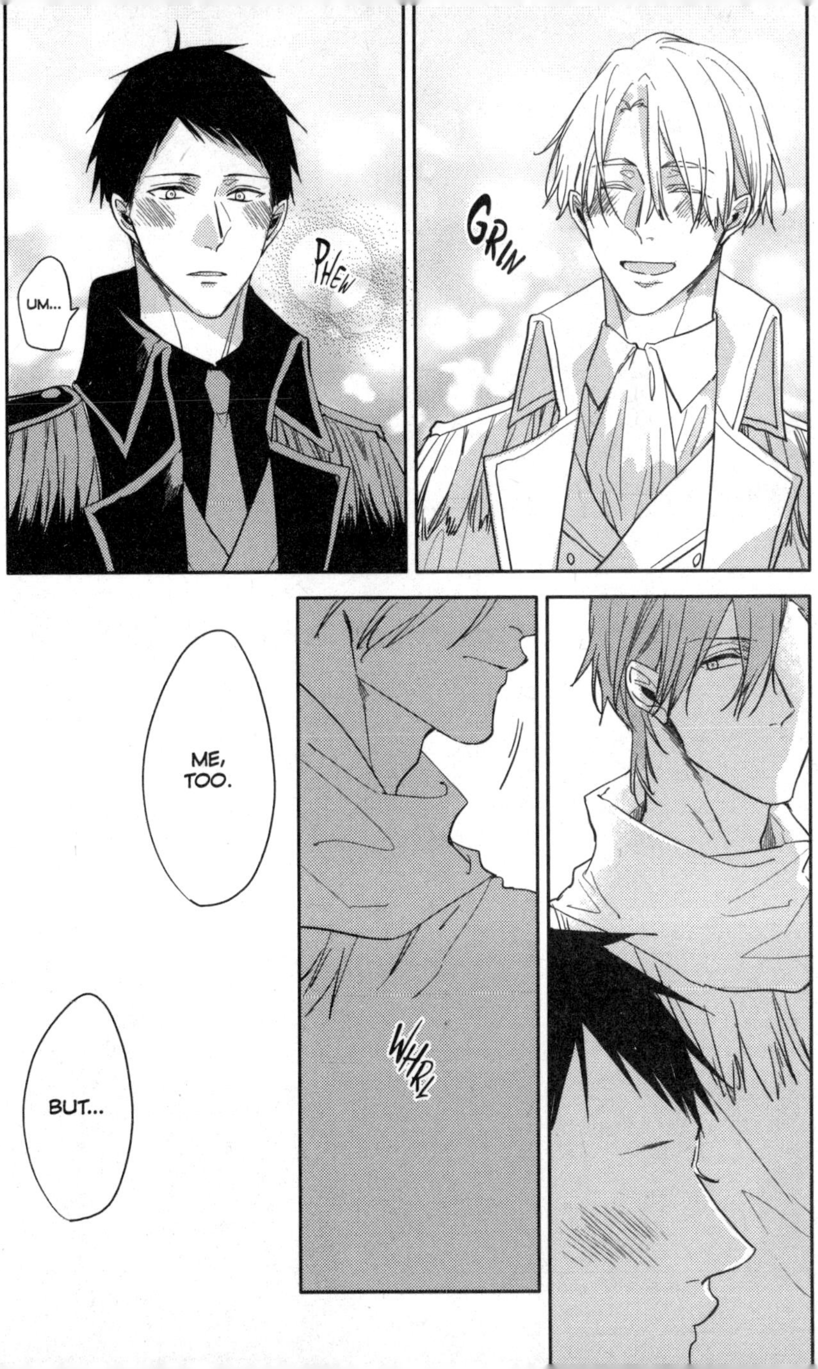
GRIN
UM...
PHEW
WHIRL
ME, TOO.
BUT...

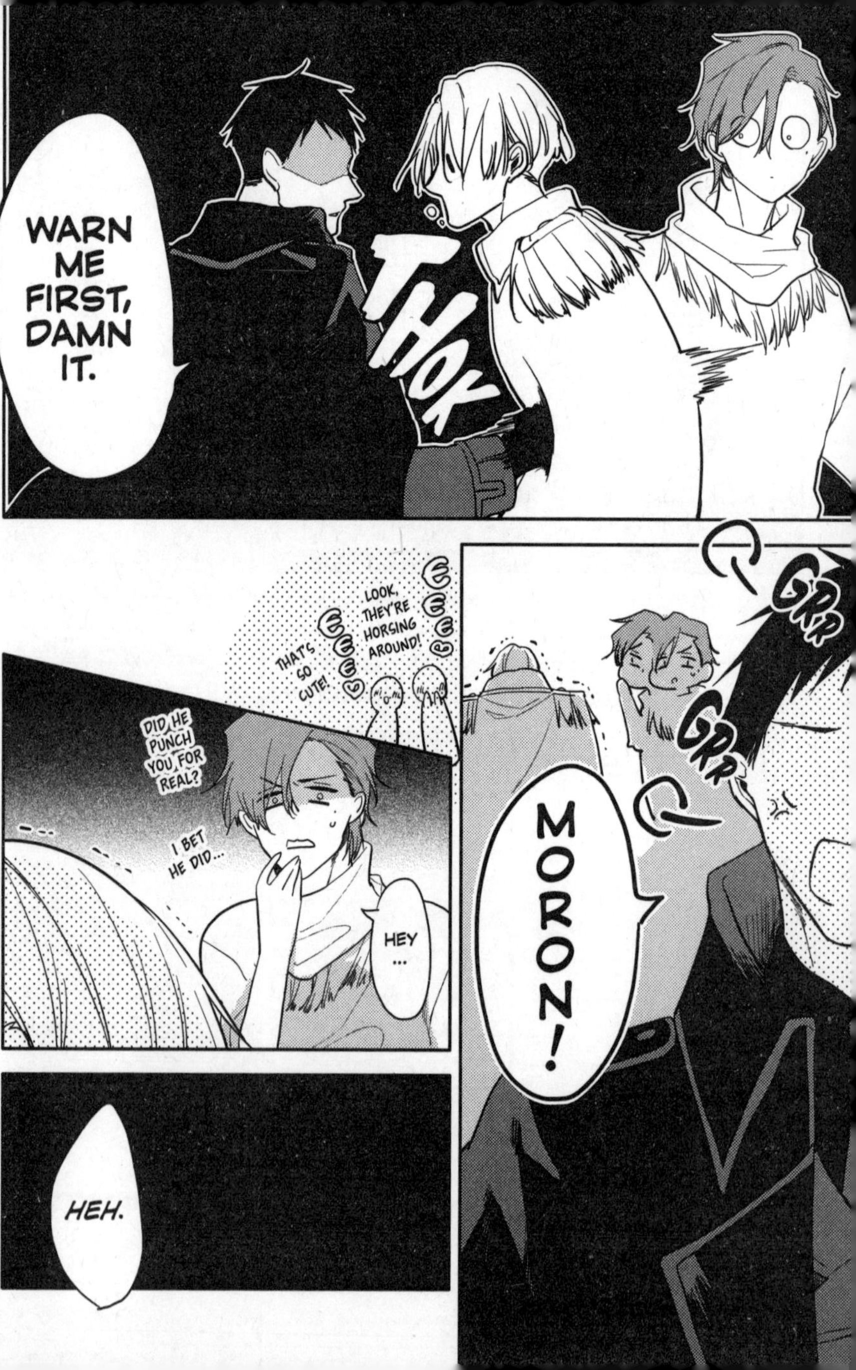
WARN ME FIRST, DAMN IT.
THOK
GRR
GRR
MORON!
LOOK, THEY'RE HORSING AROUND!
THAT'S SO CUTE!
DID HE PUNCH YOU FOR REAL?
I BET HE DID...
HEY ...
HEH.

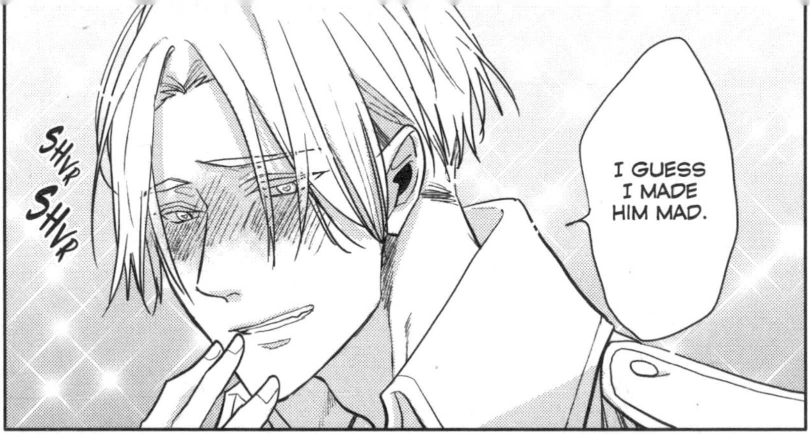
I GUESS I MADE HIM MAD.
SHVR SHVR

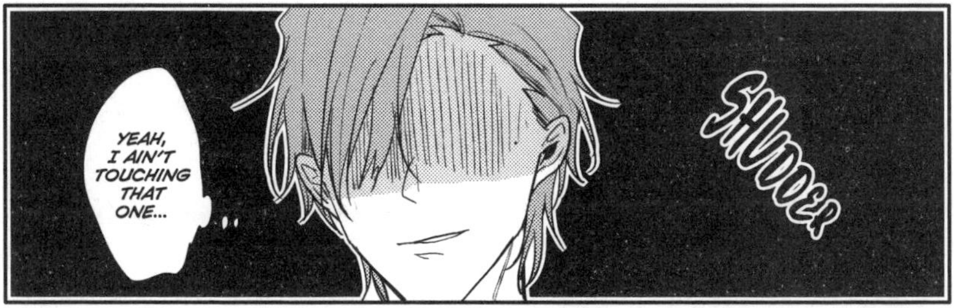
SHUDDER
YEAH, I AIN'T TOUCHING THAT ONE...

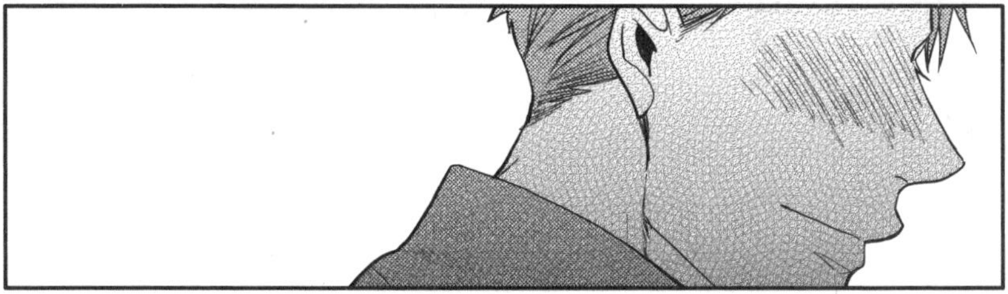

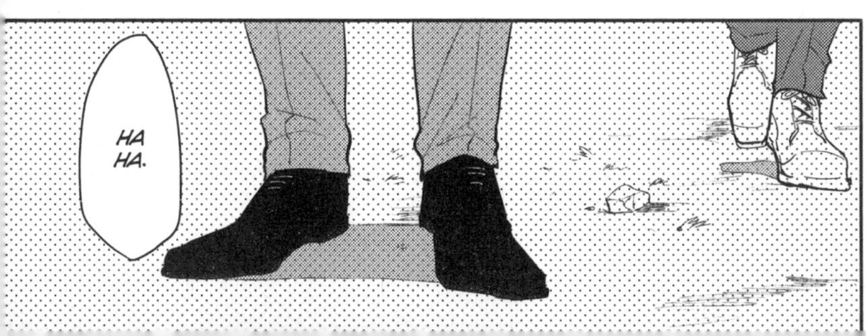
HA HA.

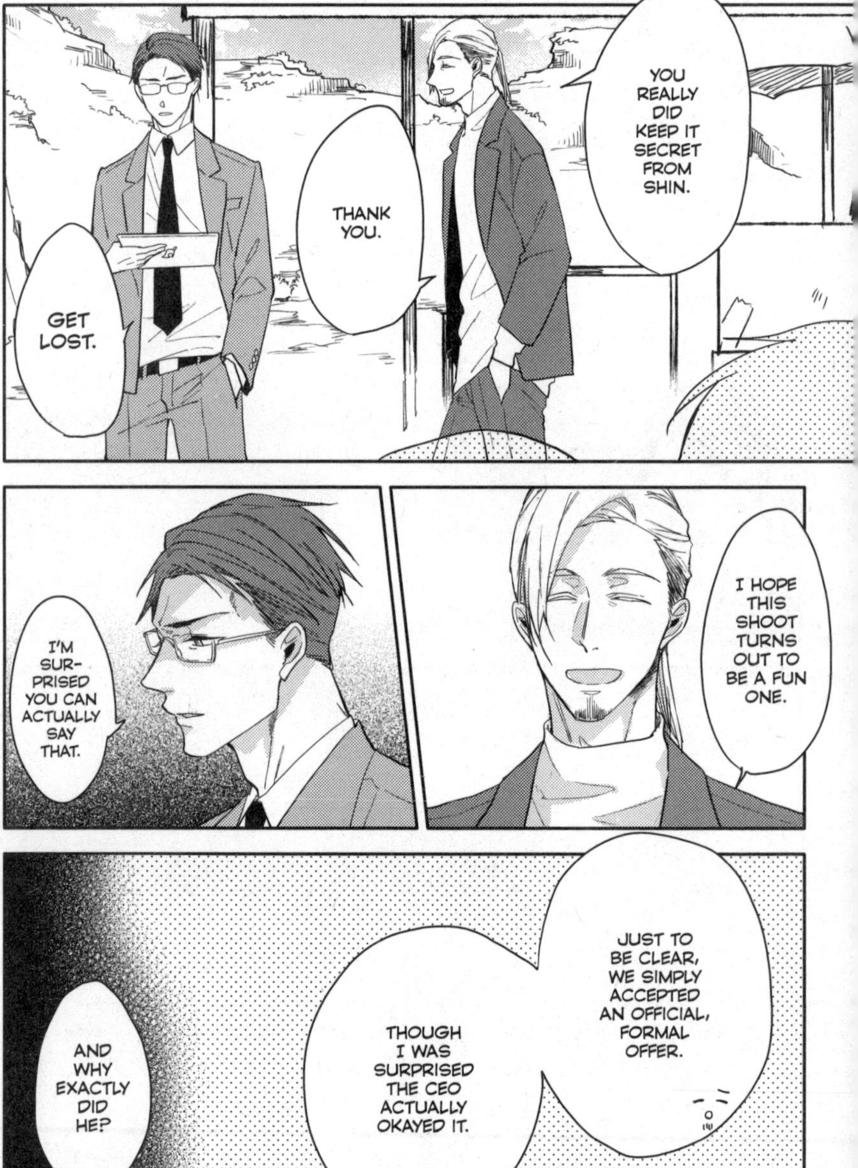
YOU REALLY DID KEEP IT SECRET FROM SHIN.
THANK YOU.
GET LOST.
I HOPE THIS SHOOT TURNS OUT TO BE A FUN ONE.
I'M SUR-PRISED YOU CAN ACTUALLY SAY THAT.
JUST TO BE CLEAR, WE SIMPLY ACCEPTED AN OFFICIAL, FORMAL OFFER.
THOUGH I WAS SURPRISED THE CEO ACTUALLY OKAYED IT.
AND WHY EXACTLY DID HE?

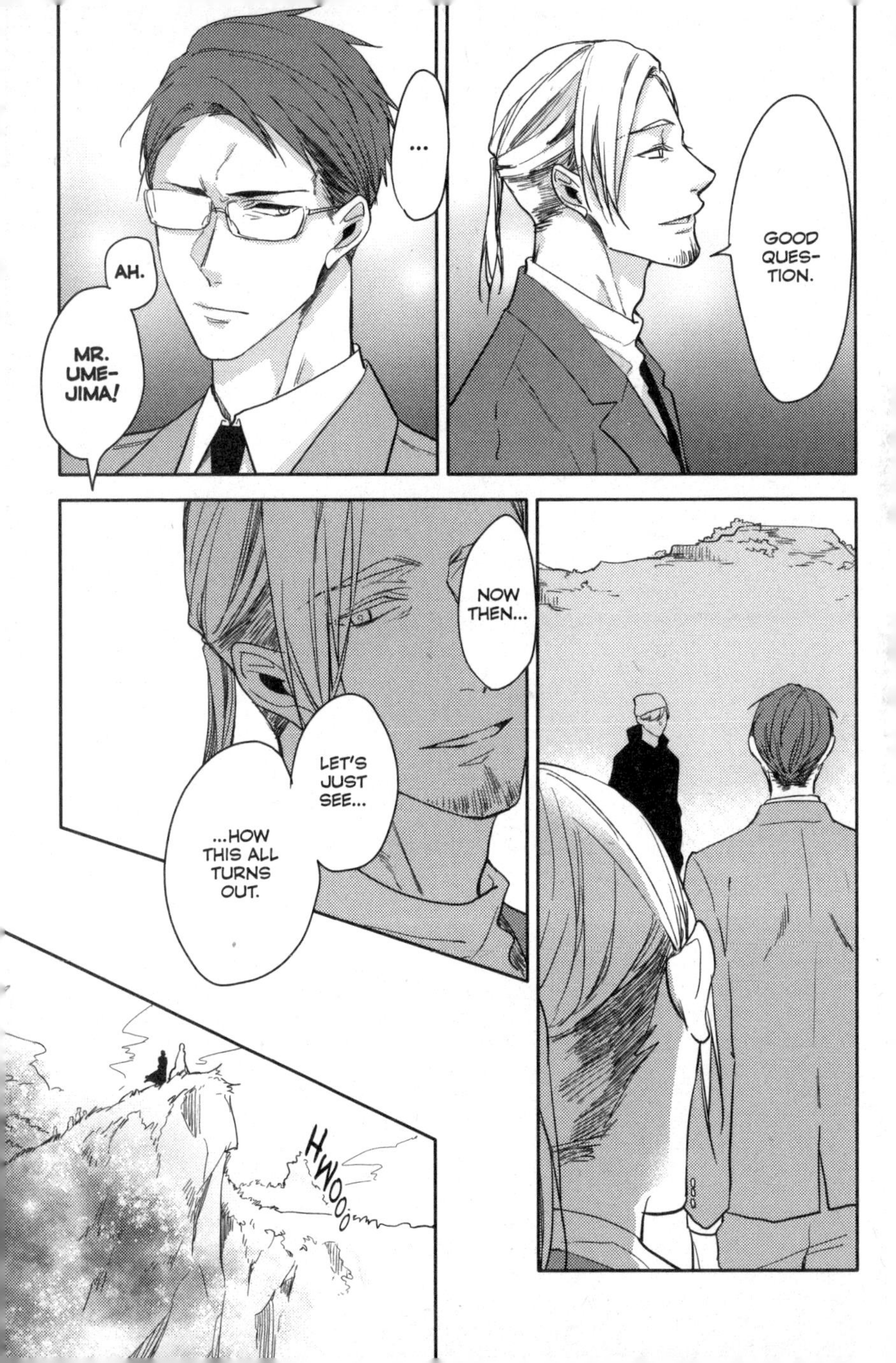
GOOD QUESTION.
...
AH.
MR. UMEJIMA!
NOW THEN...
LET'S JUST SEE...
...HOW THIS ALL TURNS OUT.
HWOOO

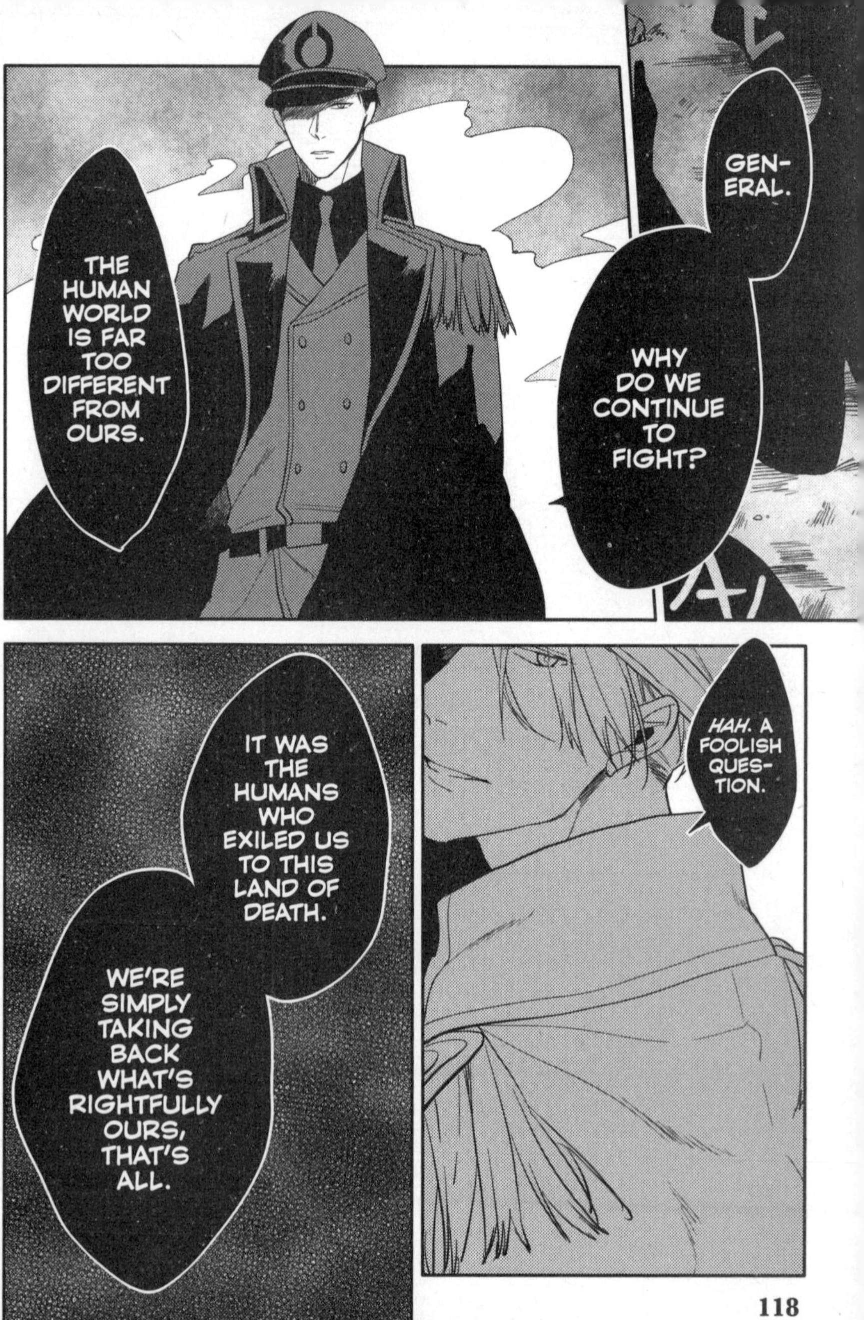
GEN-ERAL.
WHY DO WE CONTINUE TO FIGHT?
THE HUMAN WORLD IS FAR TOO DIFFERENT FROM OURS.
HAH. A FOOLISH QUES-TION.
IT WAS THE HUMANS WHO EXILED US TO THIS LAND OF DEATH.
WE'RE SIMPLY TAKING BACK WHAT'S RIGHTFULLY OURS, THAT'S ALL.

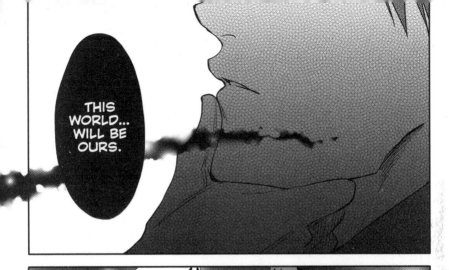

THIS WORLD... WILL BE OURS.

DON'T YOU AGREE...

...CAPTAIN DARK?

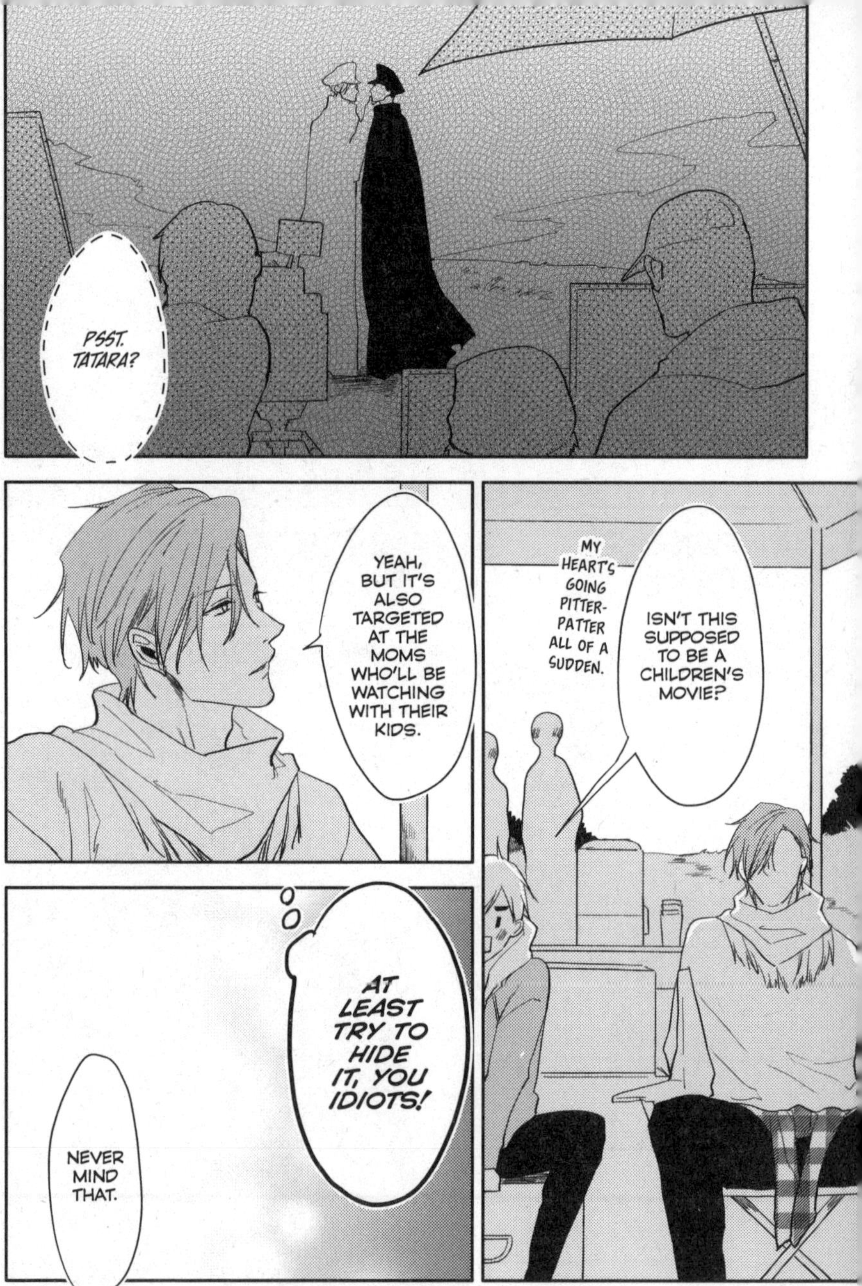

PSST. TATARA?
ISN'T THIS SUPPOSED TO BE A CHILDREN'S MOVIE?
MY HEART'S GOING PITTER-PATTER ALL OF A SUDDEN.
YEAH, BUT IT'S ALSO TARGETED AT THE MOMS WHO'LL BE WATCHING WITH THEIR KIDS.
AT LEAST TRY TO HIDE IT, YOU IDIOTS!
NEVER MIND THAT.

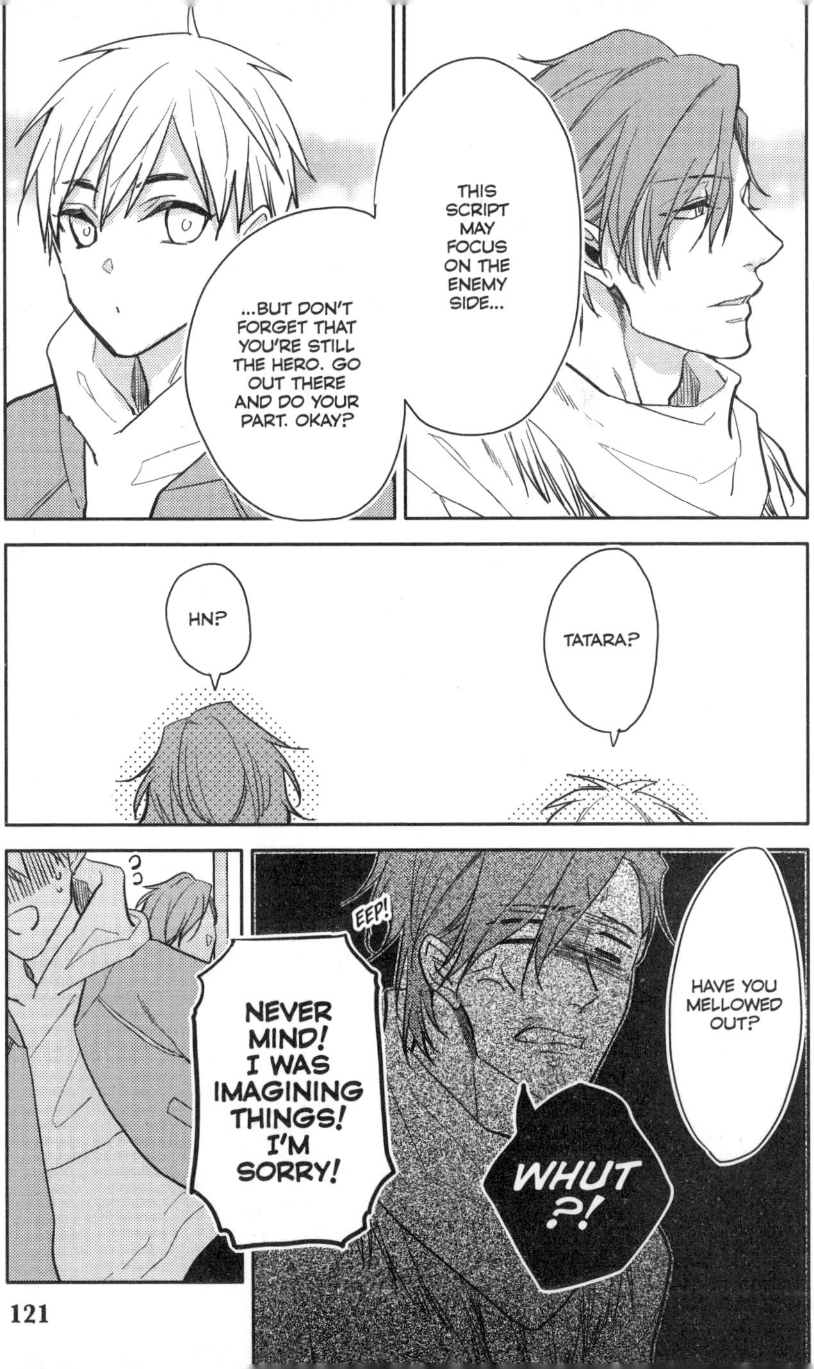
THIS SCRIPT MAY FOCUS ON THE ENEMY SIDE...
...BUT DON'T FORGET THAT YOU'RE STILL THE HERO. GO OUT THERE AND DO YOUR PART. OKAY?
TATARA?
HN?
HAVE YOU MELLOWED OUT?
WHUT?!
EEP!
NEVER MIND! I WAS IMAGINING THINGS! I'M SORRY!

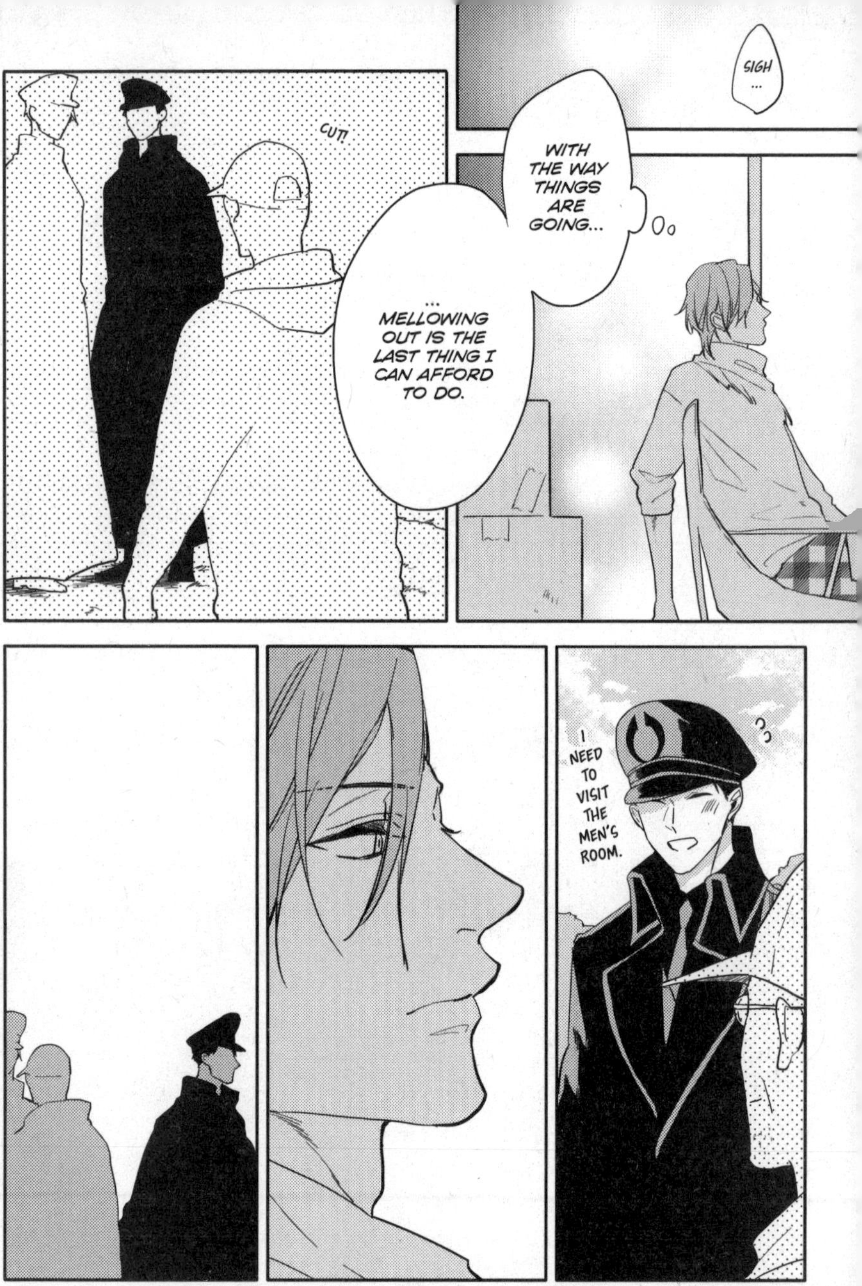
SIGH...
WITH THE WAY THINGS ARE GOING...
... MELLOWING OUT IS THE LAST THING I CAN AFFORD TO DO.
CUT!
I NEED TO VISIT THE MEN'S ROOM.

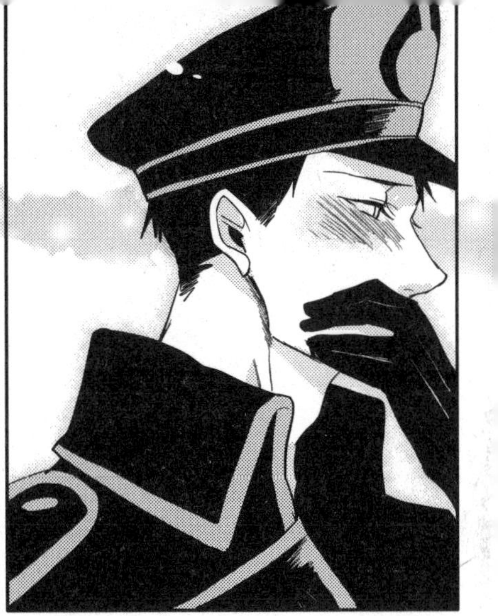

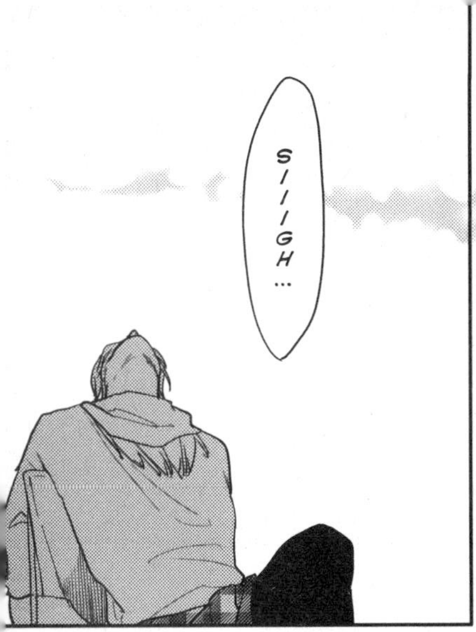
S///GH...

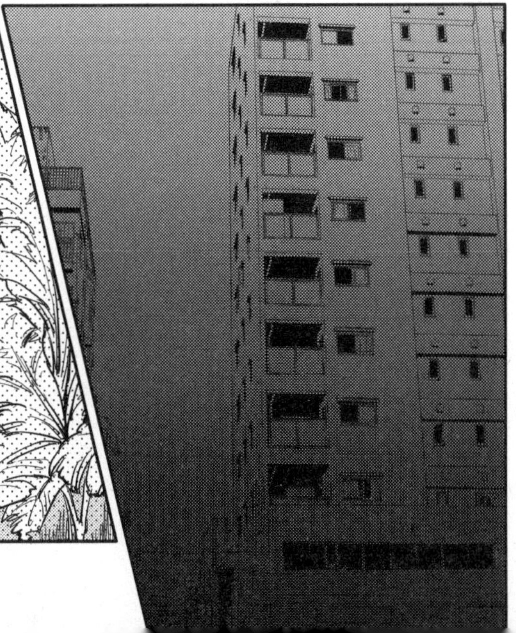

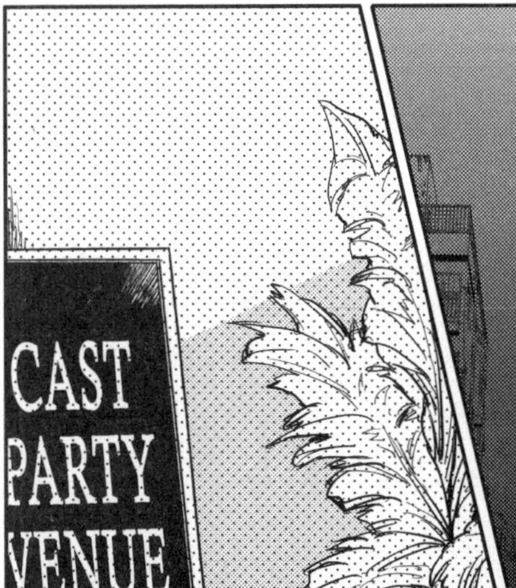
CAST
PARTY
VENUE

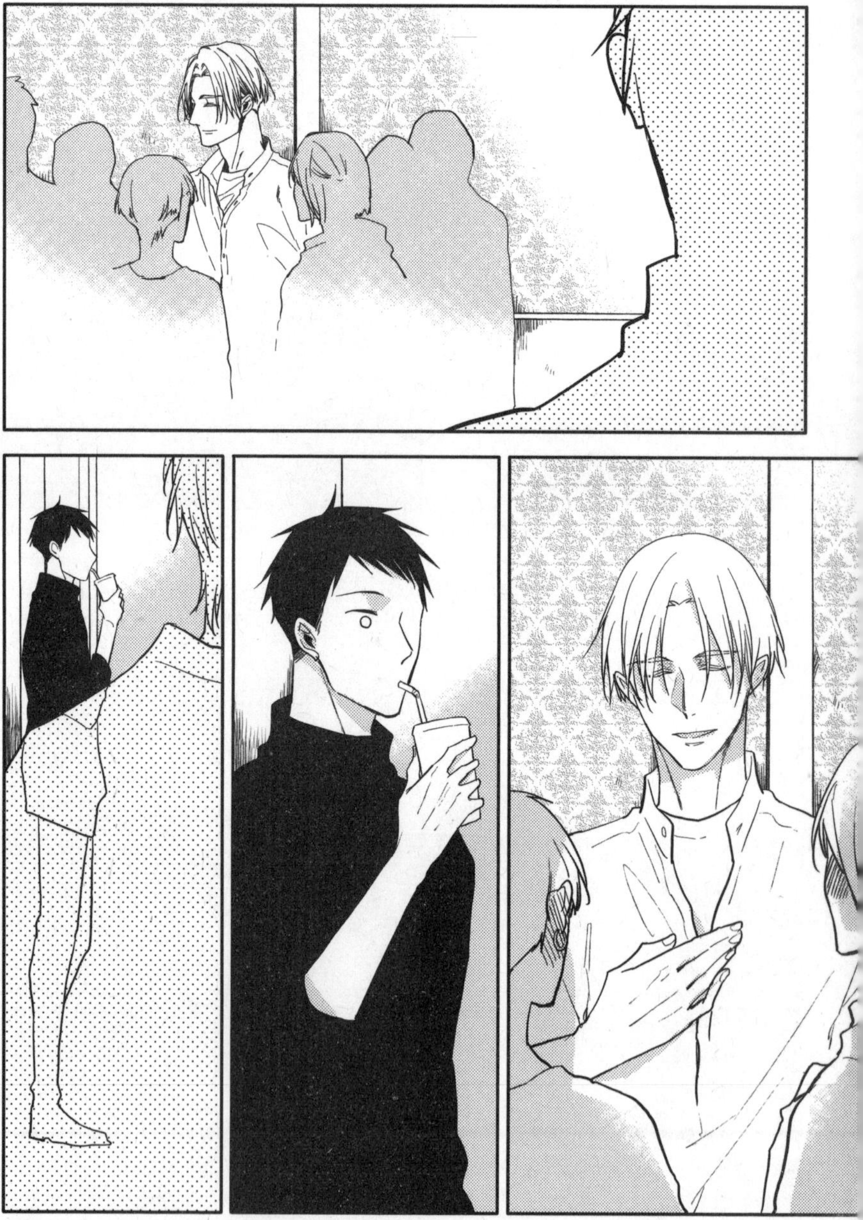

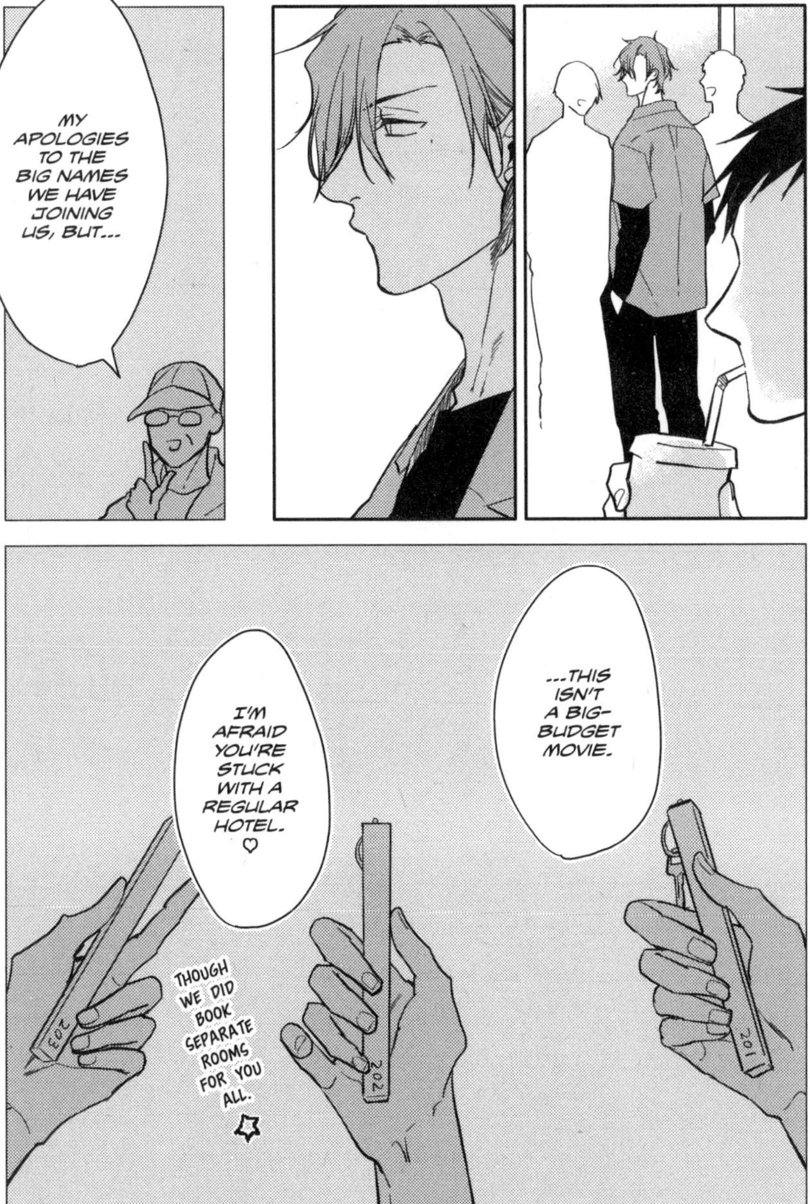
MY APOLOGIES TO THE BIG NAMES WE HAVE JOINING US, BUT...
...THIS ISN'T A BIG-BUDGET MOVIE.
I'M AFRAID YOU'RE STUCK WITH A REGULAR HOTEL. ♡
201
202
THOUGH WE DID BOOK SEPARATE ROOMS FOR YOU ALL.
203

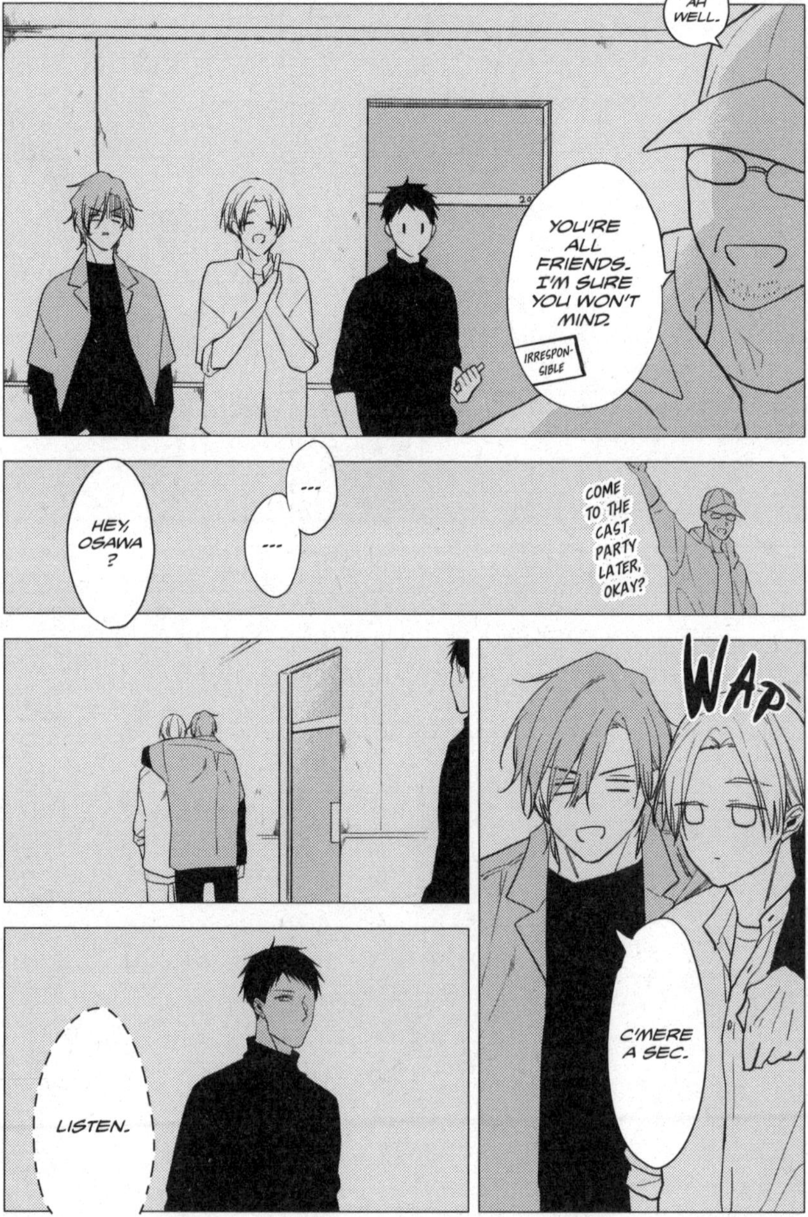
AH WELL.
YOU'RE ALL FRIENDS. I'M SURE YOU WON'T MIND.
IRRESPONSIBLE
COME TO THE CAST PARTY LATER, OKAY?
...
...
HEY, OSAWA?
WAP
C'MERE A SEC.
LISTEN.

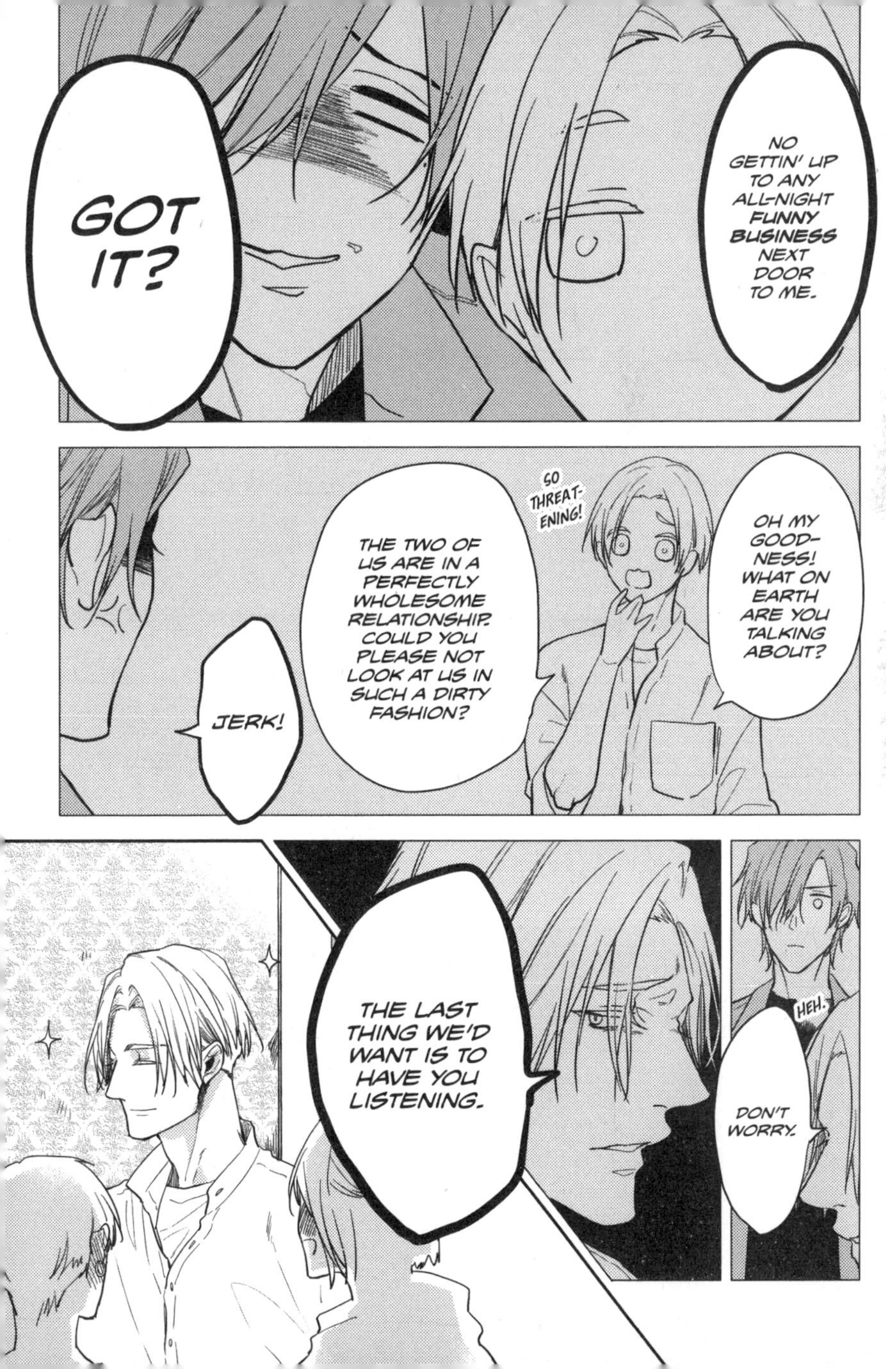
NO GETTIN' UP TO ANY ALL-NIGHT FUNNY BUSINESS NEXT DOOR TO ME.
GOT IT?
OH MY GOODNESS! WHAT ON EARTH ARE YOU TALKING ABOUT?
SO THREAT-ENING!
THE TWO OF US ARE IN A PERFECTLY WHOLESOME RELATIONSHIP. COULD YOU PLEASE NOT LOOK AT US IN SUCH A DIRTY FASHION?
JERK!
HEH.
DON'T WORRY.
THE LAST THING WE'D WANT IS TO HAVE YOU LISTENING.

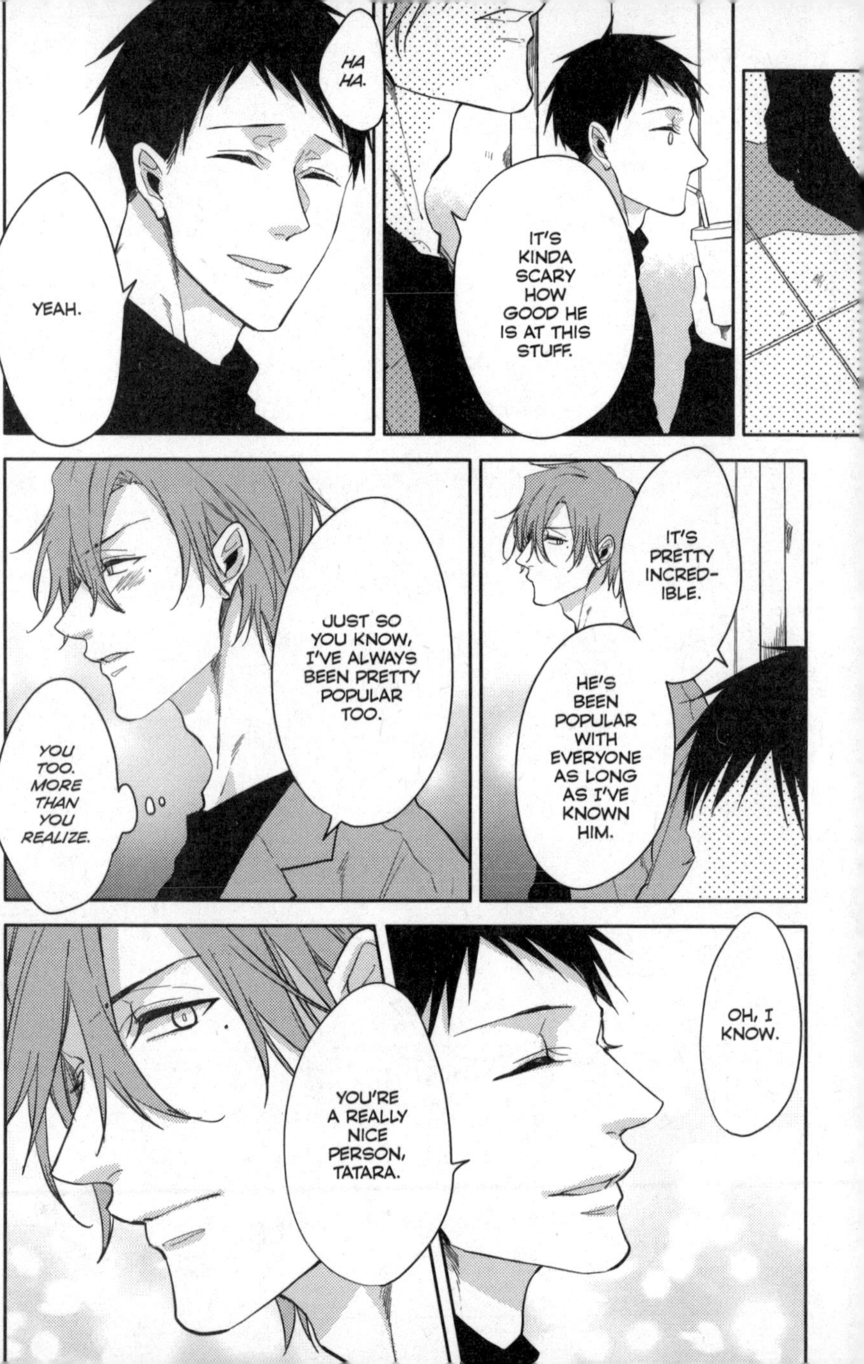
IT'S KINDA SCARY HOW GOOD HE IS AT THIS STUFF.
HA HA.
YEAH.
IT'S PRETTY INCRED-IBLE.
HE'S BEEN POPULAR WITH EVERYONE AS LONG AS I'VE KNOWN HIM.
JUST SO YOU KNOW, I'VE ALWAYS BEEN PRETTY POPULAR TOO.
YOU TOO. MORE THAN YOU REALIZE.
OH, I KNOW.
YOU'RE A REALLY NICE PERSON, TATARA.

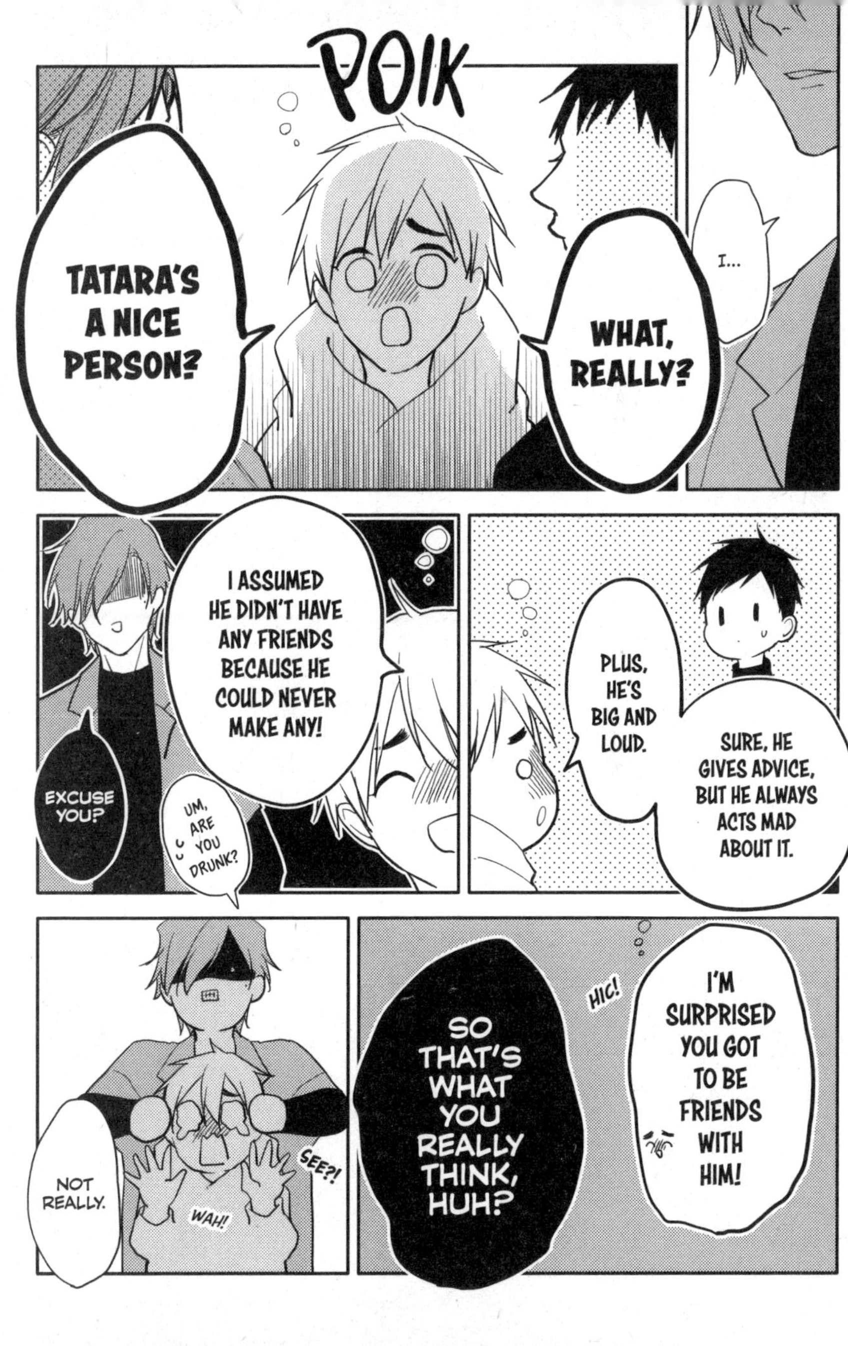
I...
POIK
WHAT, REALLY?
TATARA'S A NICE PERSON?
SURE, HE GIVES ADVICE, BUT HE ALWAYS ACTS MAD ABOUT IT.
PLUS, HE'S BIG AND LOUD.
I ASSUMED HE DIDN'T HAVE ANY FRIENDS BECAUSE HE COULD NEVER MAKE ANY!
UM, ARE YOU DRUNK?
EXCUSE YOU?
I'M SURPRISED YOU GOT TO BE FRIENDS WITH HIM!
HIC!
SO THAT'S WHAT YOU REALLY THINK, HUH?
SEE?!
WAH!
NOT REALLY.

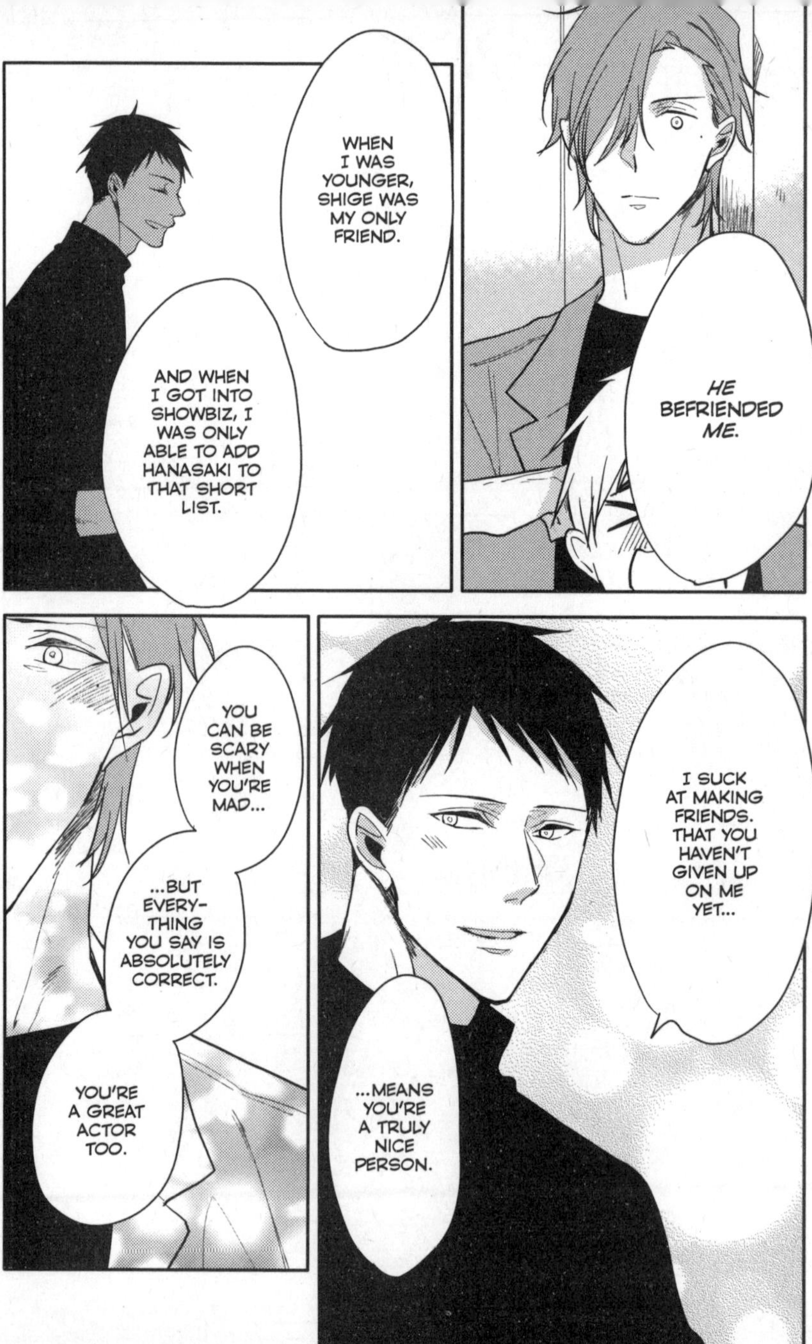
HE BEFRIENDED ME.
WHEN I WAS YOUNGER, SHIGE WAS MY ONLY FRIEND.
AND WHEN I GOT INTO SHOWBIZ, I WAS ONLY ABLE TO ADD HANASAKI TO THAT SHORT LIST.
I SUCK AT MAKING FRIENDS. THAT YOU HAVEN'T GIVEN UP ON ME YET...
...MEANS YOU'RE A TRULY NICE PERSON.
YOU CAN BE SCARY WHEN YOU'RE MAD...
...BUT EVERYTHING YOU SAY IS ABSOLUTELY CORRECT.
YOU'RE A GREAT ACTOR TOO.

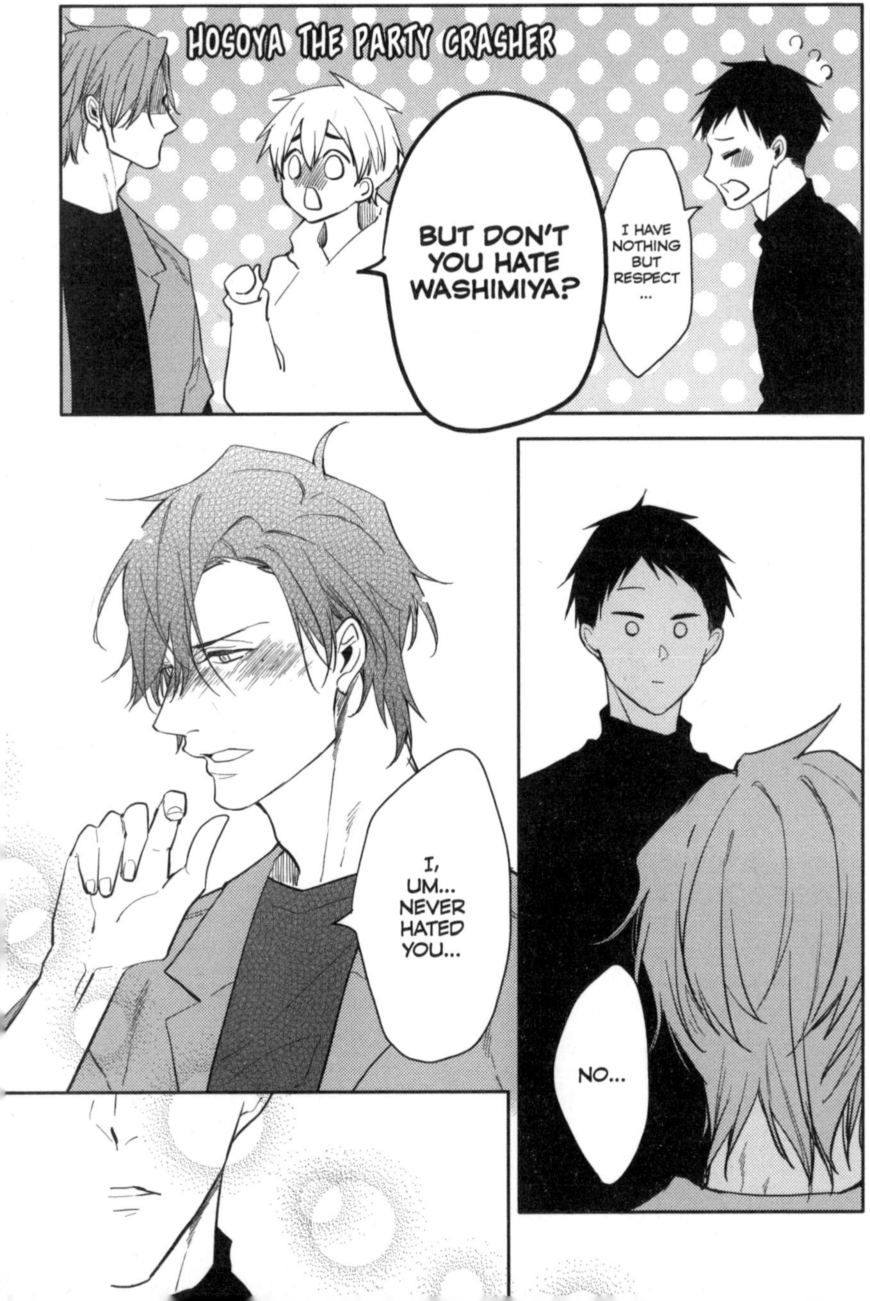
HOSOYA THE PARTY CRASHER
I HAVE NOTHING BUT RESPECT...
BUT DON'T YOU HATE WASHIMIYA?
NO...
I, UM... NEVER HATED YOU...

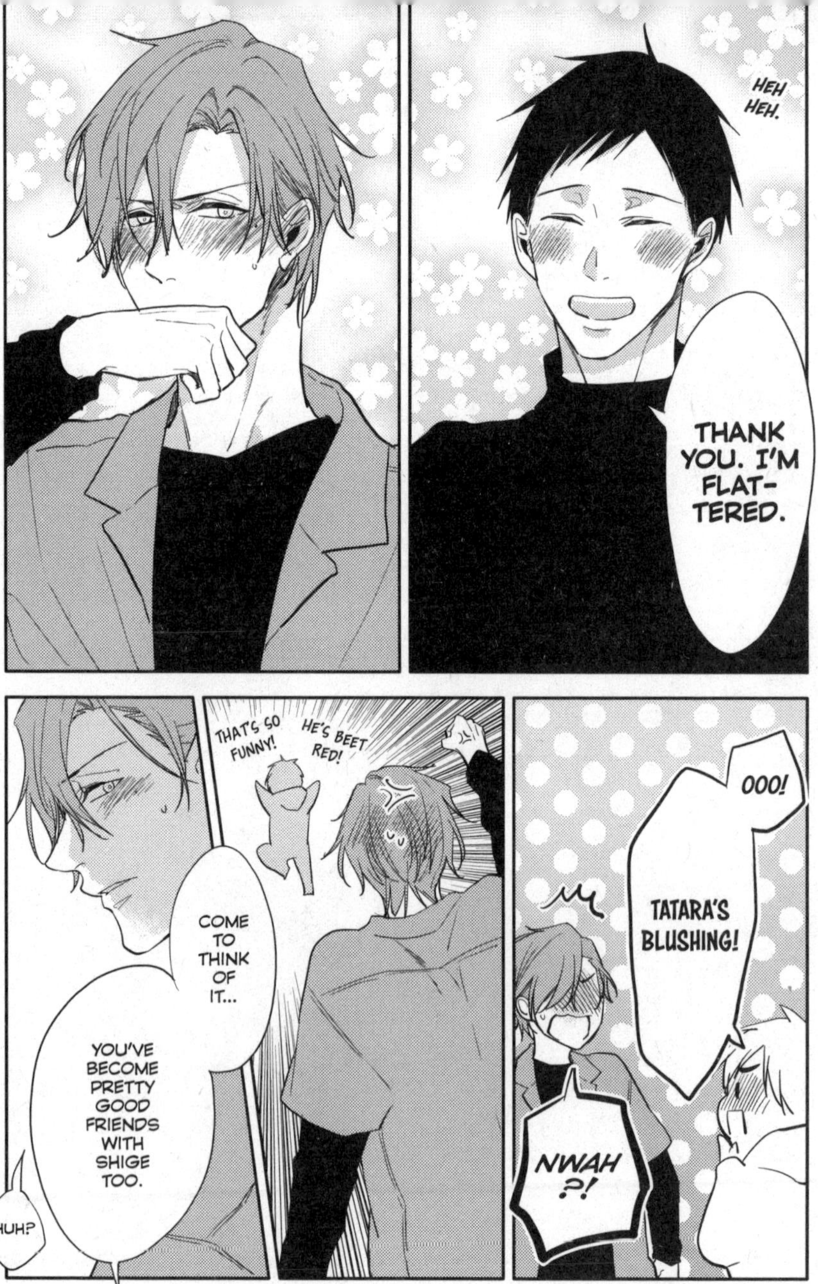
HEH HEH.
THANK YOU. I'M FLAT-TERED.
OOO! TATARA'S BLUSHING!
NWAH ?!
HE'S BEET RED!
THAT'S SO FUNNY!
COME TO THINK OF IT...
YOU'VE BECOME PRETTY GOOD FRIENDS WITH SHIGE TOO.
HUH?

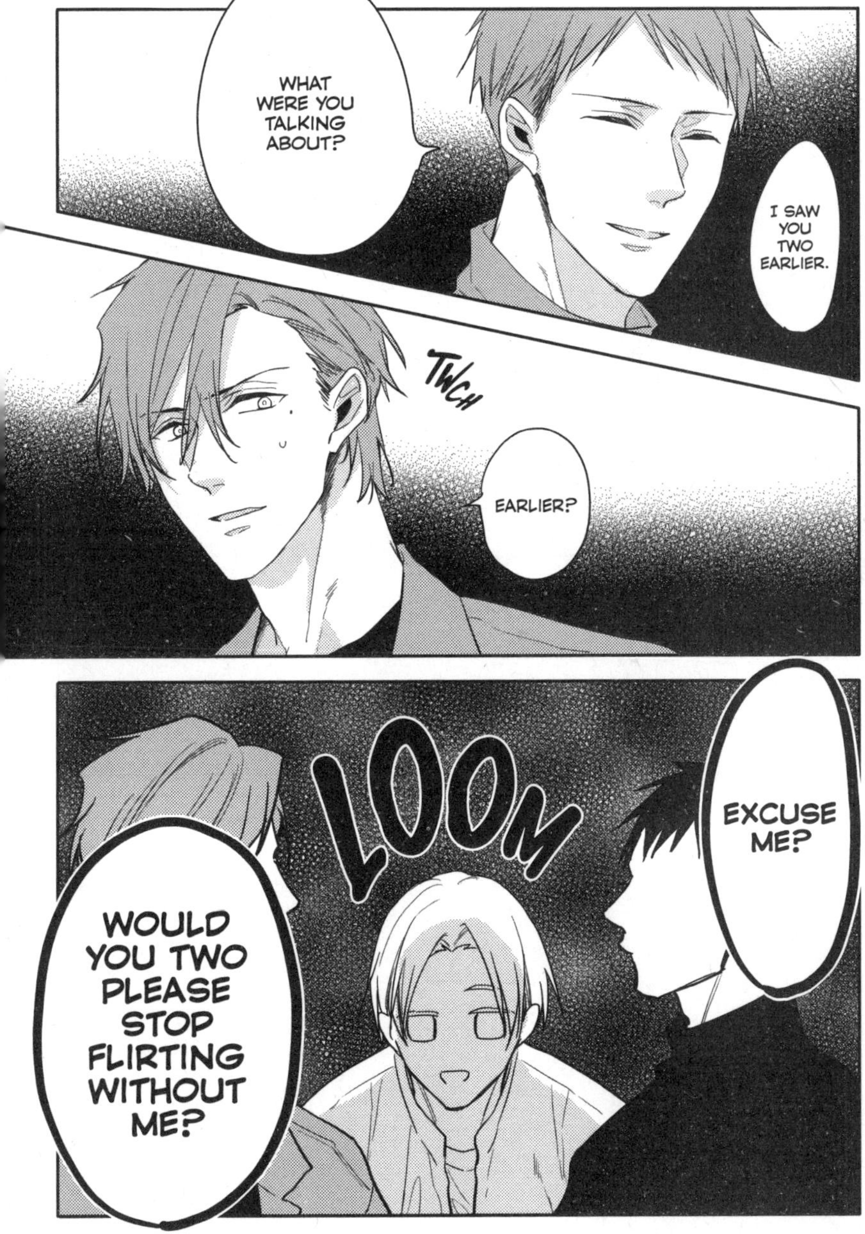
I SAW YOU TWO EARLIER.
WHAT WERE YOU TALKING ABOUT?
TWCH
EARLIER?
EXCUSE ME?
LOOM
WOULD YOU TWO PLEASE STOP FLIRTING WITHOUT ME?

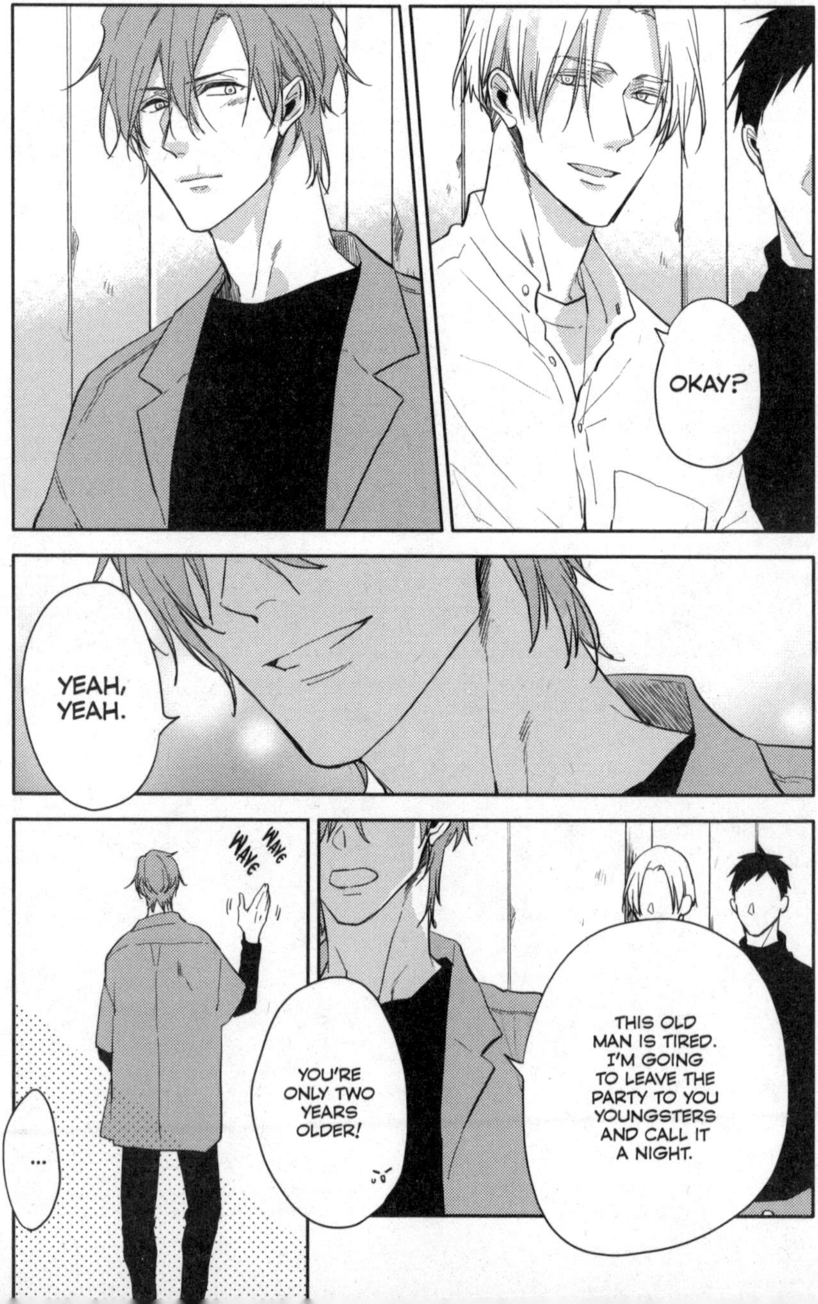
OKAY?
YEAH, YEAH.
THIS OLD MAN IS TIRED. I'M GOING TO LEAVE THE PARTY TO YOU YOUNGSTERS AND CALL IT A NIGHT.
YOU'RE ONLY TWO YEARS OLDER!
WAVE WAVE
...

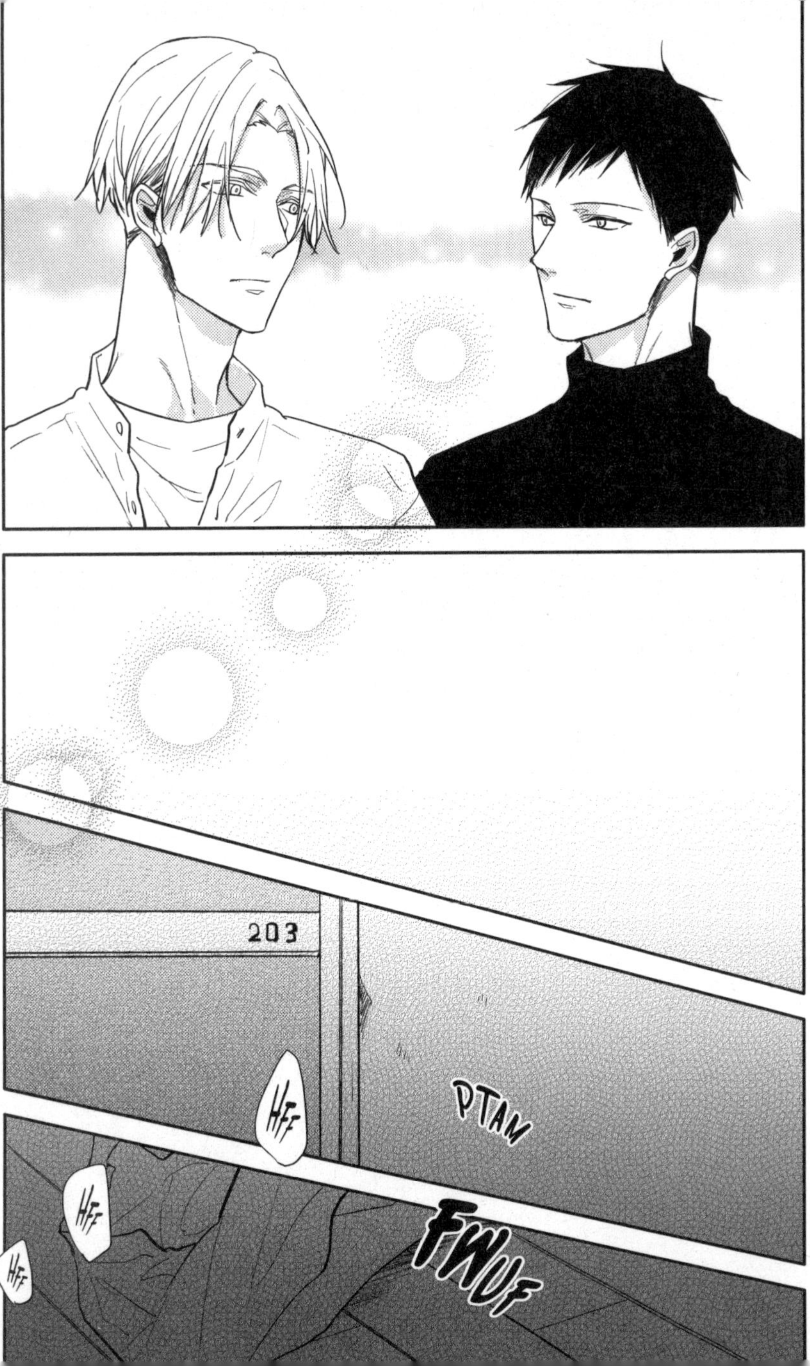
PTAM
HFF
203
FWUF
HFF
HFF

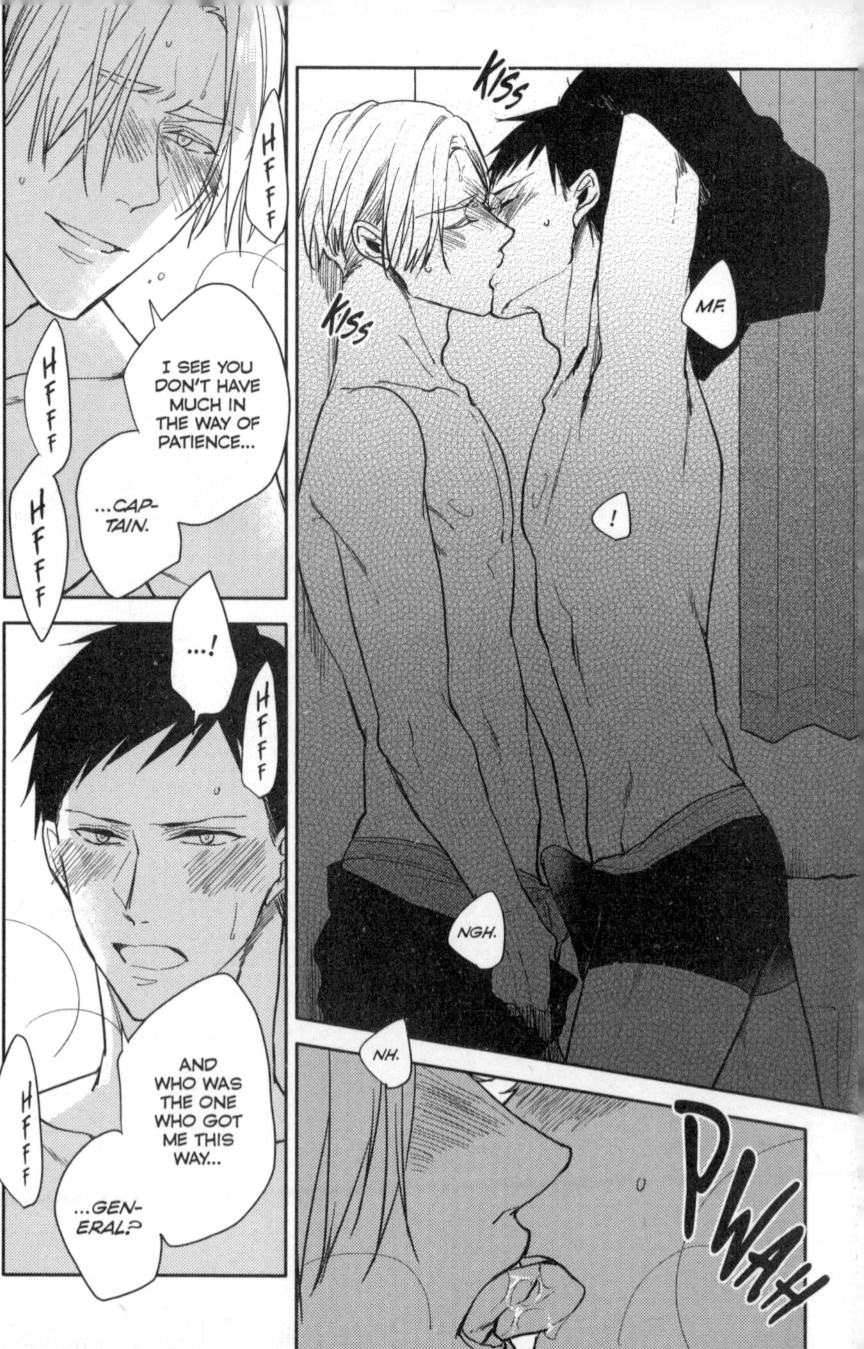
KISS
MF.
KISS
!
NGH.
NH.
PWAH
HFFF
I SEE YOU DON'T HAVE MUCH IN THE WAY OF PATIENCE...
HFFF
...CAP-TAIN.
HFFF
...!
HFFF
AND WHO WAS THE ONE WHO GOT ME THIS WAY...
...GEN-ERAL?
HFFF

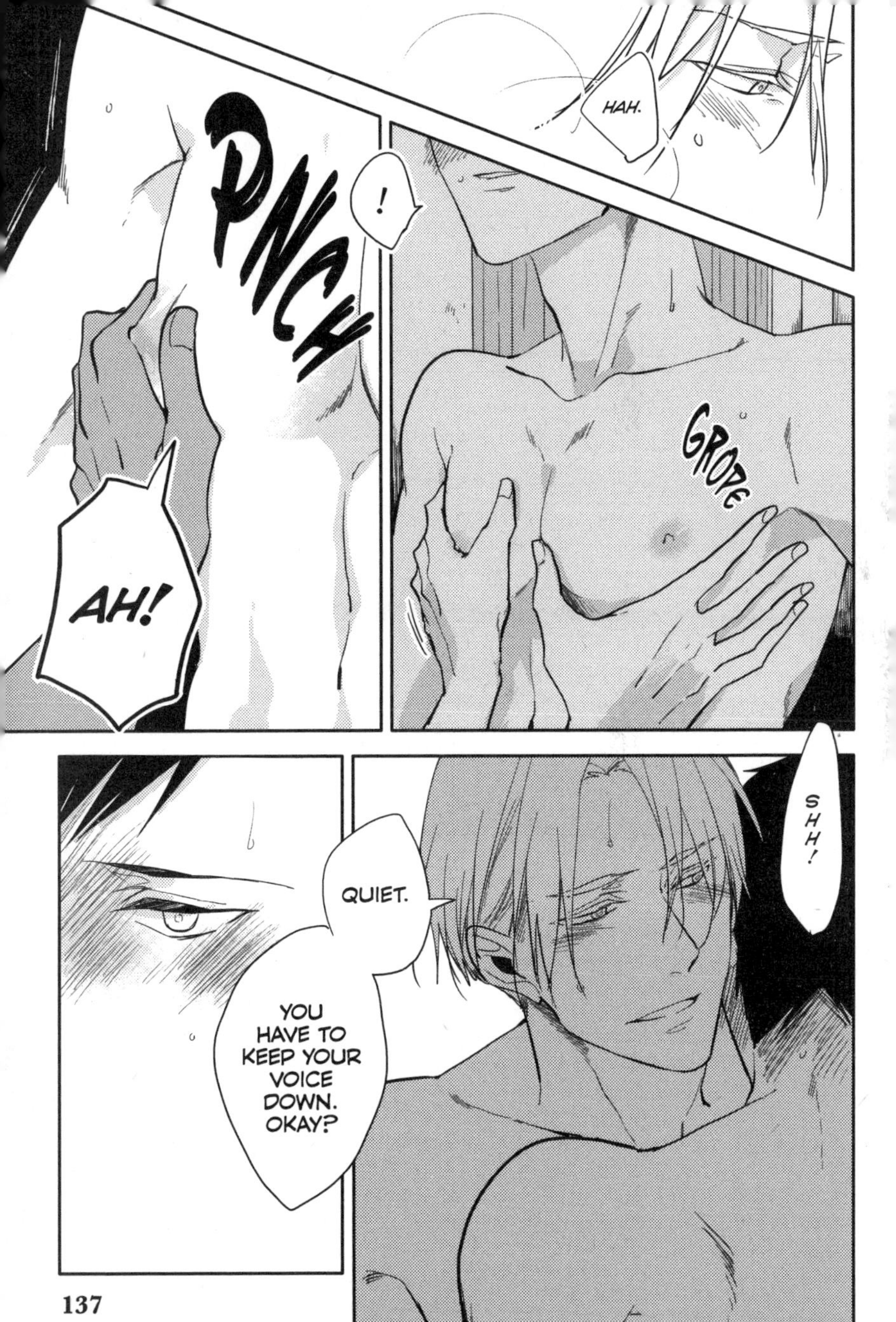
HAH.
!
GROPE
PINCH
AH!
SHH!
QUIET.
YOU HAVE TO KEEP YOUR VOICE DOWN. OKAY?

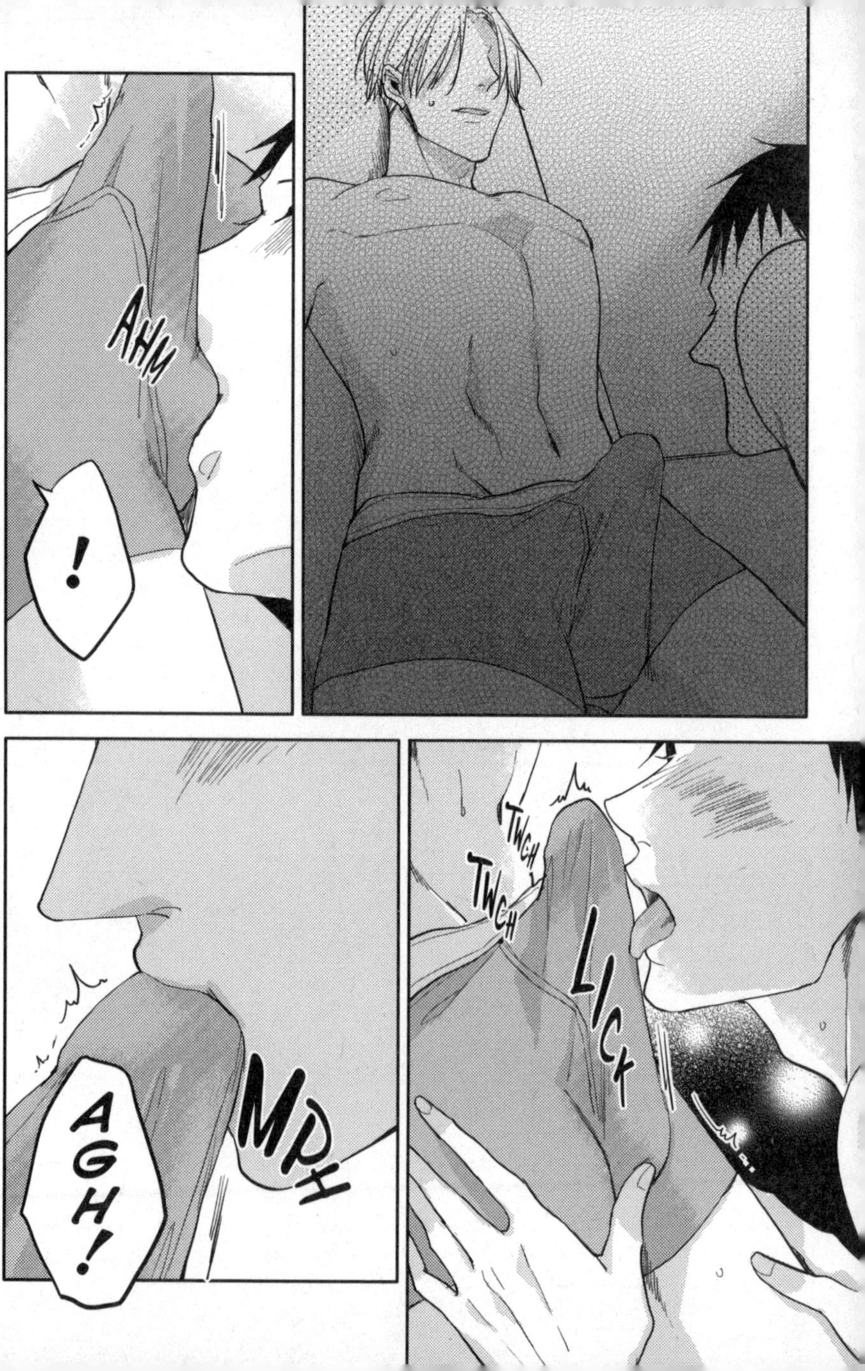
AHM
!
TWCH
TWCH
LICK
MPH
AGH!

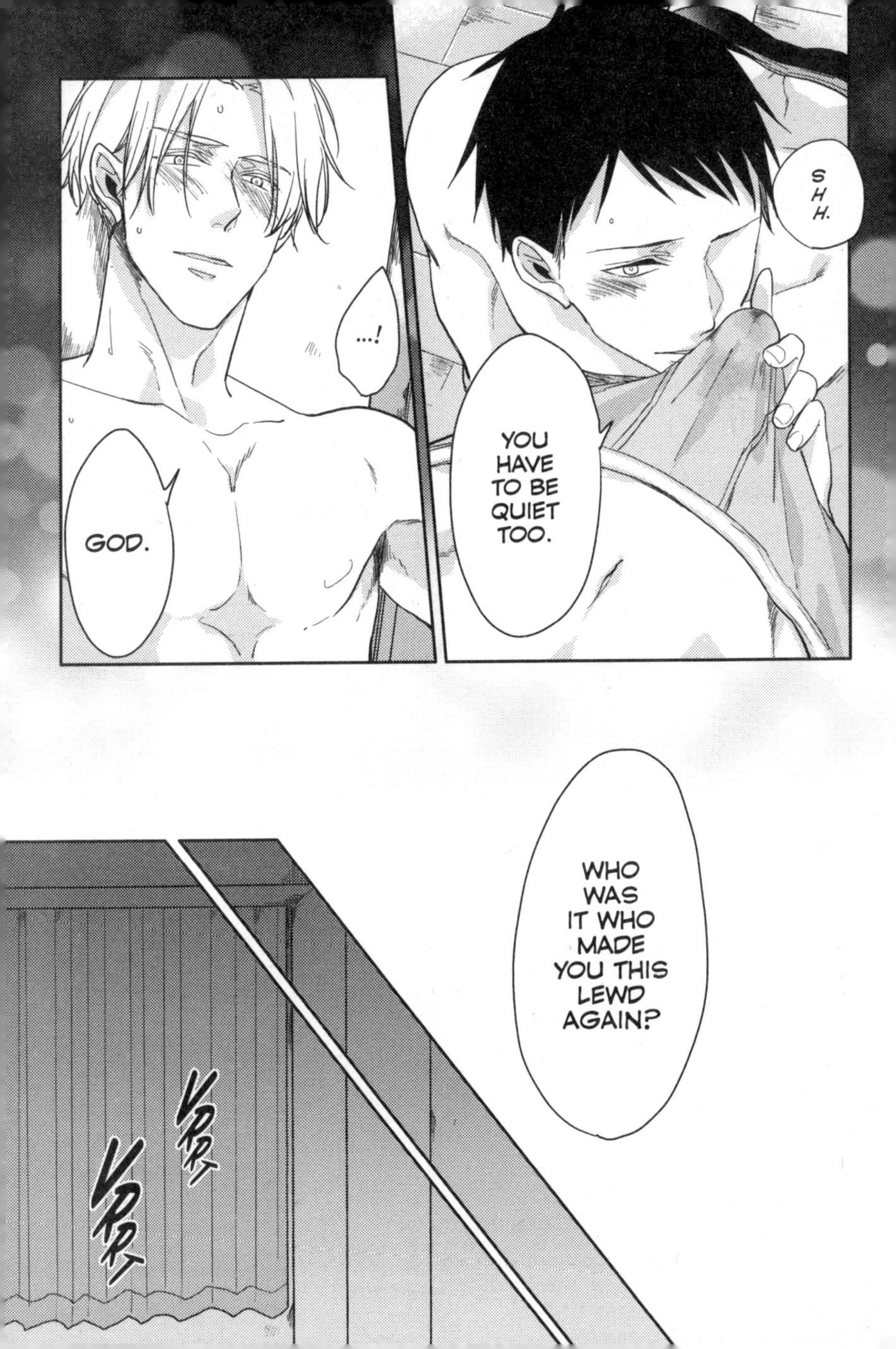
SHH.
YOU HAVE TO BE QUIET TOO.
...!
GOD.
WHO WAS IT WHO MADE YOU THIS LEWD AGAIN?
VRRT
VRRT

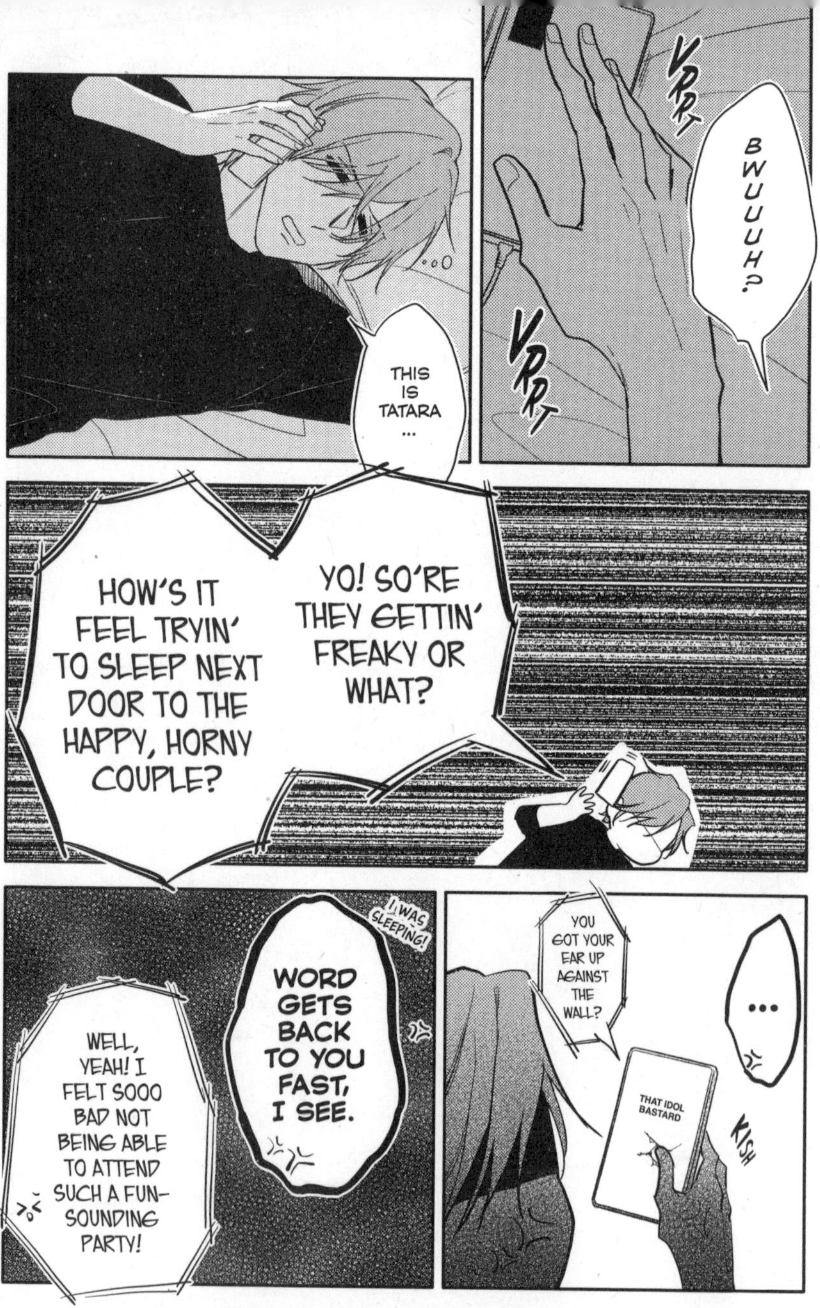
VRRT
BWUUUH?
VRRT
...oO
THIS IS TATARA ...
YO! SO'RE THEY GETTIN' FREAKY OR WHAT?
HOW'S IT FEEL TRYIN' TO SLEEP NEXT DOOR TO THE HAPPY, HORNY COUPLE?
YOU GOT YOUR EAR UP AGAINST THE WALL?
...
THAT IDOL BASTARD
KISH
I WAS SLEEPING!
WORD GETS BACK TO YOU FAST, I SEE.
WELL, YEAH! I FELT SOOO BAD NOT BEING ABLE TO ATTEND SUCH A FUN-SOUNDING PARTY!

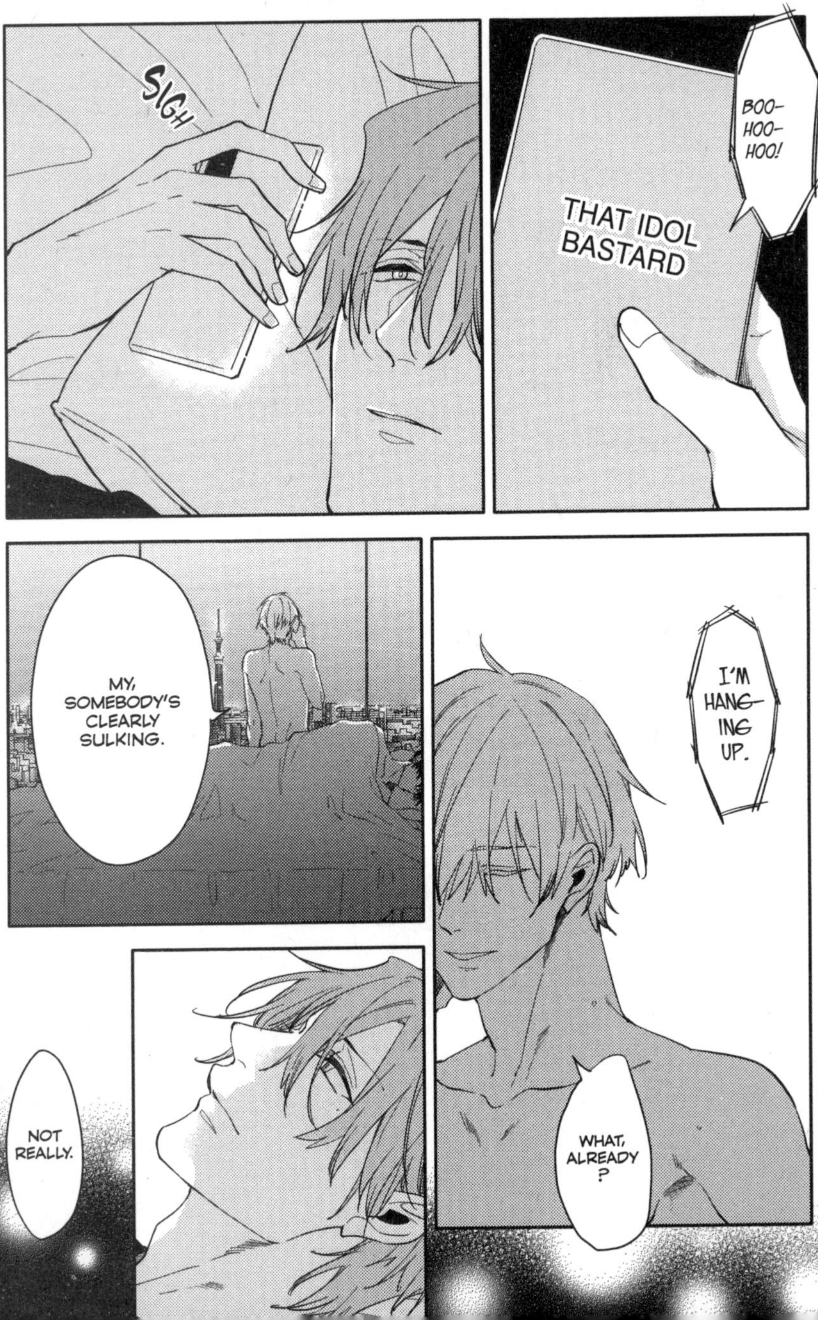
BOO-HOO-HOO!
THAT IDOL BASTARD
SIGH
I'M HANG-ING UP.
WHAT, ALREADY?
MY, SOMEBODY'S CLEARLY SULKING.
NOT REALLY.

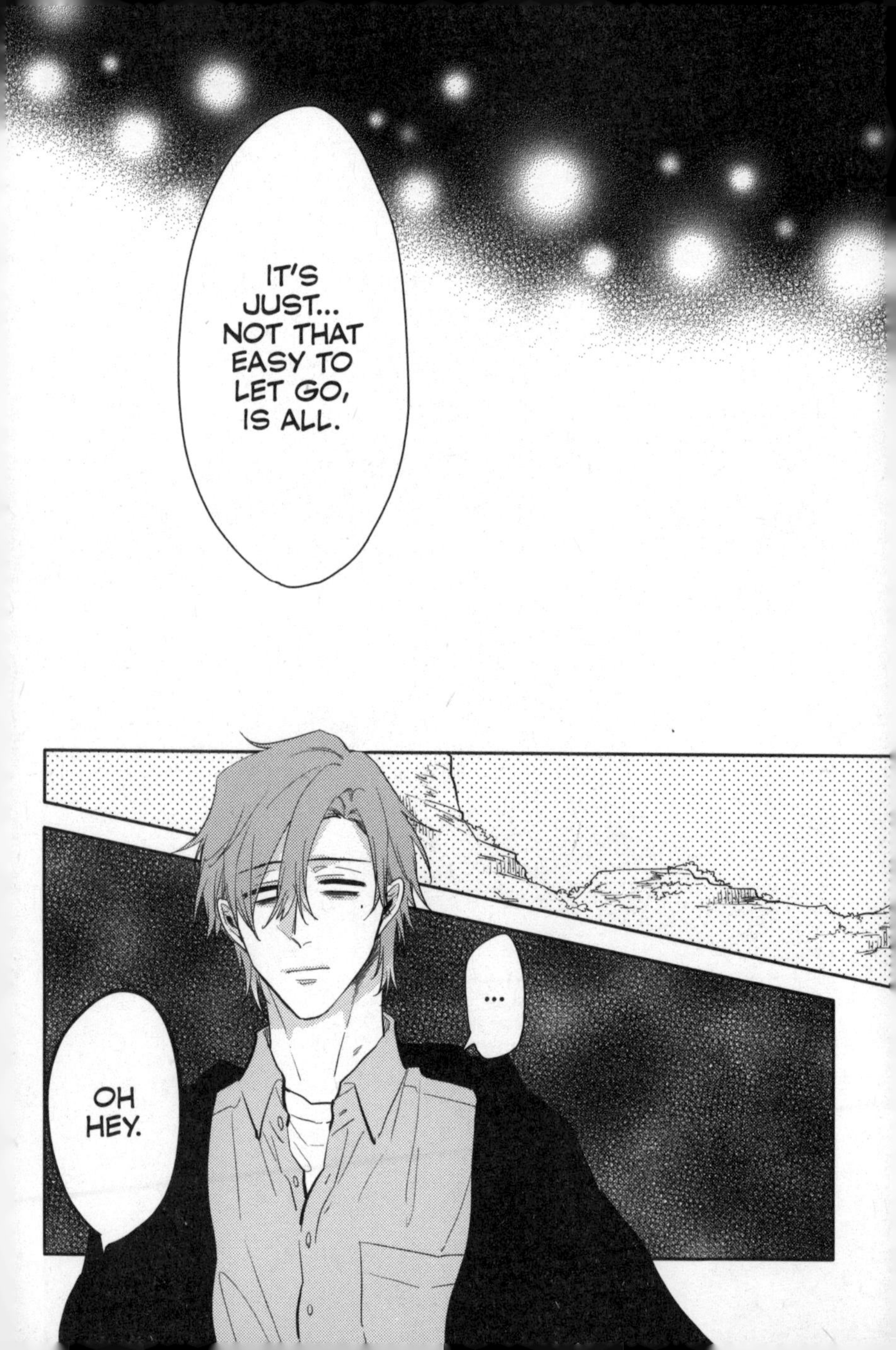
IT'S JUST... NOT THAT EASY TO LET GO, IS ALL.
...
OH HEY.

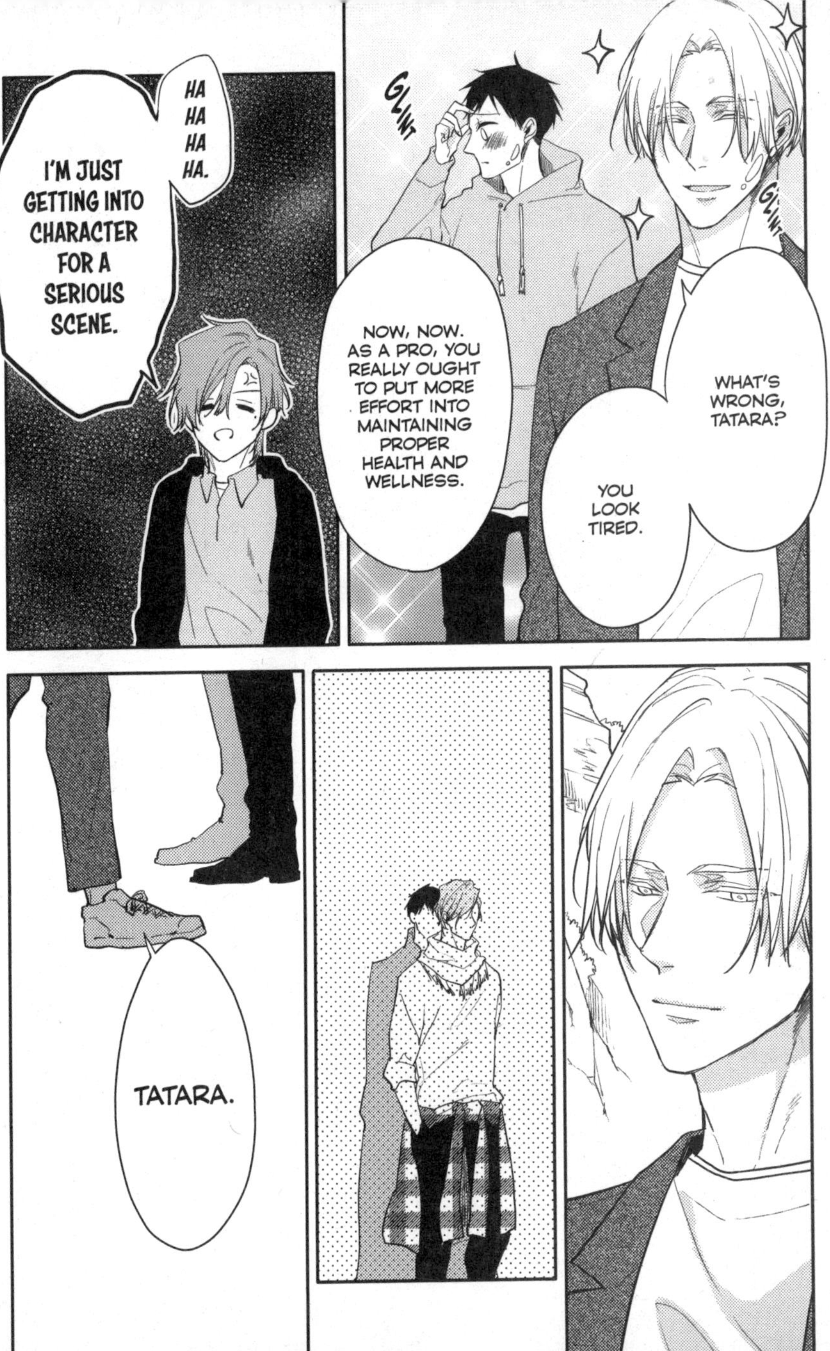
GLINT
WHAT'S WRONG, TATARA?
YOU LOOK TIRED.
GLINT
NOW, NOW. AS A PRO, YOU REALLY OUGHT TO PUT MORE EFFORT INTO MAINTAINING PROPER HEALTH AND WELLNESS.
HA HA HA HA.
I'M JUST GETTING INTO CHARACTER FOR A SERIOUS SCENE.
TATARA.

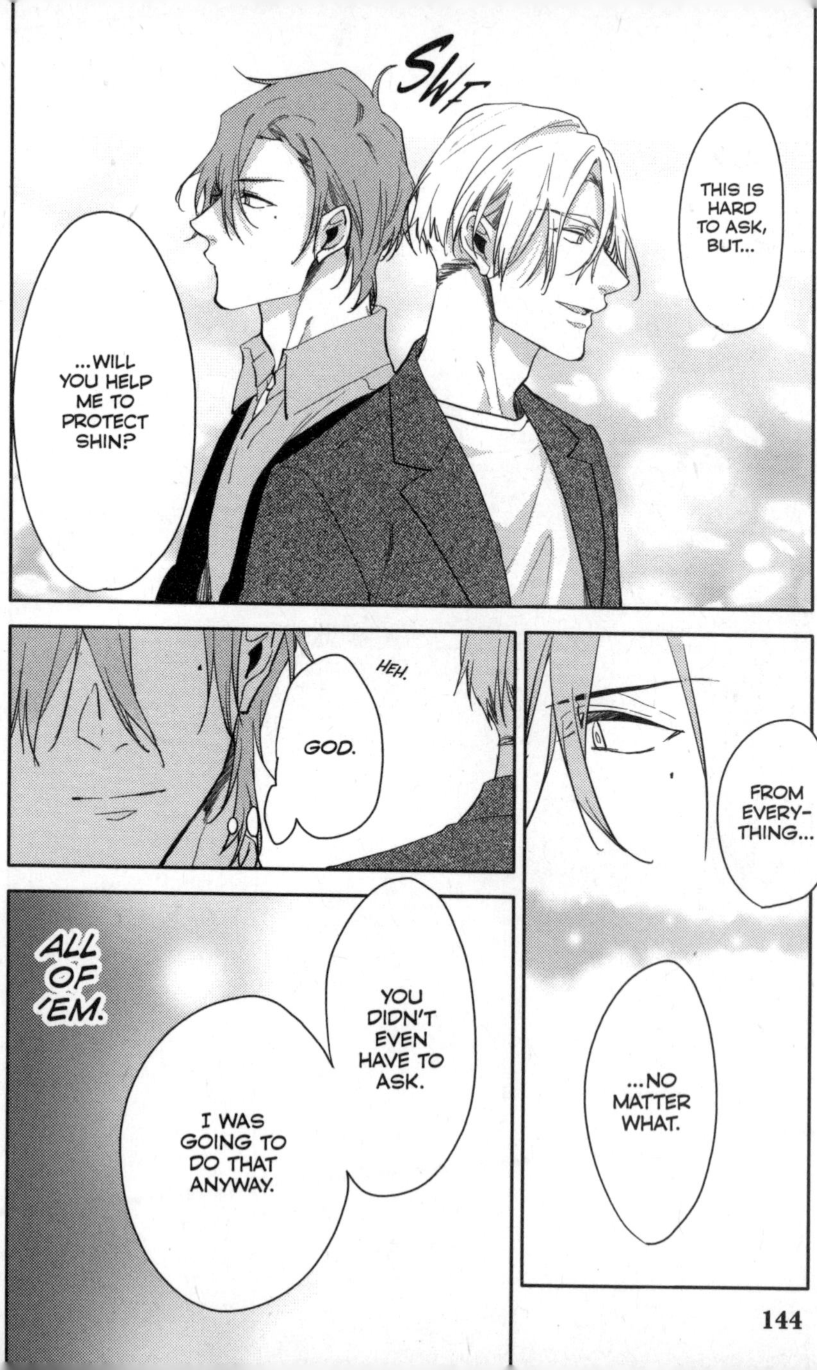
SWF
THIS IS HARD TO ASK, BUT...
...WILL YOU HELP ME TO PROTECT SHIN?
FROM EVERY-THING...
...NO MATTER WHAT.
HEH.
GOD.
YOU DIDN'T EVEN HAVE TO ASK.
I WAS GOING TO DO THAT ANYWAY.
ALL OF 'EM.

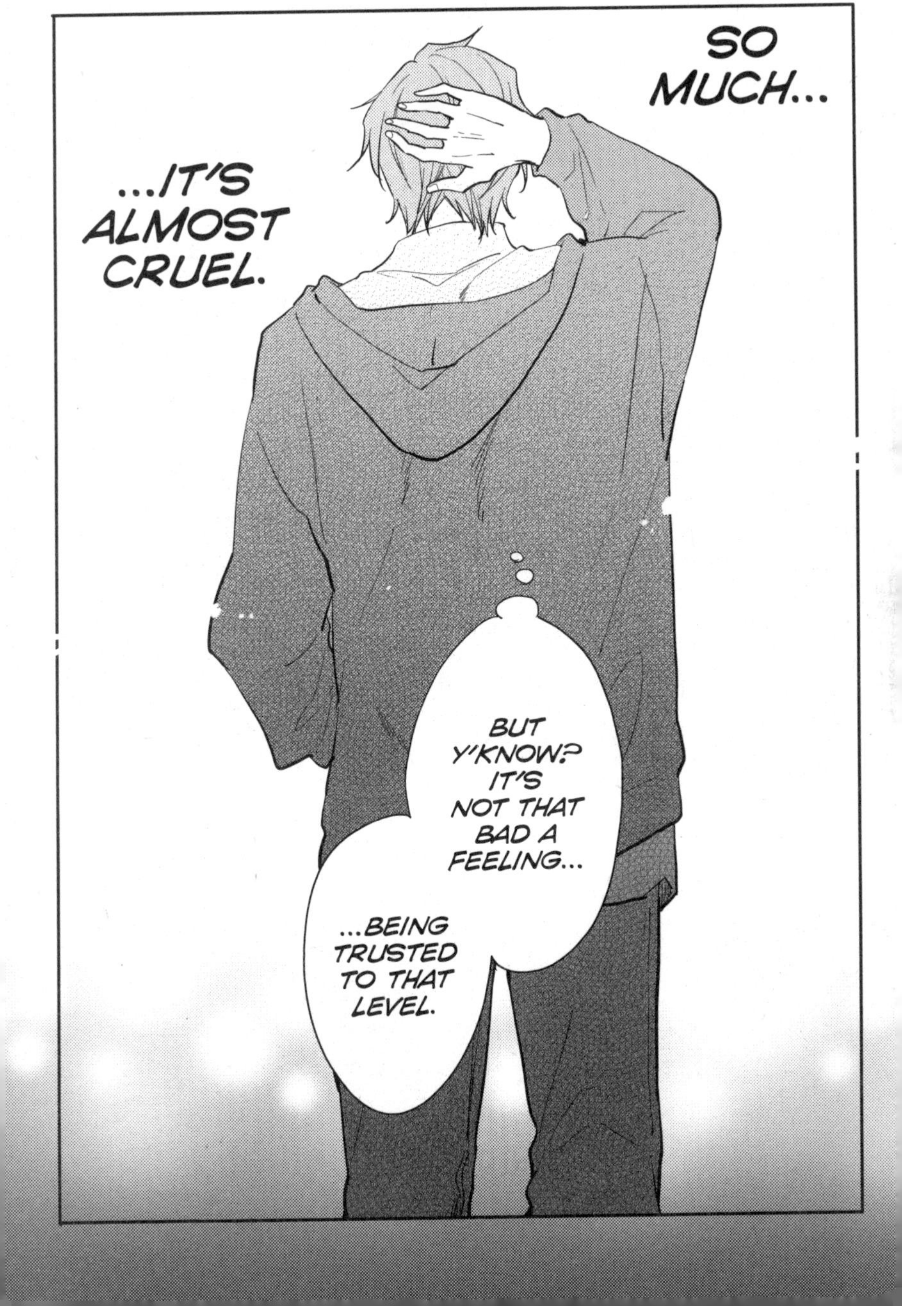
SO MUCH...
...IT'S ALMOST CRUEL.
BUT Y'KNOW? IT'S NOT THAT BAD A FEELING...
...BEING TRUSTED TO THAT LEVEL.

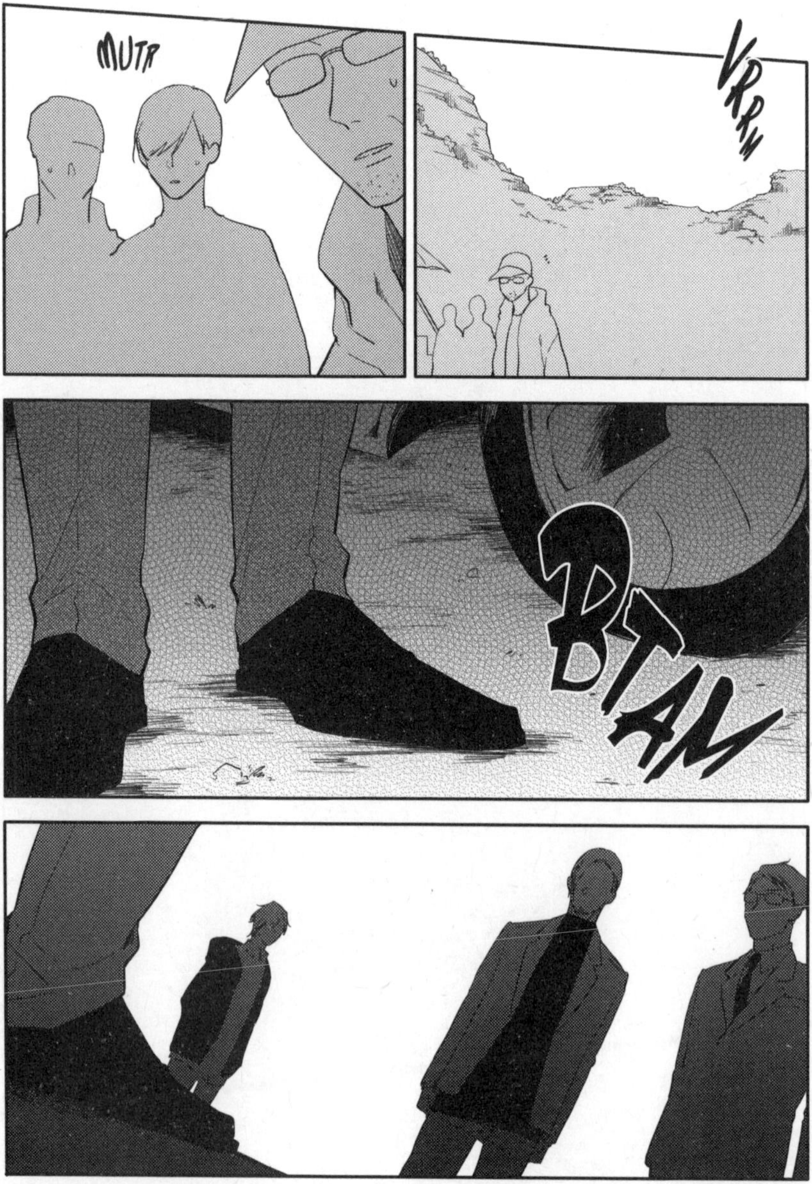
VRRM
MUTR
BTAM

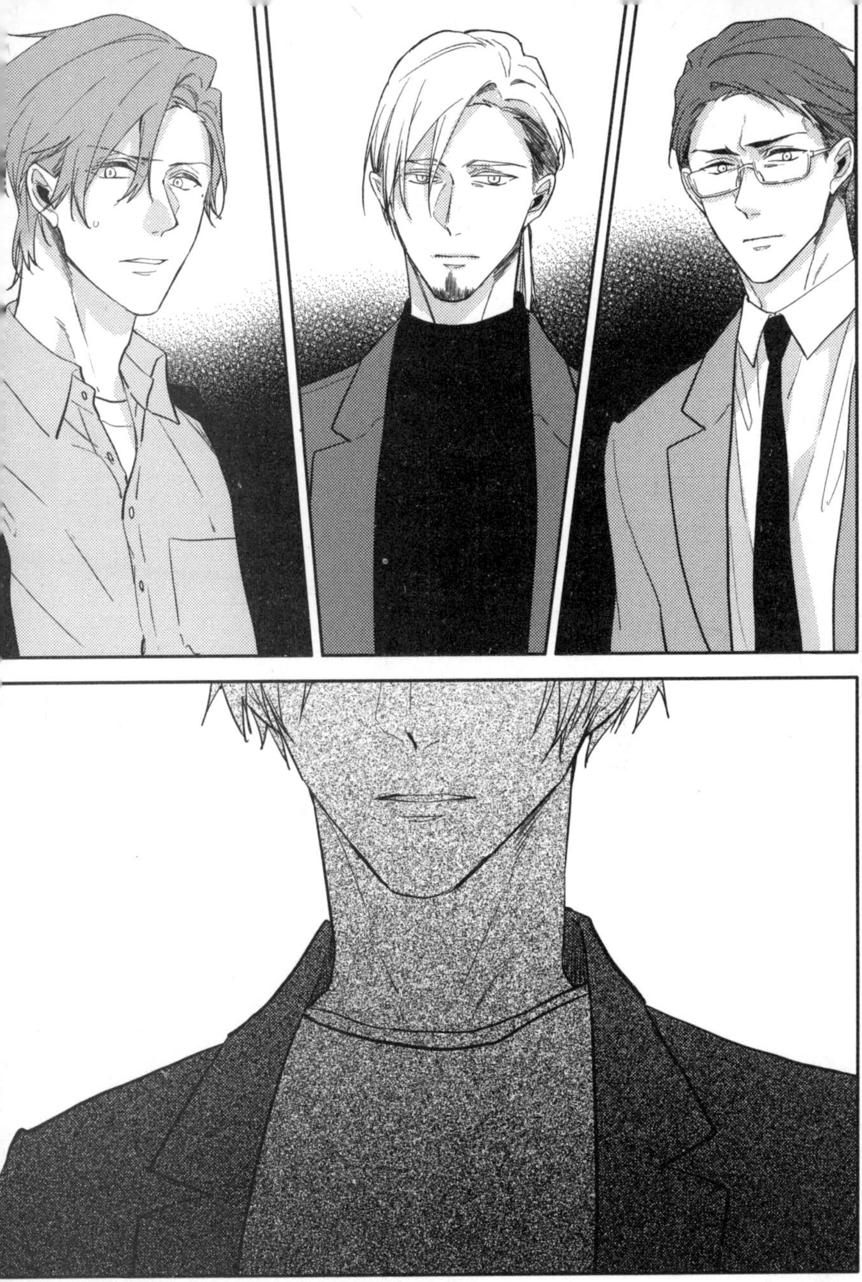

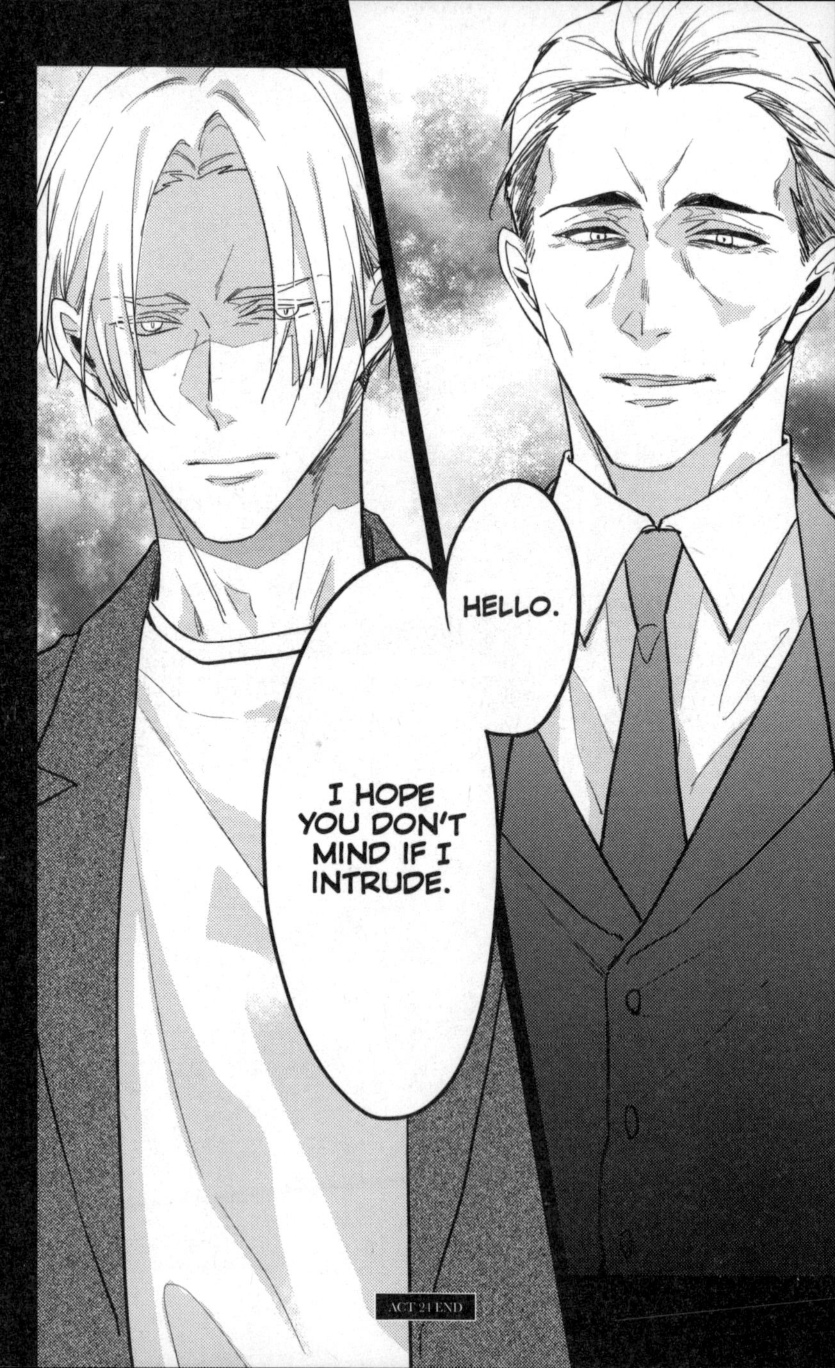
HELLO.
I HOPE YOU DON'T MIND IF I INTRUDE.
ACT 24 END

Black
or White

Black
or White

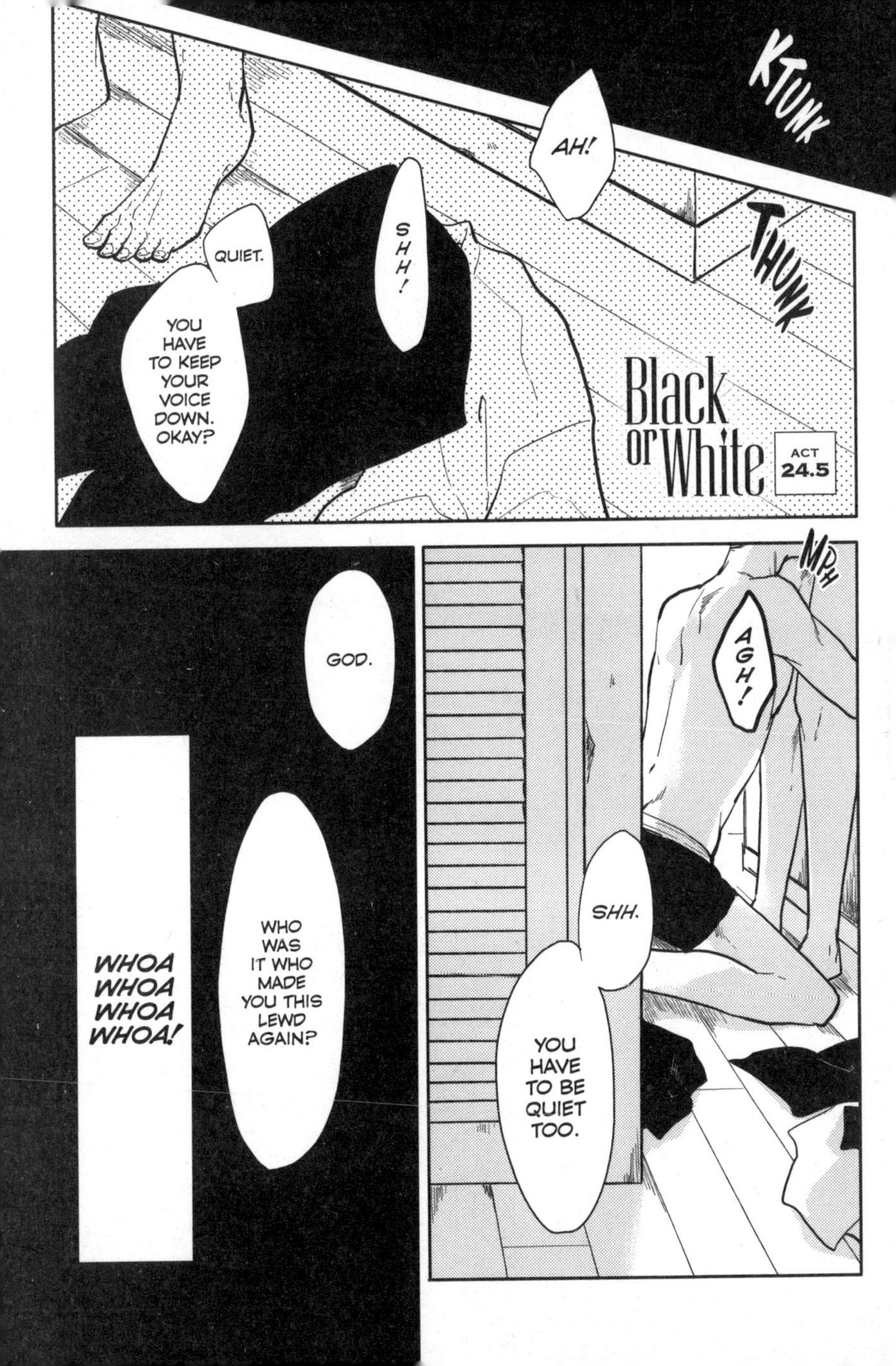
KTUNK
THUNK
AH!
SHH!
QUIET.
YOU HAVE TO KEEP YOUR VOICE DOWN. OKAY?
Black or White
ACT 24.5
MPH
AGH!
SHH.
YOU HAVE TO BE QUIET TOO.
GOD.
WHO WAS IT WHO MADE YOU THIS LEWD AGAIN?
WHOA WHOA WHOA WHOA!

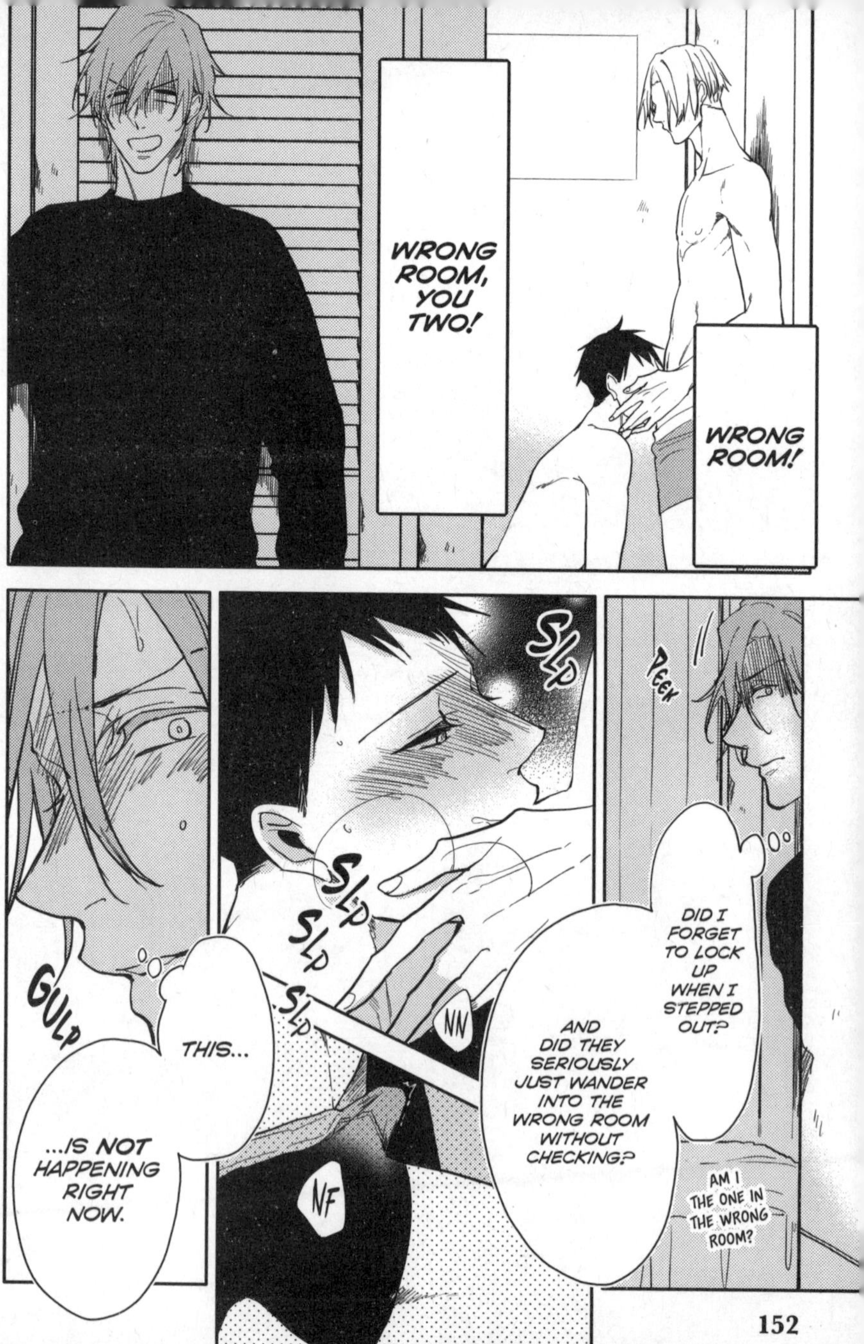
WRONG ROOM!
WRONG ROOM, YOU TWO!
PEEK
DID I FORGET TO LOCK UP WHEN I STEPPED OUT?
AND DID THEY SERIOUSLY JUST WANDER INTO THE WRONG ROOM WITHOUT CHECKING?
AM I THE ONE IN THE WRONG ROOM?
SLP
SLP SLP SLP
NN
NF
GULP
THIS...
...IS NOT HAPPENING RIGHT NOW.

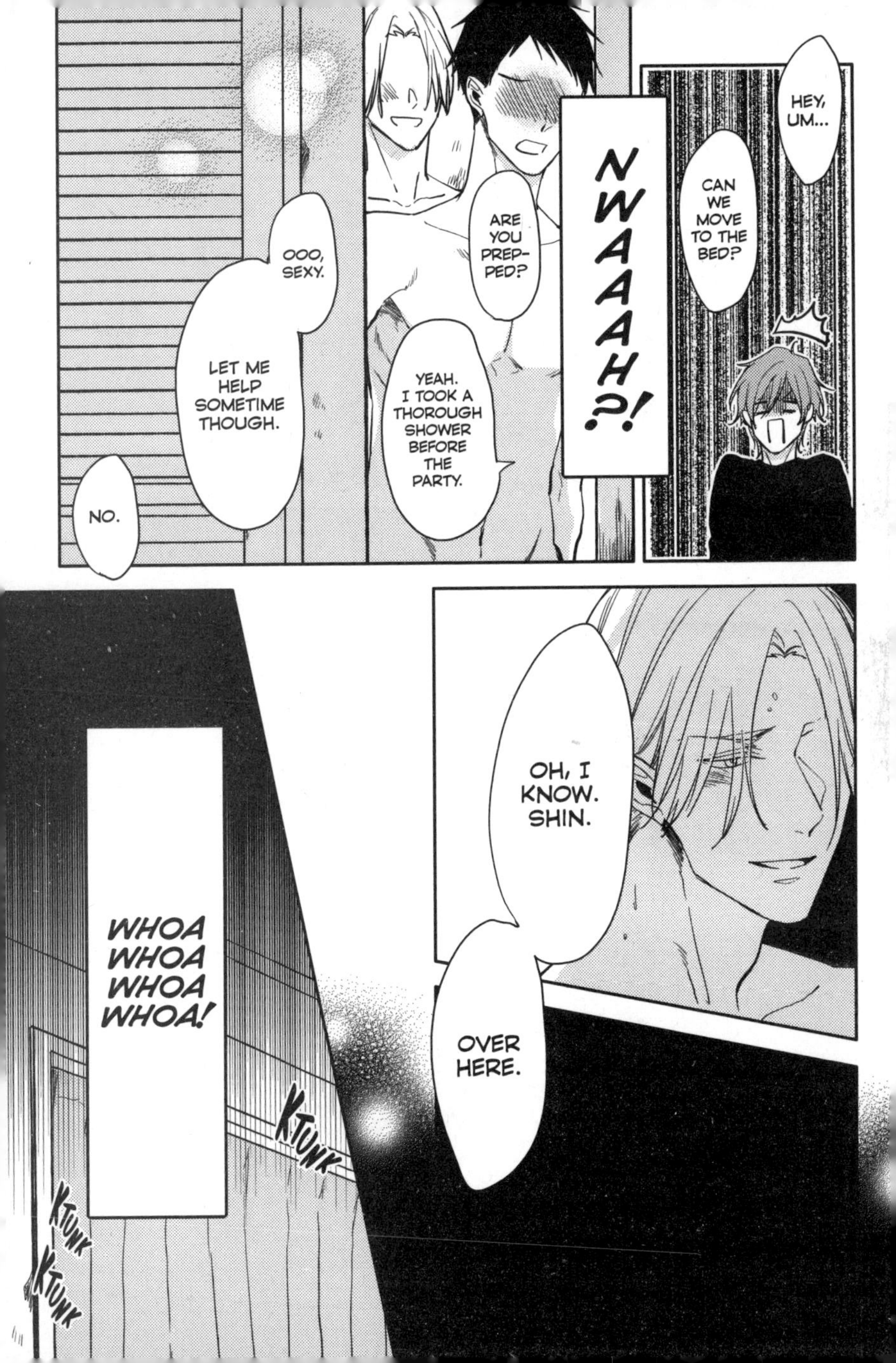
HEY, UM...
CAN WE MOVE TO THE BED?
NWAAAAH?!
ARE YOU PREP-PED?
YEAH. I TOOK A THOROUGH SHOWER BEFORE THE PARTY.
OOO, SEXY.
LET ME HELP SOMETIME THOUGH.
NO.
OH, I KNOW. SHIN.
OVER HERE.
WHOA WHOA WHOA WHOA!
KTUNK
KTUNK
KTUNK

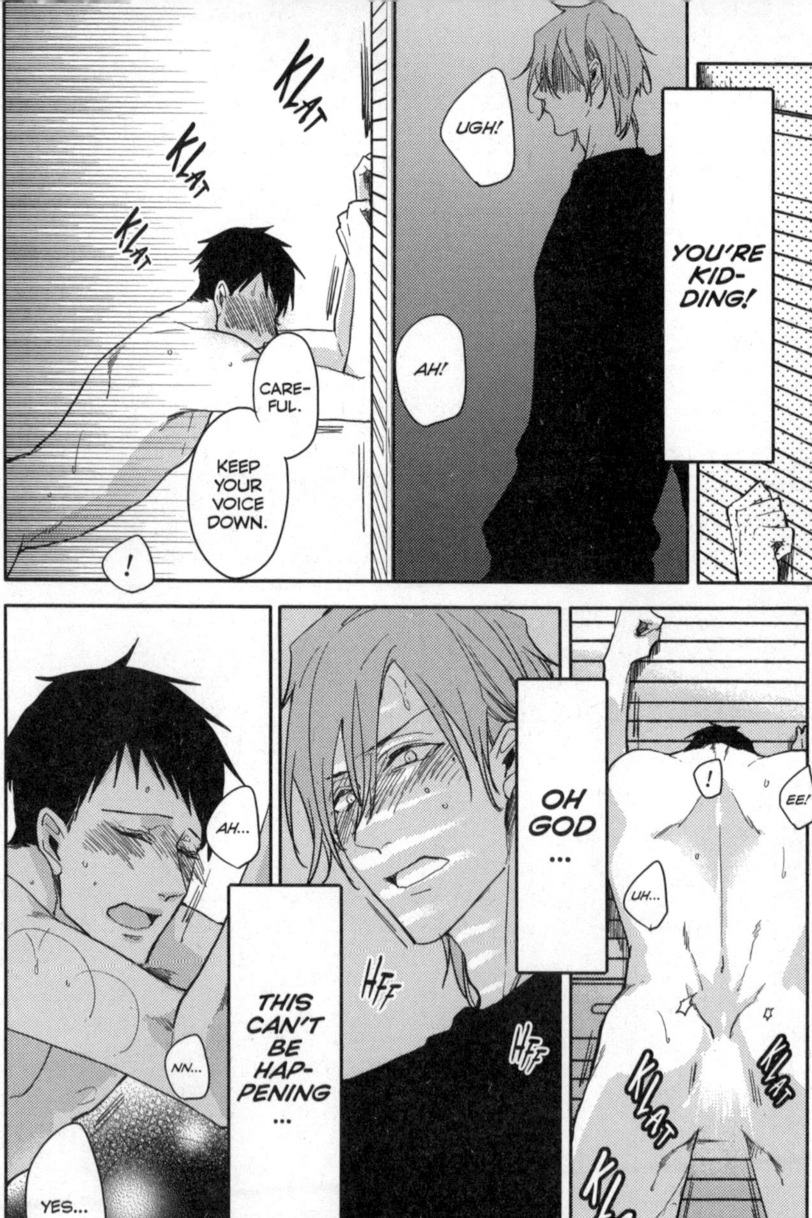
YOU'RE KID-DING!
UGH!
AH!
KLAT
KLAT
KLAT
CARE-FUL.
KEEP YOUR VOICE DOWN.
!
OH GOD ...
!
EE!
UH...
KLAT
KLAT
KLAT
KLAT
HFF
HFF
AH...
THIS CAN'T BE HAP-PENING ...
NN...
YES...

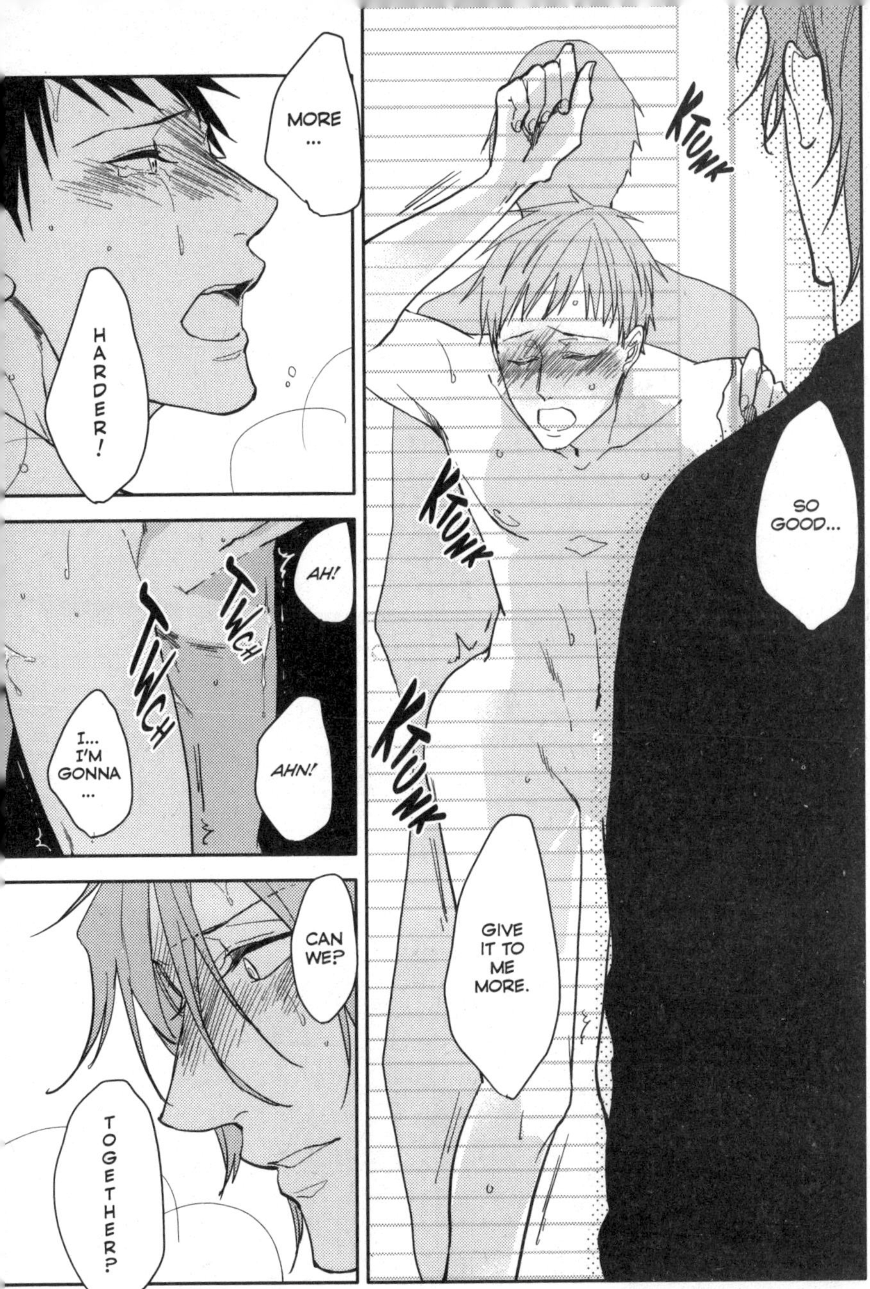
KTUNK
SO GOOD...
KTUNK
KTUNK
GIVE IT TO ME MORE.
MORE ...
HARDER!
AH!
TWITCH
TWITCH
AHN!
I... I'M GONNA ...
CAN WE?
TOGETHER?

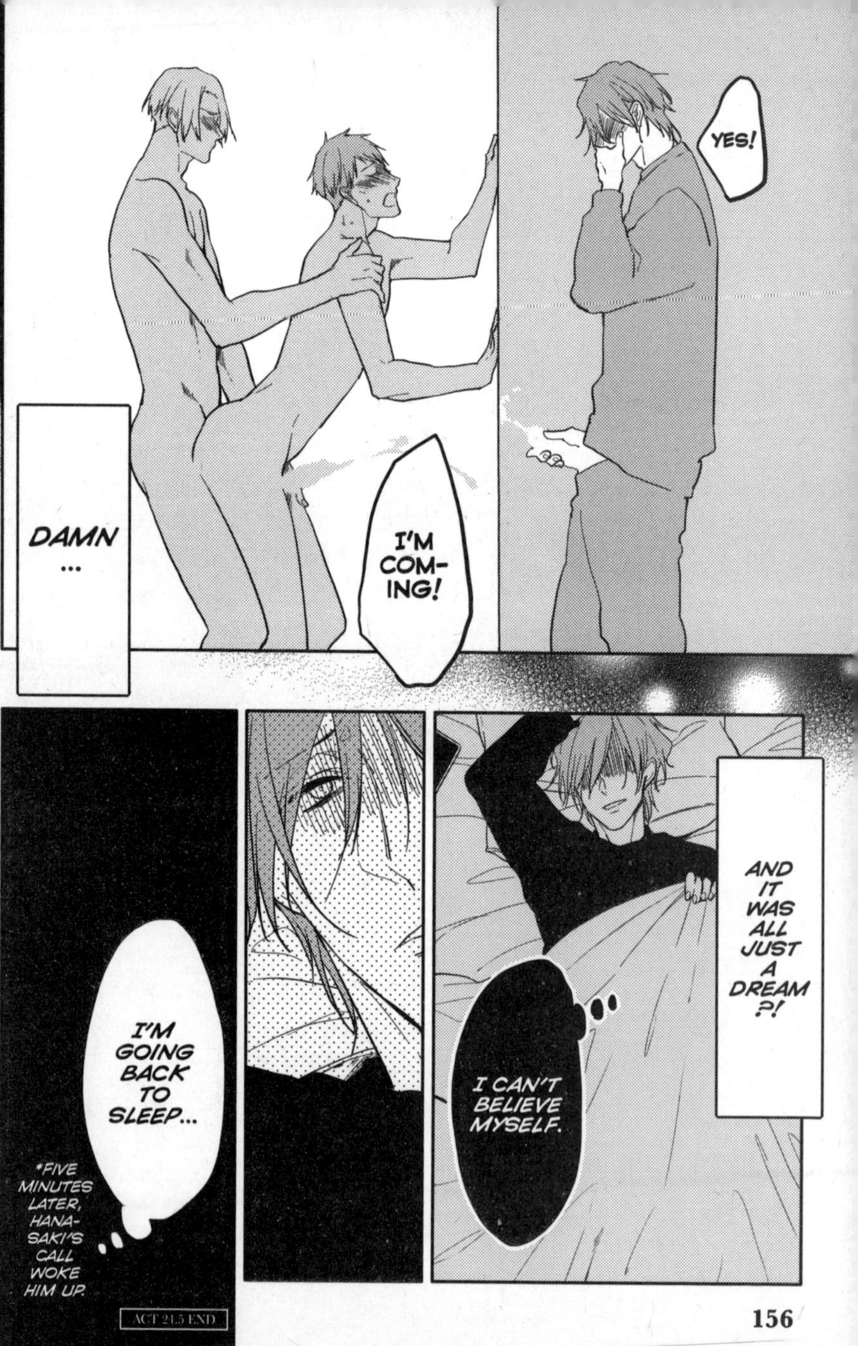
YES!
I'M COMING!
DAMN...
AND IT WAS ALL JUST A DREAM?!
...
I CAN'T BELIEVE MYSELF.
I'M GOING BACK TO SLEEP...
...
*FIVE MINUTES LATER, HANASAKI'S CALL WOKE HIM UP.
ACT 21.5 END

AFTERWORD

HELLO. I'M SACHIMO.

EVERYBODY HATES THAT CEO. I HATE HIM TOO. BUT I LOVE DRAWING THE GUY. IT'S COMPLICATED. I DON'T HAVE MUCH EXPERIENCE WITH WRITING CHARACTERS THAT ARE MEGA VILLAINS, SO THIS IS KIND OF FUN. BUT I STILL HATE HIM.

I HOPE OUR TWO MAIN CHARACTERS WILL FIND HAPPINESS NEXT VOLUME!

さちも。
SACHIMO

AND THAT!

TAKE THAT!

BIF

BIF

ON BEHALF OF ALL READERS EVERYWHERE, I SHALL PUNCH YOU!

About the Author

Sachimo
DOB August 17
Blood Type O
Born in Saitama Prefecture

Black or White
Volume 8
SuBLime Manga Edition

Story and Art by **Sachimo**

Translation—**Adrienne Beck**
Touch-Up Art and Lettering—**Deborah Fisher, Gwen Butler**
Cover and Graphic Design—**Shawn Carrico**
Editor—**Jennifer LeBlanc**

BLACK or WHITE Vol. 8
© Sachimo 2022
First published in Japan in 2022 by KADOKAWA CORPORATION, Tokyo.
English translation rights arranged with KADOKAWA CORPORATION, Tokyo.

ASUKA
COMICS
CL$_X^D$

Printed in the U.S.A.

Published by SuBLime Manga
P.O. Box 77010
San Francisco, CA 94107

10 9 8 7 6 5 4 3 2 1
First printing, April 2024

SuBLimeManga.com

For more information

on all our products, along with the most up-to-date news on releases, series announcements, and contests, please visit us at:

 SuBLimeManga.com

 twitter.com/**SuBLimeManga**

 facebook.com/**SuBLimeManga**

 instagram.com/**SuBLimeManga**

 SuBLimeManga.tumblr.com

Sparks fly in this *Secret XXX* spin-off featuring the brothers of Shouhei and Itsuki after a drunken fling!

therapy game

Story and Art by
Meguru Hinohara

COMPLETE IN 2 VOLUMES!

Shizuma only drank that night to forget his heartbreak. He didn't intend to also forget Minato, the one-night stand who soothed his broken heart. And since Minato's not one to be forgotten, he hatches a plan of seduction...and revenge!

M
MATURE

SUBLIME
SuBLimeManga.com